WORLD HISTORY

WORLD HISTORY

DR. IAN BARNES

CARTOGRAPHICA

A CARTOGRAPHICA BOOK

This book is produced by
Cartographica Press
6 Blundell Street
London N7 9BH

Copyright © 2007 Cartographica Press

This edition printed 2007

ISBN: 978-1-84573-323-0

QUMWOHI

Printed in Singapore by
Star Standard Industries Pte Ltd

CONTENTS

INTRODUCTION 6

PART 1: HUMAN ORIGINS TO FIRST CIVILIZATIONS 23

PART 2: THE CLASSICAL WORLD 47

PART 3: DIVIDED REGIONS 73

PART 4: EXPLORATION AND FIRST CONTACT 105

PART 5: THE AGE OF EMPIRE 115

PART 6: GLOBALIZATION 133

MAP AND RECONSTRUCTION LIST 160

INTRODUCTION

THE BIRTH OF CIVILIZATION

The birth of civilization is always said to have coincided with the advent of mankind on Earth. Prior to this all creatures existed by instinct, but mankind introduced a whole new dimension; for the first time there were creatures capable of creative thought.

HUMAN ORIGINS

The origin of the human race has always been the subject of intense speculation. Evidence can only be gathered from scraps of fossilised bone and although it is now possible to date these with reasonable accuracy, the actual location of mankind's origin remains a mystery.

There are two main theories. The first is that various species of humanoid developed in parallel in different parts of the world, while the second, more commonly accepted theory places mankind's origin several million years ago in Africa, with subsequent moves to Asia and Australia, then Europe and finally the Americas.

What is beyond doubt is that over a considerable period of time, the early *Homo erectus* were replaced by the present *Homo sapiens*. Early groups such as the cave dwelling Neanderthals and Cro Magnas gradually died out.

The rise of *Homo sapiens* occurred between 130,000 to 200,000 years ago. These early humans were hunter-gatherers who lived in a hostile world. Much of Europe at that time was covered by ice and these nomadic people would follow game trails and river valleys to obtain fish. In order to survive they needed fire, shelter, clothing and weapons.

An effect of this extreme cold was that much of the water in the northern hemisphere was locked in glaciers, causing the sea level to fall. This created land bridges between Eurasia and the Americas, enabling wider migration.

At the same time much of Indonesia was linked to south-east Asia; Australia was also linked to New Guinea. Australia could therefore be reached relatively easily. The actual movement of various groups continues to be subject to a considerable amount of speculation. It is assumed that the Bering Land Bridge allowed north-eastern Asians to migrate into Alaska and then further inland. Biological anthropologists place the arrival of Stone Age Indians in three waves around 15,000 years ago, yet campfire remains in Mexico have been carbon dated to 21,000 BC.

According to recent research Australian Aboriginal genes still exist in Tierra del Fuego and it is speculated that Japanese could have reached America via the Japanese current or via Hawaii. The warrior armour of the Tlingit people of Alaska has

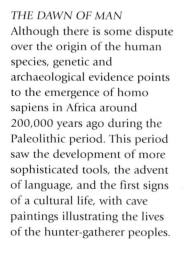

THE DAWN OF MAN
Although there is some dispute over the origin of the human species, genetic and archaeological evidence points to the emergence of homo sapiens in Africa around 200,000 years ago during the Paleolithic period. This period saw the development of more sophisticated tools, the advent of language, and the first signs of a cultural life, with cave paintings illustrating the lives of the hunter-gatherer peoples.

a very Japanese look about it and the Japanese Jomon pottery bears a strong resemblance to the Valdivia pottery of Equador.

EARLY CIVILIZATIONS

Over a period of time this hunter-gathering lifestyle evolved into a more settled way of life. The first ancient settlements of note developed between 8000 and 6000 BC.

They were along the banks of four major rivers; the Huang Ho, the Tigris, Euphrates, and the Nile. These all possessed rich alluvial soil that spread around the surrounding areas as a result of regular inundations. A system of irrigation and field terracing was developed in each area, allowing cereals and other crops to be grown. Animals were tamed and used for meat, dairy products, and motive power. Wealth was created and societies developed hierarchical organizations of kings, priests, merchants, artisans, and peasants.

EGYPT

Early Egyptians settled along the Nile, building irrigation ditches and terraces to enable the cultivation of emmer, wheat, barley, flax, lettuce, onions, pulses and fruit. The earliest known kings of the First Dynasty ruled from about 2900 BC; the first one is thought to have been King Narmer. These early Pharaohs were interred at Abydos. The early dynasties developed a court life and archaeologists have uncovered evidence of gods and mining in Sinai supported by military defenses.

Egypt at that time stretched as far south as Elephantine at the First Cataract of the Nile. Military governors stationed there traveled south into Nubia, occasionally conducting raids. Egyptian state defense relied on native levies, with Nubian mercenaries sometimes waging war in Sinai against nomads and into southern Palestine. Politically, Egypt suffered from tension between kings and powerful provincial governors. However, Montjuhotep II unified Egypt from his base at Thebes.

The Egyptian Middle Kingdom maintained international trade through Crete, Palestine, Syria, Anatolia, and Babylonia, the products exchanged being Lebanon timber, jewels, metals, ivory, spices, and gold. After Mentuhotep II consolidated the kingdom, he expelled foreigners from the Nile delta and campaigned against Libyans in the West and nomads in the East. The Sinai frontier was strengthened with a fortress, known as Walls of the Ruler. This dominated all routes across northern Sinai, while acting as an entrepôt and staging post for the Sinai mines.

In the south, Nubia was controlled via skilfully placed fortifications, such as Semna. Thus, Egypt dominated the southern trade routes, and occasionally attacked Kush. Under the 11th Dynasty, ships voyaged to Punt, Ethiopia, probably to buy incense, and mining expeditions were made to the Wadi Hammamat. Egyptian mines produced gold, amethyst and turquoise. The 12th Dynasty moved the capital north to Itj-towy and the rulers built their pyramids at Fayyum. Over time, the dynasties weakened and eastern invaders, known as the Hyksos, invaded. These Semitic horsemen and charioteers captured Memphis, established a capital at Averis, and made the rest of Egypt pay tribute. This dynasty lasted from about 1648–1540 BC.

THE HARAPPANS OF THE INDUS VALLEY

Meanwhile in Asia the earliest known civilization flourished amidst the alluvial soil of the Indus Valley. For a thousand years this civilization existed at the same time as those in Bronze Age Egypt, Mesopotamia, and Crete. This Harappan culture was based on wheat and rice production. Animals were domesticated, including elephants, and hunting supplemented the diet. Major urban developments took place, major cities being at Harappa, Mohenjo-Daro and Rohn. Archaeologists have uncovered grid patterns of streets with elaborate drainage systems and defenses including walls and citadels. Cotton textiles were manufactured and goods were traded with Persia and Afghanistan. Bahrain was used as a way-station. Evidence suggests that priests or merchants held the main power not kings. This civilization collapsed in around 2000 BC when river courses changed, destroying fields and trade patterns.

MESOPOTAMIA

The Tigris–Euphrates river system of Mesopotamia created a fertile region that lead to the growth of several civilizations. The Sumerians built complex cities constructed from clay-brick. Ziggurats were built, with religious edifices like that at Uruk. A large number of gods were worshipped, including Anu, the god of heaven, Enki the water god and Enlil, the god of earth. Clay writing tablets recorded the Epic of Gilgamesh where the King of Uruk searches in vain for immortality. Clay tablets also record commercial transactions, and later, works covering religion and science.

The Sumerian civilization came to an end when they were overthrown by the Akkadians, a Semitic people from the Zagros Mountains. United by Sargon (c. 2334–2279 BC) in a quest for loot, the Akkadian Empire stretched from the Persian Gulf to the Mediterranean, lasting until it was overthrown by the Gutians. A new Sumerian dynasty established a well-organized empire in the last century of the 3rd Millennium.

THE CRADLE OF CIVILISATION
Ancient Mesopotamia, the region now occupied by modern Iraq, parts of eastern Syria, southeastern Turkey, and southwest Iran, is often referred to as the "cradle of civilisation," since it was here that the first sophisticated, literate societies emerged in the late 4th millennium BC. Though the land close to the Euphrates and Tigris rivers was highly fertile, land further away was arid and largely uninhabitable. The Mesopotamians solved this problem through the development of irrigation systems, as well as the control of water by dams and the use of aqueducts. Besides agricultural breakthroughs, the Mesopotamians made significant leaps forward in language, writing, science, mathematics, astronomy, economics, politics, and law, laying the foundations for modern society as we know it today.

CLASH OF CIVILISATIONS
The Hittite empire emerged in Anatolia, part of modern day Turkey, but spread into Syria, Lebanon, and Armenia. During the period 1750 BC – 1160 BC, the Hittite empire was just one of a number of civilizations vying for power in the period before Greek dominance, its most significant rival being Egypt. Hittite expansionism led eventually to the Battle of Kadesh against the Egyptians in 1274 BC, significant for concluding with one of the first peace treaties in history.

The Babylonian Empire followed later, its most well-known King being Hammurabi who ruled from around 1728 to 1686 BC. He was renowned for his Code of Laws, the first such code in recorded history. Eventually Babylon grew weaker, as it came under attack from the Hittites.

The Indo-European Hittites, who probably originated from beyond the Black Sea, invaded Anatolia in the 2nd Millennium BC. The Empire's political structure shows a collection of client kings all owing their loyalty to the Great King in the capital, Hattusas. Clients were often linked to the royal dynasty by marriage and were required to furnish the King with troops and supplies in times of need. The monarch was a storm god's representative on earth, this deity co-existing with a sun god. Hittite power conflicted with the Mitanni state, destroying it but retained Ugarit, Carchemish, and Aleppo as tributary cities. As Hittite power grew, penetrating Armenia, it also swept into Syria and the Lebanon ending in battle with the Egyptians at Kadesh. After a peace treaty involving dynastic marriage, both the Hittites and Egypt were savaged by the Sea Peoples, the former suffering destruction as its cities were burnt and the state collapsed. Additionally, Phrygians invaded across the Dardanelles and over-ran much of Anatolia. Some cities managed to emerge from this chaos still retaining a Hittite identity, Carchemish being the most important.

CHINA

Chinese civilizations were developing along the River Huang Ho and other waterways. The Shang state based its power on bronze weapons and chariots, with culture and political dominance being spread southward by a warrior noble class, working on behalf of priest-kings. Authority was based upon force and kings had ultimate power of life over death. Dynastic alliances were important and wisdom and foresight were based on the ability to interpret indications given by bones and turtle shells.

Over 100,000 inscribed oracle bones have been found at Anyang. In one tomb at Anyang a King was found to have been buried along with 90 retainers who had allowed their own deaths in order to accompany him into the afterlife. Shang culture reached the crossroads of the Bronze and Iron Ages with the use of iron weapons. Noted for a form of feudalism whereby a tribal nobility was given land for military service, the Shang perfected bronze casting.

The Shang were overthrown by the Chou. The Chou leader, WuWang, claimed that Shang Zhou Xin had lost the mandate of heaven. The Chou ruled a series of territories controlled by family and allies, the Qiang. Eventually Chou China

disintegrated into two states (841–771 BC). A new weaker dynasty was formed that was bedeviled by a virtually independent vassal nobility as China entered the Period of Warring States (403–221 BC).

THE EMPIRE OF SOLOMON

At the eastern end of the Mediterranean, Solomon's Empire was fairly short-lived. It became a powerful mini-state after the death of King David of Israel when weakened regional superpowers had left a power vacuum. Solomon, King David's son, constructed the state from a confederation of opposing northern and southern Hebrew tribes.

As well as building a huge Temple and state fortifications, Solomon enhanced state power through trade across Arabia and through the Red Sea to Ophir (Abyssinia) and Sheba (Yemen). Caravan and sea routes carried the output of a large-scale copper mining industry. He continued David's alliance with Hiram, King of Tyre, and these allies traded together. Allegedly, their fleets sailed throughout the known world, some voyages taking three years.

Solomon enslaved the Canaanites in his Empire, using them as building labor. Ultimately, he used his own people too for forced labor, generating great resentment. On Solomon's death in around 931 BC, the state split into Israel and Judah, ruled by Solomon's sons, Jereboam and Reheboam respectively. These smaller states became easy prey for Assyria and Babylon in years to come.

EARLY LANGUAGE

Linguistic research has shown that many languages have a common origin in a ProtoIndo-European tongue, spoken by Aryans. These nomadic people moved in different directions, and with each separation from others the language mutated into different language families, such as Slav, Balt, German, Celtic, Greek, and Tocharian.

The Aryans also spread into the Indus Valley, possibly wiping out existing civilization as they spread their Vedic religion and culture. The Indo-Iranian subgroup of language families includes Median, Persian, Hindi, Urdu, Marathi, Bengali, and Gujerati.

Some link words are still comprehensible. The Vedic fire-god, Agni, can be found in the Latin ignis (fire), which is the root for the English "'ignition." The word for father (English) has similarities with vater (German), pater (Latin), and pacer (Tocharian).

THE CLASSICAL WORLD

The civilizations of the Classical World, as opposed to those of the Ancient World, are characterized by their generally higher level of culture. The classical world saw the creation of a series of important civilizations in Persia, Greece, Etruria, Macedon, Celtic Europe, Rome, China, and India. All of these ultimately suffered from imperial overstretch and the threat of invasion by neighbors or nomadic tribes.

PERSIA

The years 550–330 BC saw the birth of the Persian Achaemenid Empire. The Persians were subject to the Medes but broke free under Cyrus who then ruled both peoples, using his enhanced power to conquer Anatolian Lydia in 547 BC, before annexing central Asia and Babylonia. Cyrus's son, Cambyses, acquired Egypt and Lydia. His successor, Darius I who ruled from 521 to 486 BC, consolidated the Empire into carefully governed satrapies linked by a vast road network. He added Thrace and areas of India west of the River Indus.

GREECE, CRETE AND THE AEGEAN

Further west, Cretan and Greek cultures were becoming developing societies. Minoan Crete was a highly important Aegean civilization, together with the Cyclades, and its successor, Mycenae. The legend of Theseus and the Minotaur, brought great fame to Knossos, Crete's capital. As a maritime nation, a considerable amount of international trade developed. Markets were found in Egypt, Syria and Cyprus, and Cretan workmanship was praised in letters found in Mesopotamian Mari. Additionally, colonies were created at Rhodes, Anatolian Miletus, and Cytheran Kastri. Crete imported metals and jewels while exporting textiles, pottery, lamps, and daggers.

Eventually Crete succumbed to Mycenae. Bronze Age Mycenaean cities included Tiryns, Pylos, Thebes, and Argos. These fortified settlements were arguably the homes of Homeric heroes like Agamemnon and Menelaus who campaigned against Troy to regain Queen Helen of Sparta.

Mycenae was the dominant power of the Aegean. Its riches were evidenced by its Lion Gate and grave finds. Its formidable sea-power enabled it to colonize Crete, Cyprus, the Cyclades, and Dodecanese islands, northern Greece, Macedonia and western Anatolia, but for some unknown reason Mycenaean culture simply collapsed around 1100 BC. This could have been as a result of Dorian invasion, pirates, or famine.

The Greek Bronze Age fell to the iron weapons of invaders who surged into Greece between 1200 and 1000 BC. A map depicts where the new Dorians, Ionians, Arcadians, Aeolians and North-West Greeks settled. They were all differentiated by their Greek dialects. These early Greeks traded throughout the Mediterranean and along the Levantine coast. The geographically divided Greece, full of mountains and valleys, allowed the growth of city states with a strongly individualistic identity and differing political forms: aristocracies, oligarchies, despotic tyrannies, and early Athenian democracy.

Greece eventually faced the might of the Persian Empire. Darius I crossed the Hellespont into Thrace to attack the Scythians. He seized the Greek islands of Lemnos and Imros but an invasion of Greece was defeated at Marathon by the Athenians and their Plataean allies. Xerxes, heir to Darius, re-attempted the conquest of Greece but was held up by King

ATHENIAN DOMINANCE
The Persian Wars in the 5th century BC ushered in a period of Athenian hegemony over Greek affairs. Its naval dominance and commercial power during this time attracted the most talented people to Athens, and a cultural and intellectual golden age began, led by figures such as the dramatists Aeschylus, Aristophanes, Euripides, and Sophocles; the philosophers Aristotle, Plato, and Socrates; the historians Herodotus, Thucydides, and Xenophon; the poet Simonides; and the sculptor Pheidias.

ROMAN POWER
Trajan's Column is a
monument in Rome raised by
Apollodorus of Damascus at
the order of the Senate. The
freestanding column, completed
in 113, commemorates the
Roman Emperor Trajan's
victory in the Dacian Wars,
in which the Roman army
defeated the Dacian army near
Tapae. It was during Trajan's
reign that the Roman Empire
reached its greatest territorial
extent.

Leonidas of Sparta at the pass of Thermopylae and defeated on land at Plataea in 479 BC and at sea at Salamis in 480 BC.

The Greeks had always used ships for trade and this also applied to colonization. The destruction of Mycenae led to a migration of refugees to Cyprus and western Asia Minor, as evidenced by the writings of the historian, Thucydides. Population pressure, political unrest and the quest for trade explain the movements. The desire for raw metals, especially precious ones, saw colonies being established on the Black Sea coastline, Anatolia, Naukratis in Egypt, Kyrene, Sicily, southern Italy, Illyria and Massilia.

Expansion in the search for iron introduced the Greeks to the Etruscans. The Etruscan culture, established between 800 and 400 BC, comprised 12 city states in central Italy, based upon modern Tuscany, whose power flooded into the Po Valley and to the Adriatic at Spina and Adria. The Bay of Naples and Campania saw the Etruscans capturing Greek colonies, especially Capua and Pompeii. Emergent Roman power, allied with Greek interests, hastened an Etruscan decline. This was followed by the complete Roman conquest of Etruria by 283 BC.

MACEDON

Another Greek success story was the rise of Macedon under usurper King Philip II who ruled from 359 to 336 BC. During this time he conquered Chalcidice, Thrace, Paeonia, and Thessaly. His extremely ruthless son, Alexander the Great, ruling from 336 to 323 BC, consolidated his Greek lands before attacking Persia. Victories at Issus and Gaugamela gave him the Persian Empire, stretching from Egypt to India and Sogdiana to the Arabian Sea. His early death, aged 33 years, saw his Empire divided between his generals and their dynasties. The most powerful were the Seleucids but the Ptolomies were the most successful in Egypt.

THE CELTS

In central Europe, a Celtic Hallstatt culture grew between 750 and 450 BC, eventually spreading to the Balkans, France, Spain, and probably Britain. Grave finds suggest links with a Russian Steppe homeland and trade with Greece and the Etruscans. The Celts were agriculturalists but susceptible to internecine strife and war with neighbors. They developed salt mines at Hallstatt, some 1300 feet deep. Celtic society comprised chiefs, druids, warriors, artisans, farmers, servants,

and slaves. A grave at Vix has evidence that aristocratic women probably had complete equality with men.

A later development of Celtic culture is the La Tène variant, lasting from 450 BC to the conquest by Julius Caesar in 56 BC. The Celts expanded from their ancestral lands into northern Italy where they encountered the Romans, the Carpathians with acquisitions in Thrace and Galatia. Squeezed by Teutonic peoples from the north and Romans from the south, Celtic independence was endangered. These Celts were noted for their art in silver, bronze and enamels, which they later developed in Ireland.

THE ROMAN EMPIRE

The most momentous classical civilization in Europe was the Roman Empire. Founded in 735 BC, Rome was under Etruscan influence for two hundred and fifty years. Eventually, controlling a strategic ford over the River Tiber, Rome brought neighboring tribes under control, threw off Etruscan influence, established a republic, and conquered Etruria.

Using a combination of warfare and diplomacy, the Samnites were defeated and by 266 BC Rome ruled all of Italy south of the Rubicon. Rome then intervened by invitation into the political affairs of Messina in Sicily and ran up against Carthaginian interests. War ensued. Success in Italy was accompanied by naval campaigns that secured Sicily, Corsica and Sardinia during the first Punic War in 238 BC.

Roman dominion in the Mediterranean forced Carthaginian armies under Hannibal in the second Punic War to move overland, complete with his elephants and cross the Alps into Italy. Sixteen years of war ended with Scipio's victory at Zama in 202 BC, allowing Rome to acquire most of Spain. A third war with a two year siege of Carthage gave Rome ultimate victory. Carthage was destroyed; its population enslaved and its lands were ploughed with salt. Rome now gained a Punic inheritance in Tunisia and North Africa.

By the time of Julius Caesar's death in 44 BC, Rome had spread throughout the Mediterranean.

Macedonia had backed Carthage and its defeat lead to it becoming a Roman province. Caesar had conquered Gaul, invaded Britain briefly and became part of the civil war against Pompey and Crassus. He was assassinated in 44 BC. Pergamon was bequeathed to Rome becoming the province of Asia. The 1st Century BC also saw the acquisition of Bithynia, Cyrene, Syria, and Egypt. Rome was now the mistress of the Mediterranean.

Caesar Augustus, 27 BC to AD 14, ended the civil war. This first Roman Emperor established a powerful, centralized government and reorganized the Empire with power based upon control of finance and the army. He presided over an expansion in the Alps and Balkans to the Danube, while Galatia was inherited. Elsewhere, campaigns were conducted in Germany by Augustus's stepsons. Tiberius was eventually adopted by Augustus.

CHINA

In China after the Chou Kings lost control, their feudal territories fragmented into successor states. Seven states fought against each other and against barbarian invasions, but only four became important: the Qin, Jin, Qi and Chu. Jockeying for power saw competition for dominance but western Qin, with an army hardened by conflict with the barbarian nomads, overcame the other states. King Zheng of Qin awarded himself the title of Qin Shi Huang Di. This sage-king then commenced reforming China. He standardized and homogenized the new country. Feudalism was abolished, a road network for troop movements built, and the northern defensive walls were expanded into the Great Wall of China. Campaigns were waged against the northern Xiongnu and the southern Min-Yue, with the conquest of Guangdong, Guangxi, and north Vietnam.

When the Emperor died, he was interred with the terracotta army. His dynasty was rapidly extinguished to be replaced by a rebel, Liu Bang, the first Han emperor. This new dynasty lasted from 207 BC to AD 220. The relatively stable regime internally was expansionist. The Viet tribes around the Gulf of Tonking were defeated and Chinese civilization and control acquired most of Korea.

Westward expansion brought the acquisition of larger horses into China allowing for the creation of heavy cavalry to defeat the Xiongnu. The Han also developed foreign trade, importing goods from India, Parthia, Japan, and the Roman Orient while the seizure of Xinjiang strengthened Han's hold on the Silk Road. This caravan route crossed from China through central Asia into Asia Minor and the Mediterranean coast, exporting mainly silk and importing western luxury goods.

INDIA

In India, the Mauryan Empire, founded by Chandragupta, emerged from the Kingdom of Magadha. This northeastern state expanded and under Asoka reached its greatest extent, extending deep into southern and western India. Asoka was a Buddhist and attempted to spread its virtues, but his state declined after being divided between his sons. New dynasties persecuted Buddhism leading to the victory of Brahmin Hinduism. The later Gupta Empire (AD 320–480) was established by Chandra Gupta I and again was founded in Magadha. Control was exerted over most of India and many states paid tribute, including Assam, Bengal, Nepal, the Punjab, Kushan and Ceylon. The Gupta state was the epitome of classical Hindu civilization. Trade flourished with Indian ships plying the Indian Ocean and the Arabian and Chinese Seas.

THE FINAL DECLINE OF THE ROMAN EMPIRE

In the year AD 324 the Roman Emperor Constantine chose Byzantium as the capital of the Roman Empire in the east. A co-ruler controlled the west while the east confronted the Sasanian Empire in conflict over Syria and Palestine. Eventually, the Byzantine section conflicted with Germanic tribes who had invaded the western Empire while facing attacks by Bulgar, Slav, and Avar incursions into Thrace, Dacia, and Dalmatia.

The western Empire was attacked by Angles, Saxons, and Jutes invading Britain, while the rest suffered invasions by Germanic Ostrogoths, Visigoths, Franks, Burgundians, Vandals, and Huns. The Germanic peoples spread throughout Italy, France, Spain and North Africa, as far as Cyrenaica. Their kingdoms comprised the Vandals in North Africa, the Visigoths in Iberia, the Franks in France and the Rhineland, the Burgundians down the Rhone Valley, while the Ostrogoths acquired Italy, western Hungary, Croatia, Serbia, Slovenia, and eastern Austria. These Visigoths were converted to Arian Christianity which conflicted with their Roman Catholic subjects in Italy. The Franks were the most successful Germans, defeating other tribes, while converting to Roman Christianity, thereby establishing a special bond between Frankish monarchy and the papacy.

THE EMPEROR AND HIS ARMY
Qin Shi Huang, the man responsible for uniting China in the 3rd century BC, remains a controversial figure in Chinese history, over two thousand years after his death. Having unified China through military victory over the competing Chinese states, he and his chief adviser Li Si introduced a series of reforms aimed at cementing unification, including the abolition of feudalism and the establishment of regional governors under the control of the central government. They also outlawed Confucianism, burying many of its scholars alive and banning all texts that weren't officially sanctioned by the state. Upon his death in 210 BC, Qin Shi Huang was buried in the huge mausoleum he had had constructed, his body guarded by over 8,000 terracotta soldiers.

POPULATION MOVEMENTS, INVASIONS, AND CONQUERORS

ISLAMIC MOVEMENTS

By the 5th Century, the Eastern Empire was threatened by barbarian incursions but Emperor Justinian resolved to regain lost lands. General Belisarius conquered North Africa and invaded Italy. Narses scored a victory over the Ostrogoths and elsewhere a foothold was established in Spai and the Persians were defeated, while invaders were confronted in the Balkans. Before long the entire region was facing fresh aggression in the form of Islam, which had been founded by Muhammad in Mecca in AD 610. Muhammad converted many Arabian tribes to Islam, which then waged jihad throughout Arabia, Syria, Persia, and Egypt. Muslim power also seized Central Asia, North Africa and much of Iberia. Attacks on Byzantium were repulsed in 718. Although religious zeal was the primary aim, looting and land-grabbing were definite attractions.

CENTRAL AMERICA

The first major civilization in Central America was the Olmec. Lasting from about 1200 to 900 BC this civilization was sited on the alluvial lands of the Mexican coast. The Olmec are renowned for the huge basalt heads with heavy features and helmets, some weighing 20 tons. The Maya followed from around 1000 BC and their most famous city-state was Palenque with its nine-tiered pyramid. Tikal and Cópal are other architectural wonders. The Mayans developed calendars, calculated the mathematical concept of zero, and utilized hieroglyphic writing. They were succeeded by the warlike Toltecs who spread from the Valley of Mexico into Central America. The site at Chichu Itzá is known for the Pyramid of Quetzalcoatl and a huge ball court, measuring 479 x 118 ft (146 x 36 meters).

THE VIKINGS

In Northern Europe the Vikings were on the move. Some four Viking voyages were made to Vinland in the Americas between 1000 and 1030. Houses and smelting works were constructed at L'Anse aux Meadows. Thorfinn Karlsefni reached there with 150 people and livestock, while others explored further south. However, after a few years the Vikings moved back to Greenland, possibly owing to the aggression of the Montaignais, Beothuk or Inuit tribes. This Vinland adventure was the culmination of a period of Viking Atlantic travel. The 8th Century AD witnessed the Norsemen reaching Britain's northern islands, and the Faroes 100 years later. A Viking administration was organized in the Orkneys in 800, before a Norse push to Iceland in 860. Greenland was colonized in 986.

Other Vikings attacked and settled in the Isle of Man in around 850 and in Dublin in 847, followed by other Irish towns. Invading armies established the Danelaw in England and were only stopped from taking over the whole country by King Alfred at Eddington in 878. Onslaughts on Francia followed with incursions into Spain and the Mediterranean. Eventually, Vikings settled in Normandy. Elsewhere, Swedish Vikings or Varangians utilized the Russian river systems to control trade to Constantinople and the Black Sea. Swedish dynasties established themselves at Novgorod, one of its princes then creating Kievan Rus.

THE HOLY ROMAN EMPIRE

The Vikings were lucky. Earlier, Charlemagne's Empire might have stopped them. Assuming the Frankish kingship in 771, his expansionist empire acquired parts of Italy, dominated the Papacy, and acquired Bohemia, Moravia, Austria and Croatia. In 800 Charlemagne was crowned Emperor of the Romans by Pope Leo III. All Christians, excepting those in the British Isles, now owed him allegiance. Following Charlemagne's death his successors allowed feudalism to develop in an Empire now weakened by decentralization and faced with foreign invaders.

KIEVAN RUS

In the east, Kievan Rus expanded under Syvatoslav against the Khazars, while also fighting the Bulgars and Pechenegs. Following Syvatoslav's death in 980, his youngest son, Vladimir, assumed rule. Vladimir had converted to Byzantine Christianity and made it Russia's official religion. He married Anne, the Byzantine Emperor's sister. Vladimir's death in 1015 led to many years of fighting amongst potential heirs. This disrupted trade and weakened Rus to the point that it was unable to resist the Tatar invasions of the 13th Century.

CHINA

In China, the Tang dynasty, founded in 626, expanded its lands across Xinjiang until the Arabs blocked their advance at the Battle of Talas in 751. An attempted usurpation damaged imperial authority allowing Uighurs and Tibetans to dispossess the Tang in central Asia. Population pressure with peasant unrest caused a Tang collapse in 907. The 53-year interlude between the Tang and Song dynasties is known as the Four Dynasties and Ten Kingdoms.

Northern warlordism co-existed with southern political fragmentation until a usurping Chou palace guard, Taizu, established the Song dynasty and reunified ethnic China. The Song state was rich in commerce, aided by developing road and canal networks. Stimulated by large-scale coal and iron industries, the wealth and civilization attracted the

A SEAFARING RACE
The sight of Viking longboats approaching the shore must have terrified the inhabitants of the many nations they visited, with violent raids or the establishment of permanent settlements real possibilities. However, the Vikings were usually content to trade with those they visited, and their reputation as a brutal and brutish race detracts from their many achievements, particularly in the fields of ship construction and exploration.

neighboring Jurchen (known as the Jin dynasty), who seized northern China. Some Song established a southern state, based on Hangzhou in Zhejiang province. Ultimately, the Song were destroyed in 1279 after Mongol invasions.

INDIA

Neighboring India was subject to numerous Muslim raids by the Ghaznavids. In 1160, they were displaced by Muhammad of Gur who campaigned in India from 1175. By 1205, Gurid forces had seized the Indo-Ganges Plain. Eventually, harsh rule incurred rebellions by both Muslims and Hindus, so weakening this Sultanate that Tamerlane defeated the Sultan at Panipat while annexing the Punjab.

JAPAN

Further east, Japan looked to the example set by Korea and China, particularly with respect to the idea of imperial rule. Local territorial lords known as daimy-lords competed with samurai warriors for power and control of the Emperor. Under Empress Suiko (593–628), a reform program commenced, including the draft of a constitution. The Fujiwara clan seized power and began the Taika Reforms aimed at strengthening the Emperor.

All arts flourished and Buddhism spread, sometimes blending with Shinto. By 1028, Fujiwara power had declined and this made way for civil wars between the Taira and Minamoto families, the latter winning and thus bringing to an end these Gempei Wars. Military government (bakafu) commenced for 700 years, developing Japanese feudalism and the samurai culture.

NORTH AMERICA

In North America, a series of civilizations developed. In the Southwest the Hohokam people inhabited southern Arizona and northern Sonora, the region lying across major continental trade routes. Key features of this culture were canal-based water management and ball courts. These ball courts had an important place in society and the game was involved in a number of ritual activities in addition to providing entertainment.

Elsewhere, the four corners of Utah, Colorado, Arizona, and New Mexico were home to the Anasazi between 100 BC and AD 1140. Noted for their adobe terraced homes and irrigation systems, powerful settlements grew at Chaco Canyon and Pueblo Bonito. Probably destroyed by drought, the former was abandoned. The Anasazi are thought to be the ancestors of the Hopi and Zuni.

The Mississippian Mound Builder culture lasted between AD 750–1500 or later. An important center was Cahokia,

Illinois, with a mound covering 160 acres (65 hectares), being 98 feet (30 meters) high. Society was a rigidly stratified religious society ruled by the Great Sun. At one time Cahokia had as many as 50,000 inhabitants but the Mississippian centers were abandoned by the early 17th Century.

Native American economies were essentially agricultural but trade grew up along well-defined routes. The Mississippi and its tributaries linked north to south while a main east–west route followed the St. Lawrence and the Great Lakes. A trail extended the length of the Appalachians. Other rivers like the Colorado and the Columbia were important. Goods were transported by canoe, dugout, and dog travois.

Some 1000 Native American languages are currently spoken in the Americas, while hundreds more have become extinct. These languages can be divided into about 62 families, but linguists disagree as to their nature. Examples are Uto-Aztecan, and Athabaskan such as Navajo. Not all languages can be fitted into a family, like the Timucuan language of Florida.

THE SPREAD OF ISLAM

By 705, Islam had spread to Morocco. The evangelized Berber population spread across the Sahara, their trade routes reaching Algeria, Ghana, the Songhay, and on into Spain. Their power moved with them. At the eastern end of North Africa, the Fatamid caliphate of Egypt maintained its influence by using Berber, Sudanese slaves, and Mamelukes (Turkish slave cavalry). The Mameluke General Saladin took over Fatamid rule, founding the Ayyubid dynasty that eventually succumbed to the Mamelukes. They ruled a vast Muslim Empire comprising Egypt, Palestine, Syria, and both Red Sea coastlines.

Muslim expansion generated a Christian reaction in Palestine and Spain. The Crusades that took place between 1095 and 1270 were motivated by a mixture of religious fervor and the desire for trade, plunder, and lands. Christian knights established a number of Crusader states at Jerusalem, Antioch, Edessa, and Tripoli. Saladin reduced Crusader territories to three coastal cities after defeating the knights at Hattin in 1187. The fight against Islam in Spain was led by Leon–Castile and Aragon. Aided by military orders of knights, pressure was exerted with a victory at Los Navas de Tolosa in 1212, which led to a general Muslim decline. Granada, the last Muslim state, was captured in 1492 by Isabella of Castile and Ferdinand II of Aragon.

In the East the Ottoman state expanded into an Anatolian power vacuum during the fourteenth century. In 1355, the Turks crossed into Europe rapidly conquering much of the Balkans, Constantinople (1453), and most of the Black Sea coast. North Africa, Egypt, Palestine, Mesopotamia, parts of the Caucasus, the edges of Arabia, Hungary, Moldavia, and

STRUGGLE FOR THE HOLY LAND
Saladin was born around 1138 in Tikrit and, through a series of military and political maneuverings, rose to become Sultan of Egypt and Syria, forming the Ayyubid dynasty. But it is for his struggles against the forces of the Crusaders in the Middle East that Saladin is best known. He was a brilliant military leader, able to inspire great loyalty in his men and great fear in his enemies, and by the late 1180s he had recaptured virtually all Crusader cities. He eventually came to a settlement with King Richard I of England, whereby the city of Jerusalem would stay under Muslim control but would be open to Christian pilgrims. This agreement was set out in the Treaty of Ramla in 1192.

Wallachia followed, with other states becoming vassals. In 1526, Suleiman I the Magnificent defeated the Hungarians at Mohacs and unsuccessfully laid siege to Vienna.

AFRICAN CIVILISATIONS

During the 8th Century, the Empire of Ghana was administered by Islamic civil servants. This state depended upon agriculture and iron work while receiving trade across the Sahara. Iron and horses made Ghana militarily strong until overthrown by the Almoravids in 1076. By 1235, a new wealthy Empire of Mali succeeded with Timbuktu becoming a cultural center and focus of the Akan goldfields.

The most extensive Malian state was the 16th-Century Songhay Empire, situated on the Niger River bend. Expansion led to the capture of Mali and control of the Hausa states and Bornu-Kanem with a northern border reaching Morocco. As well as being a commercial empire, Songhay was home to Timbuktu's center of Koranic study. Bornu-Kanem eventually shrugged off Songhay influence and the rule of Idris Alooma (1580–1603) saw trade reaching North Africa and the Ottomans. Africa also saw the Horn of Africa host an expansionist Christian Ethiopian state and a Muslim Somali Kingdom of Adal.

Africa has a complex language structure. There are four main language groups:

- the Niger–Congo, first spoken to the west of Lake Chad;
- the Nilo–Saharan negroid languages;
- Afro-Asiatic, used in the north and northeast; and,
- the Khoisan language of the San.

These groups can be subdivided and some tongues have migrated from one region to another.

INVASION FROM THE EAST
Mounted on horseback and armed with deadly arrows, Mongol archers were highly feared by their enemies. Under the leadership of Genghis Khan, who had united the nomadic tribes of Mongolia, the Mongols moved west, acquiring central Asia, Persia, Mesopotamia, Tibet, and the Viet lands. With their raids into Russia, the rest of Europe was put on alert to the new threat from the east.

THE GROWTH OF TRADE

During the Middle Ages, the European economy expanded as a result of Genoese and Venetian trade with the Near East, a result of Arab decline. Italy acquired immense wealth exchanging exotic goods with northern Europe. There, the Hanseatic League controlled the Baltic and Low Country trade, much wealth being based on wool and textile production.

Co-existing with innovations in trade and industry was the growth of the Holy Roman Empire. In Germany, after Charlemagne's Empire was divided, Saxon King Henry II, the Fowler (918–936) and his son, Otto I the Great (936–973), spread their influence through the imperial duchies, bolstered by papal support. The resultant Holy Roman Empire lasted until 1804 when it was eventually destroyed by Napoleon I.

ASIAN AGGRESSION

Christian Europe faced a major threat from the east. In Mongolia, Ghengis Khan united nomadic tribes and invaded, defeated but did not occupy northern China and Manchuria. His power grew and with his successors the Mongols acquired central Asia, Persia, Mesopotamia, Tibet and the Viet lands while revisiting and seizing northern China and Korea. Kublai Khan, Ghengis's grandson (1225–1294), conquered southern China and invaded Tibet Annam and Tonking. Successful wars were waged against Burma but two seaborne invasions of Japan in 1274 and 1281 failed badly.

In Russia, the Mongols or Tatars attacked the Volga Bulgars in 1236 before seizing nine Russian principalities, which were forced to pay tribute. Only Novgorod, Pskov and some smaller principalities maintained independence. In central Europe, Hungary was targeted. Tatar toumans swept through Poland while others ravaged Hungary forcing King Bela IV to fight at Mohi where he lost 70,000 men. Elsewhere, Poland was damaged with Cracow being burnt. A German-Polish army under Henry II of Silesia was next destroyed at Leignitz in 1241.

These early population movements came about for a variety of reasons. There was an ever-present need to secure territorial boundaries and in some cases there was simply a desire for expansion for expansion's sake, since a larger territory brought more wealth. There was also a growing interest in trade as a way of boosting wealth and this led to a developing interest in world exploration.

WORLD EXPLORATIONS

MONGOLIAN EXPANSION

The Mongolian Empire of Kublai Khan was augmented by tribute from states in Malaya, Ceylon, and southern India as well as from the Siamese kingdoms of Xieng-mai and Sukhotai. When ruling China, the Mongols were aided by Qidans, Chinese, and Jurchens. Chinese bureaucracy generally continued and under the Mongol Yuan dynasty, the Chinese economy expanded to become part of a vast trading network tied into the Near East and Europe. Safe roads and the renovation and expansion of the canal system facilitated the movement of goods. Other trade routes entered Southeast Asia. The Mongols practiced religious toleration, with Buddhists receiving special favor. Nestorian Christianity had an archbishopric in Beijing in 1275 and Muslim communities developed as trade grew between Persia and the Arab world. Artistic life flourished under the Mongols in terms of novels, poetry, and calligraphy. Zhao's pictures of horses and Qian Xuan's portrayal of insects and flowers were brilliant.

EARLY VISITORS TO CHINA

Two early visitors to China were Marco Polo and Ibn Batuta. The former traveled to China in 1271 with his father and uncle. He entered Kublai Khan's diplomatic corps and journeyed to Yunnan, Burma, Tibet and along the Yangzi, Yellow, and Mekong river systems. He recorded his observations in *Il Milione*. He was particularly impressed by paper money, the vast urban sprawl of Hangzhou, coal, the postal system, canals, and the multi-masted, multi-decked junks with bulk-headed watertight compartments.

Ibn Batuta was another world traveler. He was born in 1304 and educated in Tangier. Before he eventually arrived in China, he had made a pilgrimage to Mecca, travelled to Timbuktu in Mali, explored the east coast of Africa, visited Turkey, southern Russia, Arabia, Syria, the Central Asian oasis khanates, and explored the coasts of India and Ceylon. His travel book, *Rihlah*, details his journeys. Arriving at Quanzhou near Xiamen, he went to Beijing as Sultan Mohammed of India's envoy.

CHRISTOPHER COLUMBUS & THE CARIBBEAN

In August 1492, Columbus sailed from Spain reaching the Bahamas, with other landings in Cuba and Hispaniola. Columbus's second expedition in 1493 saw the start of the Spanish conquest of the Caribbean. The expedition called at Dominica, Guadeloupe, Antigua, and Hispaniola where the colony of Isabella was established. Columbus met Arawaks who inhabited the Greater Antilles, Cuba, Hispaniola, Jamaica, and Puerto Rico. Other groups were the Guanahatabegs and the Caribs in the Lesser Antilles.

Relations between the Spanish and the Arawaks began to break down in the face of brutal evangelization and racism. Indians were compelled to pan gold and any rebellions were suppressed with cavalry and fierce dogs. 1495 and 1496 saw European epidemics spread through the islands as well as famine. Some Indians killed their children and committed suicide rather than live under Spanish cruelty and slavery. Depopulation was so rapid that the 5 peso cost of an Indian slave in 1508 reached 150 pesos in 1509.

CHINESE EXPANSION DURING THE MING DYNASTY

The Ming dynasty between 1368 and 1647 saw China's most expansionist and innovative period. Ming prestige was raised by its fleets announcing the reign of Emperor Yanglo throughout Southeast Asia to Java and southern India. Admiral Zheng He's expeditions reached Vietnam, Java, Sumatra, Ceylon, Siam, Somalia, and the African coast to Zanzibar. The emissaries of more than thirty states paid homage to China enhancing China's diplomatic prestige.

The largest of Zheng's ships was nearly 500 feet (152 meters) long and 180 feet (55 meters) wide and carried about 1,000 men. The rudder alone of one of Zheng's capital ships was, at 36 feet (11 meters), half as long as Columbus's Nina. The Nina's displacement was a mere 100 tons compared to the 3,100 ton displacement of Zheng's largest ships. In all Zheng made seven voyages, the last comprising several hundred ships and 27,750 men. Compare this with Vasco da Gama's Portuguese expedition in 1498 with four ships and only 170 men.

EARLY ENGLISH COLONIZATION IN NORTH AMERICA

Before colonists established an English presence in North Carolina, the shoreline of the Atlantic was home to several small tribes: Poteskeet, Pasquotank, Yeopim, Chowanok, Moratoc, Roanoc, Machapunga, Hatteras, Pamlico, and Secotan. In 1578 Walter Raleigh reconnoitred the coast and during a second voyage in 1584, reached Roanoke Island, meeting the Secotans. In 1585, a colony was established there but was pulled out by Francis Drake in 1586 after a disease decimated the Secotan and Chowanoc, causing war and the slaughter of a Secotan settlement.

A third expedition established a colony, which a later expedition found to be completely deserted. Eventually, in 1607, the Virginia Company established Jamestown on Chesapeake Bay. This settlement flourished, beginning commercial tobacco production in 1612 and introducing black slaves in 1619. Here, John Rolfe was married to Pocohontas which did not prevent Powhattan confederacy attacks in 1622 and 1644. The English response was to seize land and kill Indians, the 10,000 Powhattans being reduced to hundreds.

SPANISH CONQUEST

Two Native American civilizations were completely obliterated by the Spanish Conquistadors. The Aztecs had founded their capital city, Tenochtitlan in Mexico in 1345 and by 1500, they controlled an empire stretching from the Gulf of Mexico to the Pacific, including parts of Guatemala. Aztec food is well known today: cocoa, vanilla, chillis, peppers, avocado, mango, papayas, tomatoes, beans, and squash.

Aztec religion demanded blood sacrifices and captives in war were the victims. This created many enemies and these allied with Hernan Cortés when his Spanish forces fought their way into the capital in 1521.

Meanwhile, in the Andes the Inca Empire ranged from southern Columbia, across Ecuador and Peru, to Bolivia and northern parts of Argentina and Chile. This agricultural theocracy was ruled by the Sapa Inca, believed to be an incarnation of the sun. In 1532, Francisco Pizarro landed in Peru with 180 men during a civil war between competitors for the Inca throne. Pizarro conquered the empire, strangling the Sapa Inca Atahualpa and built a capital at Lima.

THE FRENCH IN CANADA

The French first arrived in Canada around the year 1500, attracted by the rich reserves of cod to be found there. Some fish were dried onshore and fur trading took place with the native Montaignais and Beothuk. The prospect of wealth drew Cartier to the St. Lawrence where he established an unsuccessful settlement near Québec in the 1530s. In 1608, Champlain prospered at Québec by trading with the Huron and Algonquin tribes. Commercial routes were established through the Great Lakes with portages to the Saskatchewan River. The impact on Native Americans was immense. The Montagnais, the Algonquin, and the Huron inhabited the headwaters of the Saguenay, Ottawa River valley and Lake Huron respectively. These tribes waged war against the Iroquois in order to gain a monopoly over French trade by driving them south of the St. Lawrence. Champlain and French musketeers aided the Huron against the Onondaga. Angry Iroquois then turned on the Huron and New France and aided the English in subsequent colonial wars.

MARITIME EXPLORATION

The tales of Marco Polo and other travelers encouraged the mounting of expeditions to find ways of sailing to the Orient to obtain silks and spices rather than having to rely on overland routes, which were subject to Ottoman customs tolls. Prince Henry the Navigator had his Portuguese sailors explore courses to the Azores, Cape Verde, and in 1498 Vasco da Gama reached India.

Coastal fortifications secured the route and opened up slave markets. Almeida and Albuquerque built up a Portuguese commercial empire in Goa, Ceylon, Malacca and the East Indies. Other explorers such as Columbus, Vespucci and Magellan sought China by sailing west or southwest.

The Americas were found and once the Spaniards failed to find a route to China from the Caribbean, they took to plundering and enslaving urban Native American civilizations. Scientific expeditions sometimes motivated exploration, especially in the Pacific, with voyages by Captains Wallis, Cook, and Clarke.

AMERICAN COLONIZATION

Many countries attempted to colonize North America, the major ones being the French and English, but there was also a small Dutch and Swedish presence. France confined its activities to Canada and the Mississippi being mainly interested in the fur trade rather than permanent colonization. Many English settlers went for religious reasons in order to practice their faiths without interference. These included Protestants, Roman Catholics, and Quakers.

English settlers increased rapidly, but there was competition for land with Native Americans as the newcomers encroached on the latter's fields and hunting grounds. Bitter conflicts developed, such as the Pequot War of 1636 to 1637 and King Philip's War from 1675 to 1676. Likewise, the Dutch fought the Delaware and Esopus peoples in various wars between 1639 and 1664.

On the Mississippi, the French destroyed the Natchez, an aristocratic theocracy. A Natchez remnant took refuge with the Chickasaw then the Cherokee. Meanwhile, the Spaniards faced a major uprising in northern New Mexico in the area inhabited by the Pueblo Indians, especially the Tiwa, Tano, Towa, Tewa, Hopi, and Zuni nations.

The Caribbean and its surrounding lands were severely damaged by Native American encounters with Europeans. Spanish brutality virtually wiped out the Arawak and Caribs. Elsewhere, they visited Florida as a source of loot, land, and souls to convert. Their incursions were fiercely resisted by the Timucuan and Ais warriors. Survivors of the 1528 Narváez expedition fired up adventurers like De Soto and Coronado with tales of gold.

The French and English decided to interfere in the Caribbean, which up until then had been regarded as virtually a Spanish lake. The English became notorious buccaneers, raiding Spanish possessions from bases in the Greater Antilles. In 1623, the English settled on St. Kitts and then in Barbados in 1627.

Plantations relied on South American natives imported by Dutch and Spanish slavers as well as indentured labor. African slaves were preferred, especially in Jamaica, which had been captured from Spain by the English in 1655. The island became a staging post for the Atlantic slave trade in the slave triangle.

The Spanish Empire in the Americas stretched deep into the heart of the north, through Central America and down the Andean chain to Chile. The Mexican lands were opened up by Jesuit and Franciscan missions. They forced Indians to pay tribute in maize, skins, and eventually labour.

The Spanish colonial system had a social hierarchy based upon the amount of Spanish blood a person had. After creoles, mestizos and zambos came the Indians and finally the black slaves. The agricultural economy was based on domestic animals and grains while silver was exploited in Mexico and Peru.

Although some Spaniards such as Bartolomé de Las Casas tried to protect them, in general the Indians were ruthlessly exploited, either by providing a servile labor pool in the mines or by giving tribute, labor or service to the Spanish.

EUROPEAN INTEREST IN AFRICA

European encounters in Africa followed the Portuguese formula by creating fortified trading stations, originally around the coast of Guinea. Portuguese influence and control centered on Luanda on the west coast, but there were many enclaves on the east coast, especially around Kilwa, Mombasa, Mozambique, and the Zambesi River.

England, France, Denmark, and Brandenburg were other competitors for trade in goods and slaves. The French dominated Senegal and Gambia while the others were settled on the gold and slave coasts.

Many African peoples profited by selling other Africans to Europeans, exemplified by the Mandingo and Fulani.

Eventually, the Dutch annexed all the Portuguese trading posts on the Atlantic coast of Africa through the good offices of the Dutch East India Company. In 1652, the Company founded a way station at the Cape of Good Hope to act as a market garden for Company ships.

Although often against the Company wishes, Dutch settlers began to move inland to farm. The Dutch word for farmer is "boer" and the Boers were the original white colonists of Africa. A new era had begun.

THE AGE OF COLONIAL EXPANSION

The eighteenth and nineteenth centuries saw the emergence of European empires, which competed for land, trade, and strategic bases.

THE AMERICAS

The English colonies in North America ran from Maine southward to Georgia, comprising thirteen states. The colonies raised cattle and grain, tobacco, rice, and indigo, with a growing ironwork and ship-building industry. The colonies were important sources of food for the West Indies and southern Europe.

Central and southern America were divided into Spanish vice-royalties, while the Portuguese had Brazil. Imports of Spanish silver into Europe caused serious inflation.

East coast America saw considerable population growth. More people arriving required more land and this continued expansion soured relations with Native Americans. The Tuscaroras attacked European settlers and other tribes alike. Their slave trade generated a Swiss-English-Indian counterattack leading to the enslavement of a thousand Tuscaroras.

Enmity between Huron and Iroquois led them and other tribes to join either France or England in a series of wars: King William's War from 1689 to 1697, Queen Anne's War from 1701 to 1713, King George's War from 1743 to 1748 and the French and Indian War of 1755 to 1763. These all brought the European balance of power firmly into the Americas.

Colonial frontiers in North America had been fairly static until colonial trade demonstrated that Atlantic commerce was important to European states. In 1699 the French added Biloxi in Louisiana to the population centers that they already controlled at Québec and Montréal. The Treaty of Utrecht saw British sovereignty recognized over the Hudson Bay, Newfoundland, and Nova Scotia.

When the French began the construction of forts in the Ohio Valley this was a precursor to a war in which the English acquired Canada. The subsequent seizure of French territories led Britain to realize that it should generate an imperial policy rather than just allowing its colonies to look after themselves.

During these early years the North American colonies were the destination of numerous migrants. Southern England supplied many, especially from Protestant East Anglia. Dutch settlers moved to New York state and a growing Swedish population was located on the River Delaware. Many German Lutherans arrived and some Moravians founded Salem. Scots-

KING WILLIAM'S WAR
King William III claimed the thrones of England and Scotland during the Glorious Revolution of 1689, a coup d'état in which the Catholic King James II was deposed from power. On becoming king, one of William's first moves was to resist French power, and he formed the Grand Alliance against the French with Leopold I of the Holy Roman Empire. As part of the resulting War of the Grand Alliance, the English opposed the French presence in North America, and this struggle on the American continent is known as "King William's War."

AMERICAN CIVIL WAR
The four-year civil war fought in the United States between 1861 and 1865 remains the most traumatic event in the nation's 230-year history. Concerned by President Abraham Lincoln's opposition to slavery, 11 southern states declared their intention to break from the union and form the Confederate States of America under a new president, a move that sparked hostilities between the Confederates and the northern Union states. The decisive battle came at Gettysburg in 1863, after which the Confederates were always on the back foot. The war ended in 1865, with Confederate General Robert E. Lee surrendering to Union General Ulysses S. Grant at the Battle of Appomattox Courthouse.

Irish abounded in the interior borderlands while dispossessed Highland Scots poured into North Carolina.

To this must also be added the enforced migration of many Africans who were entering America into the world of slavery.

Meanwhile, further south the influence of Spain was on the decline, mainly due to a combination of activity by pirates and the English government. European wars spread to Spanish possessions and the 1763 Treaty of Paris awarded Florida to Britain. Elsewhere, Spanish missions had secured Texas but in 1751 missionary activity in Arizona faced Apache, Yavapai, and Pima rebellion. 1752 witnessed the construction of the Tubac presidio in Arizona to re-establish Spanish control. However, the missions incubated diseases and as a result the Tekesta, Calusa and Ais tribes were completely wiped out.

British governmental interference in its American colonies was gradually growing. There had been general resentment against the Proclamation of Indian Territory in 1763, while in 1765 the oppressive Stamp Act caused riots in Boston. The Townshend Acts and the Québec Act eventually caused the first Continental Congress at Philadelphia in 1774. In 1775 open rebellion broke out at Lexington and Concord and with the Battle of Bunker Hill the real conflict began.

The American War of Independence finally ended when the Treaty of Paris granted the United States of America full sovereignty in 1783.

80 years later the United States was locked in a bitter Civil War Lasting from 1861 to 1865. The Southern Confederates believed that Republican President Lincoln's election would lead to economic ruin and political domination with a loss of the investments in slavery.

The old order was broken and African-Americans were admitted into the US Army units for the first time since the War of Independence, although not in integrated units. Native Americans fought on each side in Indian Territory, with Chief Stand Watie of the Cherokee Nations being the last Confederate general to surrender. Civil war battles were horrendous and Gettysburg in1863 was the turning point. By now Confederate fortunes were so damaged that Southern armies were always on the defensive. At the end of the war in his Gettysburg Address, Abraham Lincoln defined democracy as "government of the people, by the people, for the people."

AFRICA

By 1600, the majority of Black Africa was tied into trade networks linked to the outside world. The Arabs established routes in the Sahel, northern Sudan, and the east coast. Portuguese vessels connected the European Atlantic states to Africa and Portugal gained Mombasa after its devastation by Zimba cannibals. The Sahel and Sudan imported horses, textiles, salt, glassware, and metalware and occasionally tobacco and alcohol. Africa exported mainly gold and slaves.

The Atlantic slave trade flourished from the late seventeenth to early nineteenth centuries. Typically it followed a triangular route. English goods were shipped to Africa, especially Guinea and the Bight of Benin and exchanged for slaves. These were taken to the West Indies and America where they were exchanged for goods such as molasses, sugar, rum, and tobacco, which was then brought back to ports such as Bristol.

The Americans sailed from Boston and Newport with rum and other goods, collecting slaves who were transported to Brazil and the West Indies. Again, the slaves were swapped for molasses and sugar, which were distilled into rum. The Southern colonial economy was underpinned by slave labor, whereas further north slaves were generally used either as domestic servants or artisan labor.

About 1830, Africa witnessed the time of troubles when the Zulu leader, Shaka, who expanded his empire by displacing other tribes who fled to Mozambique or the high veldt. The British had acquired coastal enclaves at Freetown, the Gold Coast, and Cape Colony, while the French had gained Senegal with the Portuguese remaining in Mozambique and Angola.

African rulers were expanding their borders as the West African jihad states developed and Mohammad Ali in Egypt took on his Turkish masters. Elsewhere, Sultan Sayyid of Oman acquired control of the East African coast and Zanzibar.

ASIAN COLONIZATION

Asia in the late sixteenth century experienced many changes in fortune. Ming China was under attack from revived Mongol power while 1592 saw the Japanese military dictator Toyotomi Hideyoshi invading Korea, with a further invasion in 1597–98. His troops advanced to the Yalu River but were repulsed by a Ming counterattack.

Muslim strength in India manifested itself in Babar's invasion. His Mughal Empire was consolidated by Akbar between 1556 and 1605. He acquired Bengal, Sind and much of the Deccan with the Rajput princes forced to pay tribute. Akbar's marriage to a Rajput princess introduced a tolerance towards Hinduism.

Akbar's descendants continued his expansion but Shajahan's son, Aurangzeb, usurped the throne and persecuted the Hindus causing a rebellion. The Sikhs, Marathas and Jats attacked the empire, which collapsed following Aurangzeb's death in 1707.

India had long been a center of war between Britain and France. 1696 saw the British East India Company possessing three fortified trading centers at Calcutta in Bengal, Madras on the Carnatic coast and Bombay on the west coast. Imperial competition with France commenced when French trade penetrated India after the War of Austrian Succession from 1740 to 1748. Anglo-French rivalry weakened the Company with each side supporting different candidates for the Nizam of the Deccan and the Nawab of the Carnatic.

Robert Clive halted the French with the seizure of Arcot in 1751, the capture of French Chandernagor in 1757 and the defeat of the French-backed Nawab Siraj-ud-Daulah at Plassey also in 1757. British supremacy was underlined by defeating the Dutch in 1759 and seizing French Pondicherry. This was all ratified by the terms of the 1763 Treaty of Paris.

A mixture of force, bribery, and diplomacy was used to create further British expansion in India. The Company became a British administrative agency in 1773 and Governor Wellesley made Hyderabad a virtual protectorate and Mysore a vassal. Half of Oudh was seized, the Carnatic was annexed and Ceylon captured. Other acquisitions were Assam, Tennasserim and Burma while the Marathas and Rajput states and the Sikhs were subjugated. The "doctrine of lapse," the acquisition of territories on the demise of a native ruler, secured other states.

Western policies helped generate the Indian Mutiny between 1857 and 1858. This was brutally crushed and 1858 witnessed India becoming a British viceroyalty with Victoria dubbed Empress of India in 1876. However, Indian discontent manifested itself in the foundation of the Indian National Congress in 1885.

Elsewhere, the Jurchen, under Nurhaci, attacked Ming China and won control over much of Manchuria, and acquired Korea as a vassal. Renamed as Manchus, their Qing dynasty gained northern China during a rebellion, annexing the south later. In Japan, the Tokugawa Shogunate remained prosperous and isolationist.

JAPAN

Japanese imperial expansion came to the fore in 1884 with the Sino-Japanese War. This admirably demonstrated Chinese weakness. The war was fought over who should be dominant in the Chinese client state, Korea. Japan wanted Korea for its strategic value and iron and coal deposits, while supporting modernizing groups in Korea. War broke out and Japan enjoyed swift victories. The 1895 Treaty of Shimonoseki forced China to recognize Korean independence while ceding to Japan Formosa, the Pescadores Islands, and the Liaotung peninsula. German, French, and Russian intervention forced Japan to reject the latter. China's defeat encouraged Western powers to seize parts of China while Japan built a large naval fleet and signed a defensive alliance with Britain (1902) and then went to war with Russia in 1904.

IMPERIALIST ASIA

The nineteenth century saw Asia colonized by imperialist powers. The British now dominated India, having annexed the Punjab and Burma. The British also dominated the Malay states and Borneo while having spheres of influence in Persia and Tibet, as well as having acquired treaty ports in China.

The French acquired Indo-China and penetrated Yunnan economically while Dutch power exerted itself throughout the Indonesia islands. The Americans defeated Spain and grabbed the Philippines. Russia seized Chinese coastal provinces southward from Siberia to Vladivostock and influenced Mongolia and Xingjiang. Britain and France divided Siam into spheres of influence while Russia joined Britain in Persia.

The Russians also expanded into Central Asia. The Kazakhs were brought under control with Russian settlements and bases established. The khanates were attacked with Uzbek territory acquired between 1853–55 and 1865 saw the capital, Tashkent, captured. The Bukharans suffered a similar fate being defeated in 1873. The Russians consolidated their imperial gains by building the Trans-Siberian railway, which required temporary occupation of Manchuria to reach Vladivostok by a branch line rather than traverse the Amur region.

GLOBALIZATION & TWENTIETH CENTURY CONFLICT

THE LEAD-UP TO WORLD WAR I

In 1900 world power rested in the hands of the European states and their respective empires. The USA and Japan were nothing more than bystanders, albeit ones that were becoming increasingly powerful themselves. On the face of it everything was peaceful, but behind the scenes lay considerable animosity. This animosity amongst the European countries sucked in new and old states into a system of conflicting alliances.

Germany had been unified into a Prussian controlled empire by a series of wars. The defeats of Denmark (1864), Austria (1866), and France (1870) had allowed Chancellor Bismarck to reform the German Confederation by annexing some states north of the River Main and Alsace-Lorraine, which were all joined to the southern states in the new Reich. This was strengthened by a German alliance with the Austro-Hungarian Empire in 1879.

Italy also later joined this alliance but only in a very tentative fashion. Italian unification dated from 1870. Unification was originally sponsored by the French Emperor Napoleon III who wanted Piedmont-Sardinia as a client state incorporating Lombardy-Venetia, Parma, Modena, and the Romagna within an Italian federation under the Pope. Austria lost an Italian war together with Lombardy. Plebiscites in other states together with Garibaldi's capture of Naples allowed these states to be swept into a new Italy, which gained Venice in 1866 and Rome in 1870.

Britain meanwhile allied with Japan in 1902, with France in 1904, and Russia in 1907.

GLOBAL WAR

The assassination of the Austrian Crown Prince in Sarajevo set off a chain reaction plunging Europe into a war that was eventually to involve the whole world. The Germans actioned the Schlieffen Plan but without full success. Eventually, the Western Front stabilized into 400 miles of trenches with various attempts to break through the lines.

Large set piece battles such as those at Ypres in 1915, the Somme in 1916 and Cambrai in 1917 led to thousands of casualties on both sides but achieved little. The deadlock shifted some combat to the skies and sea.

In the east, the Germans held the Russians until the latter collapsed in 1917. Various sideshows took place in the Dardanelles, Serbia, and Italy. The USA entered the war in 1917 and in 1918 the Germans sought an armistice after their army mutinied and the Kaiser abdicated. The war had been global

with the use of submarine warfare and offensives against Turkey in Palestine and one joined by T. E. Lawrence in Arabia.

Africa saw conflict in East Africa while the Japanese mopped up German possessions in Asia and the Pacific.

THE AFTERMATH

World War I had strained a fragile Russia. In February 1917 industrial unrest was rife and it continued as the soldiers refused orders to fire on the crowds. The seriousness of the revolt caused the abdication of Tsar Nicholas and liberal rule began in the Duma (parliament). The Bolsheviks sat on the sidelines biding their time and winning adherents with slogans such as "Peace, Bread, and Land." In October 1917, Lenin and the Bolsheviks grabbed power in Petrograd and then imposed rule over the whole of Russia during a Civil War.

The aftermath of World War I witnessed peacemakers at Versailles redrawing the map of Europe and the world. The German and the Austro-Hungarian Empires were divided and truncated. New states were created in central Europe and the Balkans while East Prussia was separated from Germany by a new Poland and Alsace-Lorraine was returned to France. Germany's overseas empire was split into League of Nations mandates controlled largely by Britain, France, and Japan.

20 YEARS OF DISCORD

By the 1920s China had suffered from a number of damaging wars between coalitions of warlords, which inflicted millions of casualties and destroyed civil government. The Japanese victory, foreign imperialism, and dynastic decline generated two Chinese political movements. Sun Yixian (Yat-sen) demanded the abolition of the Manchu dynasty and an end to foreign intervention and the extra-territorial rights of foreign powers. He also founded the Guomindang, the Chinese National Peoples Party. Alternatively, Kang Youwei wanted to reorganize the Chinese administration.

Sun's radical ideas overthrew the emperor and he founded a republic in 1912. However, the final arbiter of the political situation was Yuan Shikai, creator of China's modern Beijing Army, which had been used to crush unilateral declarations of independence by seven provinces. After agreeing to Japan's Twenty One Demands in 1915, Yuan proclaimed himself emperor in 1916 and died soon after. China then collapsed into warlordism in the 1920s, with Jiang Jieshi running the Guomindang forces.

Sun Yixian attempted to impose control with Jiang Jieshi purging the Communists who fled on the Long March north. In 1931, the Japanese occupied Manchuria and war with China ensued in 1937, notorious for the massacre at Nanking. Jiang's Guomindang, the Chinese Nationalists, were supplied by the

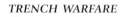

TRENCH WARFARE
The most enduring image of World War I is of soldiers fighting from trenches. Although trench warfare had been a feature of previous conflicts, it had never before been used on this scale, and the intensity of the fighting during World War I meant that about 10 percent of all soldiers died, compared to 5 percent in the Second Boer War and 4.5 percent during World War II. Machine guns, mortars, artillery, and gas were all used to devastating effect, but it was actually disease that claimed the most lives.

British and Americans from 1940.

During this period the imperialist hold on Africa was constantly subject to rebellions against all colonial powers. The Maghreb saw fierce resistance against the French in Morocco, the Spanish in the Rif, the Sanussi against the Italians, while Egyptians resisted the British. World War I had seen Germany lose its colonies and the resultant mandated territories were "guaranteed" political independence and territorial integrity.

Mussolini's Italian dictatorship commenced in 1922. He was the first fascist and he wished to reconstruct the Roman Empire in Africa by extending Italy's East African possessions into Ethiopia. After failing to get Britain to agree to divide the state he mounted an Italian invasion in 1935, the conquest being completed in 1937.

1929 saw the beginning of a Depression. This affected most countries and caused immense economic dislocation. Radical solutions were needed since impoverishment and malnutrition were beginning to take their toll. President Roosevelt's New Deal, British Keynesian economics, and Nazi Germany's economic government intervention helped ameliorate some of the ill effects but at the same time they helped to spawn extreme right-wing political parties in Europe.

The fragile European states that had been created by the Versailles Treaty began to suffer. The Depression had taken its toll, but a combination of intense nationalism, the fear of Bolshevism and political instability led to the search for a new way. People were prepared to forego individualism and democracy in order to have strong leadership, which lead to the growth in power of Hitler and Mussolini. Other countries developed fascist movements and Franco's "fascist" rebellion caused the Spanish Civil War.

WORLD WAR II

World War II commenced in Europe as a result of Hitler's desire to overthrow the Polish borders established by Versailles. Hitler conquered the European democracies and conducted a two-front war against Britain and the USSR. Eventual American involvement led to the D-Day invasion from England and Germany was squeezed between two armed forces leading to unconditional surrender on 8 May 1945.

World War II in Asia comprised a British rearguard action against Japanese expansion into Southeast Asia with its threat to India, while US intentions after Pearl Harbor in 1941 were to defeat Japanese forces in the Philippines and Indonesia. The 1942 Battle of Midway was a turning point against a Japan that was bogged down in China. Future sea battles in the Philippine Sea and at Leyte Gulf in1944 decimated the Japanese fleet while US forces island-hopped their way across the Pacific.

Meanwhile, the British fought back into Burma. Final Japanese defeat was caused by American strategic bombing and the destruction by atomic bomb of Hiroshima and Nagasaki on 6 and 9 August 1945 respectively.

WORLD WAR II – THE AFTERMATH

The 1939–45 war devastated populations, cities, and infrastructures throughout Europe. Rebuilding was essential and American aid through the Marshall Plan's European Recovery Program was welcomed by Western Europe whereas the Soviet Union regarded it as dollar imperialism. The aid stimulated European economic and political recovery with the added benefits of a collaboration aimed at a new European project as evidenced in the 1957 Treaty of Rome.

The different economic treatment meted out to Europe saw Eastern Europe, under Soviet pressure, establish the Council for Mutual Economic Assistance (Comecon) in 1949. Stalinist paranoia, the Yalta Conference in1945, the Kennan Telegram, and Churchill's Fulbright Speech helped consolidate ideological conflict and arms racing, establishing a Cold war.

This was evidenced by a nuclear standoff by two confrontational organisations, NATO (the North Atlantic Treaty Organisation) and the Warsaw Pact. Germany became a microcosm of the Cold War in Europe being divided into four zones; the west, controlled by Britain, France, and America, which later became the Federal German Republic and the east controlled by the USSR, which later became the German Democratic Republic.

Berlin was located in East Germany and that in turn was divided into four zones. In 1948 the USSR tried to force the Western powers out of Berlin by blockading all land routes to the Western sector. For the western powers this would have been a political disaster and the attempt was thwarted by an airlift operation that supplied the Western area for eleven months.

The weaknesses demonstrated by imperialist powers during World War II encouraged a struggle for independence. Britain gave independence to India and Pakistan in 1947 followed by all other Asian possessions. The Dutch and French resisted decolonizxation but were expelled from the East Indies in 1949 and Indochina in 1954. In the Middle East, Britain left Palestine to the United Nations.

African independence was rapid with most states achieving sovereignty in the early 1960s. Some anachronisms remained with Spanish and Portuguese rule continuing, Rhodesia declaring independence illegally and a white-run South Africa continuing to control South West Africa.

Aspects of the Cold War can be seen in the aftermath of decolonization in the Korean War, Cuban Missile Crisis, and

Vietnam War. 1949 witnessed Mao Zedong proclaiming the People's Republic of China and neighboring Korea was divided into North (Communist) and South (US dominated) regions. North Korea invaded the South in 1950. Ultimately, each side wanted unification on its own terms. The USA via the UN and China were sucked in with land and air battles, with an armistice finally being signed at Panmunjan in summer 1953.

In the USSR, Khrushchev engaged in international brinkmanship. Sino-Russian affairs were fraught so Khrushchev sought to project Soviet power elsewhere in the world. At Castro's request, he placed missiles in Cuba, bringing the USA within range. Determined resistance from the US with its naval blockade forced Khrushchev to back down with a quid pro quo by the USA reducing its missiles in Turkey.

When the French left Indochina, the country was partitioned along the 17th Parallel. Hostility between North and South generated war, with the USA increasingly supporting the corrupt South. Entering the fray in 1961, the USA encountered guerrilla fighting and a tough North Vietnamese army. By 1973, after sustaining large numbers of casualties, the US withdrew from Saigon, which was captured by the Communists in 1975 thus unifying Vietnam.

In 1991, the world observed the end of the Soviet Union, the final collapse of European communism commencing with the fall of the Berlin Wall in 1989. The USSR disintegrated into its constituent fifteen republics, dissolving into ethnic nationalist violence, especially in Chechnya, part of a Caucasian powder keg. With the collapse of the Warsaw Pact, some of its members joinied NATO, leaving the Russian Federation with a number of security issues still to address.

VIETNAM

Fought between 1959 and 1975, the Vietnam War was a war of unification, after the Geneva Peace Accords had partitioned the country in 1954. With the failure of political attempts to reunify the country, the Vietnamese Communist Party committed itself to revolutionary violence in order to bring about its goal of a unified nation. Determined to protect South Vietnam from falling into Communist hands, the United States committed more troops to its defense, and by 1965 around 200,000 American soldiers had been deployed, increasing to 553,000 by 1969. Despite these numbers and the huge arsenal of weaponry at their disposal, US forces faced a determined enemy in some of the harshest terrain imaginable. This, combined with widespread public opposition to the war at home, led the United States to sign the Paris Peace Accords in 1973, and by 1975 all of its soldiers had been withdrawn.

MIDDLE EASTERN CONFLICTS AND ISLAMIC EXTREMISM

Another region suffering war has been the Middle East. The creation of Israel has generated a War of Independence, the 1967 Six-Day War, the 1973 Yom Kippur War and various Lebanese crises. Only Egypt and Jordan have signed peace treaties with Israel. The issue of Palestinian independence has bedeviled regional peace. The foundation of a Palestinian Authority with some sovereignty in the Gaza Strip and the West bank has not satisfied Palestinian aspirations.

The Middle East erupted in 1991 in Gulf War. This was a postscript to the Iran-Iraq War of 1980 to 1988. Iraq, under the leadership of Saddam Hussein, wanted to reduce its foreign debt by seizing Kuwait's oil

fields. As a result of the Gulf War the Iraqi invaders were speedily removed, but immense damage was caused to Iraq's infrastructure.

In September 2001, terrorists crashed planes into the twin towers of the World Trade Center in New York and the Pentagon. Osama bin Laden and the Al Qaeda organisation were accused and they were already suspected of involvement in attacking US embassies in Tanzania and Kenya in1998 and a suicide attack on USS Cole off Yemen.

When the Afghan Taliban government refused to hand over bin Laden, US and British forces attacked Afghanistan and with local northern armies defeated the Taliban. The new government has failed to achieve full authority and 2007 witnessed US and British forces still embroiled in fights against Taliban remnants. The Al Qaeda version of terrorism has seen Muslim groups bombing in Bali, Madrid, and London. Meanwhile, in 2004, Russia suffered a terror/hostage situation at a school in Beslan, carried out by Chechen separatists.

In 2003 the USA and Britain were suspicious that Saddam Hussein was harboring Al Qaeda terrorists. He also failed to comply with UN monitoring of chemical and biological weapons. As a result a coalition of British and American forces invaded Iraq in order to bring down the Iraqi dictator and restore democracy. Although Saddam Hussein was subsequently captured and executed, reconstruction has proved difficult owing to armed conflict between Sunni and Shi'ite fighters and the inability of occupying forces to impose peace. As a result the country has descended into anarchy and in 2007 there is no foreseeable date when coalition forces will be withdrawn.

LOOKING TO THE FUTURE

Conflicts and world terrorist considerations aside, the major problem facing the world today is climatic change with global warming. Crop yields have diminished, hurricanes are more prevalent in the Caribbean, sea levels have risen, ice caps are melting. There is also evidence of increased seismic movement and a savage tsunami hit countries around the Indian Ocean in 2004, killing nearly 300,000 people. Although many scientists regard global warming as an inevitability, international discussions continue on ways to reduce this.

PART 1

HUMAN ORIGINS TO FIRST CIVILIZATIONS

THEORETICAL ORIGINS CONCERNING HUMAN origins abound, the most commonly held theory being that *Homo sapiens* developed in Africa. Penetrating the sub-Saharan barrier, hunter-gatherer man populated Europe, Asia, Australasia, and crossed the landbridge into the Americas. Cave societies developed with Neolithic humankind creating the first major civilizations along river valleys: the Nile; Tigris and Euphrates, the Indus, and the Huang Ho. In Europe, peoples spread along the Danube and eventually to the Atlantic. The development of each major civilization was linked to breakthroughs in irrigation techniques, agriculture, and the domestication of animals. Pigs, sheep, goats, cattle, donkeys, and horses were all used, providing meat, dairy products, and motive power. Developments in writing were crucial to early civilizations; Mesopotamia produced a series of societies renowned for their cuneiform script, while the Chinese Shang forged a written language based on pictograms. Language and power became increasingly connected, with highly literate societies often proving more dominant. All societies developed social stratification with elite priests and kings dominating their people. Prominent among early states were the Mitanni, the Hittites, Pharaonic Egypt, and Solomonic Israel. Societies benefited from the growth of urban civilization, differentiated labor, and metallurgy based on copper and bronze.

HUMAN ORIGINS; THE MIGRATION OF HOMO SAPIENS

THE LAST FOUR MILLION YEARS

HUMAN ORIGINS

Around four million years ago our early human ancestors were living and thriving on the grasslands of Africa.

Three million years later their descendants had developed stone tools such as axes and cutting edges. A million years on they were using fire to cook their food.

From these beginnings family groups coalesced into clans forming the earliest of societies. Their ways of life can be understood from rock paintings and some evidence of early religious belief can be gleaned from archaeological evidence found at sites such as Gambles Cave in Kenya.

The human species had begun its journey toward organized societies. Hunter gathers cooperated and controlled an area from which the essentials to maintain life could be controlled and exploited. The earliest remains that can be described as fully modern humans were unearthed in Africa; known as *Homo sapiens*, fossil remains date to around 130,000 years ago. These inventive and resourceful beings were capable of adapting to and colonizing the most marginal landscapes, displacing their Neanderthal rivals and becoming the sole surviving human species.

THE MIGRATION OF HOMO SAPIENS

Anthropologists believe that modern humans evolved in Africa and were equipped by experience and evolution to explore new environments. Approximately thirty thousand years ago humans had colonized the globe, coping with and adapting to the last ice age.

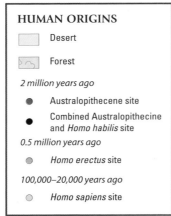

HUMAN ORIGINS

☐ Desert

☐ Forest

2 million years ago

● Australopithecene site

● Combined Australopithecine and *Homo habilis* site

0.5 million years ago

● *Homo erectus* site

100,000–20,000 years ago

● *Homo sapiens* site

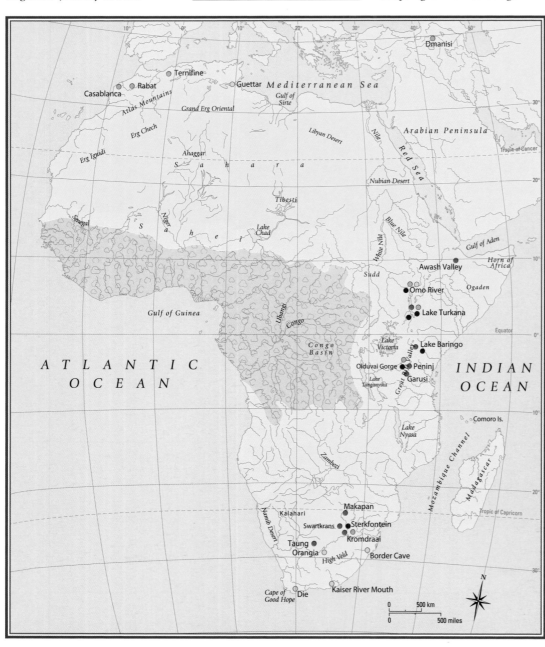

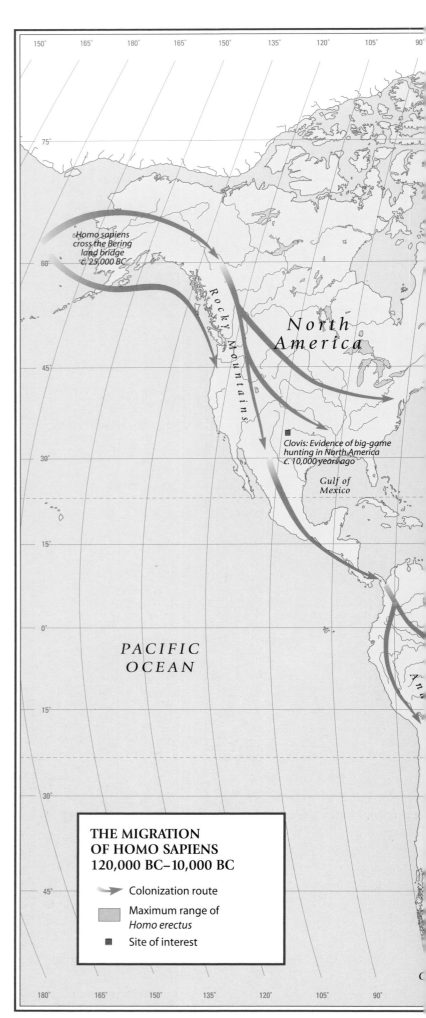

THE MIGRATION OF HOMO SAPIENS 120,000 BC–10,000 BC

→ Colonization route

☐ Maximum range of *Homo erectus*

■ Site of interest

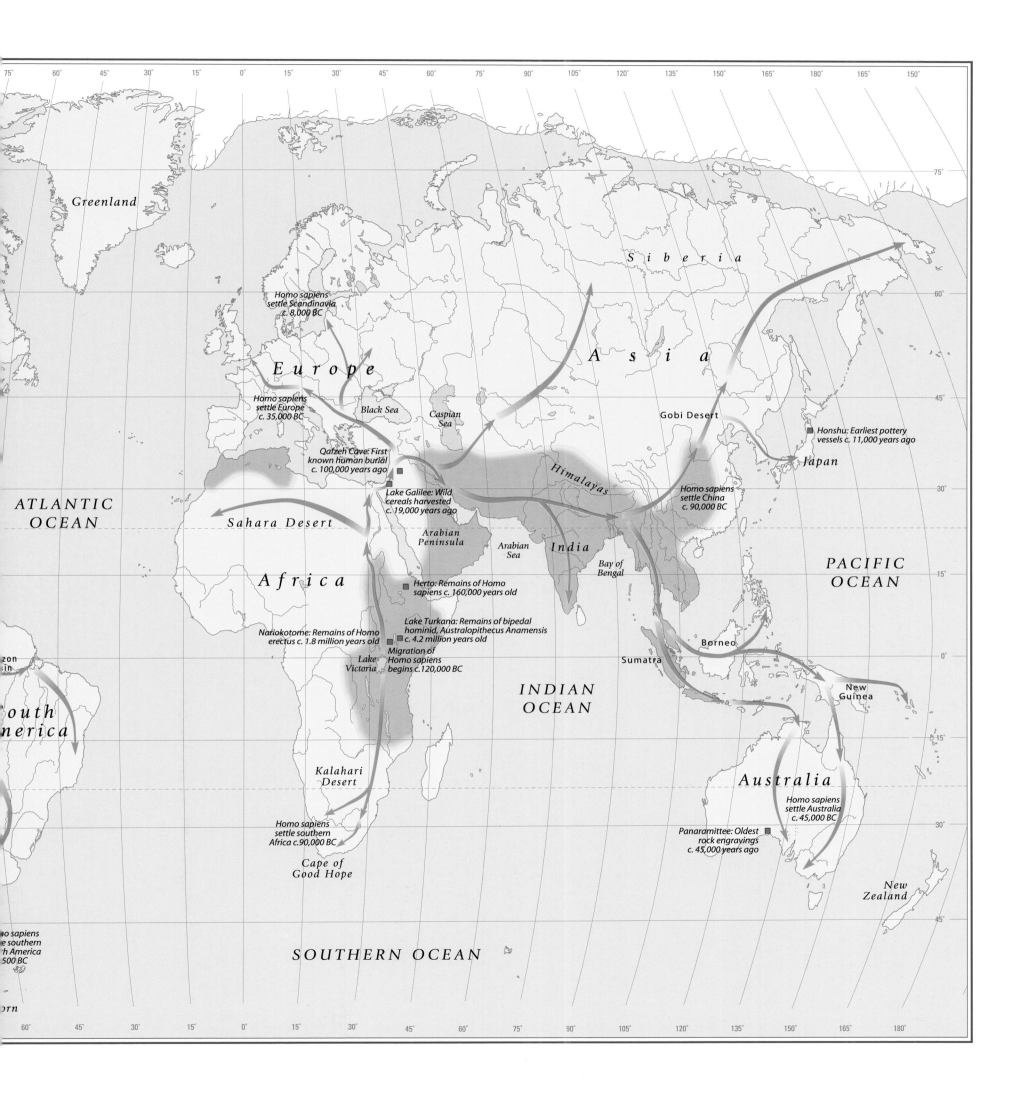

Greenland

Siberia

Homo sapiens
settle Scandinavia
c. 8,000 BC

Europe

Asia

Homo sapiens
settle Europe
c. 35,000 BC

Black Sea

Caspian
Sea

Gobi Desert

Honshu: Earliest pottery
vessels c. 11,000 years ago

Qafzeh Cave: First
known human burial
c. 100,000 years ago

Himalayas

Japan

Lake Galilee: Wild
cereals harvested
c. 19,000 years ago

ATLANTIC
OCEAN

Sahara Desert

Arabian
Peninsula

Arabian
Sea

India

Homo sapiens
settle China
c. 90,000 BC

PACIFIC
OCEAN

Africa

Bay of
Bengal

Herto: Remains of Homo
sapiens c. 160,000 years old

Nariokotome: Remains of Homo
erectus c. 1.8 million years old

Lake Turkana: Remains of bipedal
hominid, Australopithecus Anamensis
c. 4.2 million years old

Borneo

Migration of
Homo sapiens
begins c.120,000 BC

Sumatra

*outh
merica*

Lake
Victoria

INDIAN
OCEAN

New
Guinea

Australia

Kalahari
Desert

Homo sapiens
settle Australia
c. 45,000 BC

Homo sapiens
settle southern
Africa c.90,000 BC

Panaramittee: Oldest
rock engravings
c. 45,000 years ago

Cape of
Good Hope

New
Zealand

*o sapiens
e southern
h America
500 BC*

SOUTHERN OCEAN

25

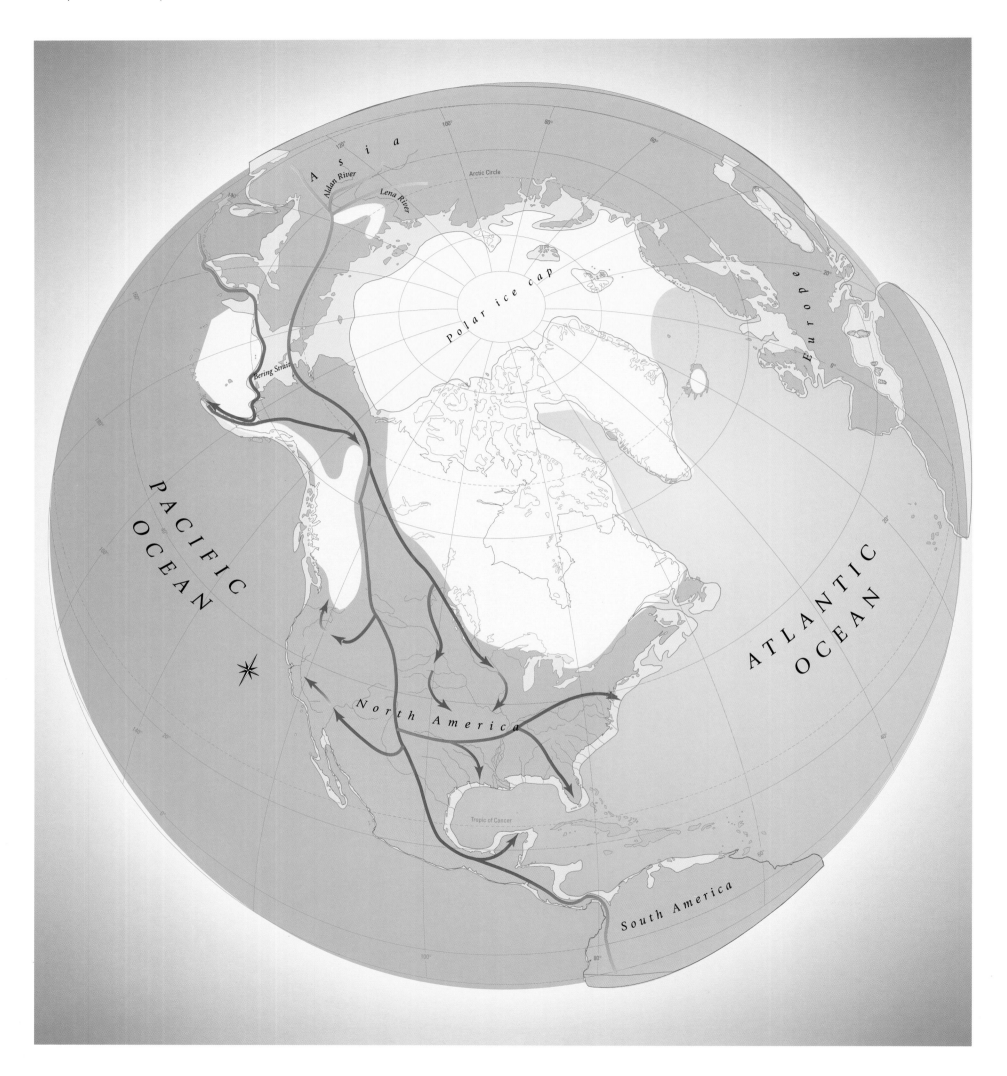

THE PEOPLING OF AUSTRALIA

LANDBRIDGE TO THE AMERICAS

There are a number of theories regarding the arrival of humans in the Americas, and the dates put forward for when this occurred range from 50,000 to 15,000 years ago.

A linguistic-based theory estimates three waves of immigration based on the language groups Amerind, Na-Dene and Eskimo-Aluit, while a model based on the study of many samples of mitochondrial DNA sequences taken from native North and South Americans supports the single wave of migration, where language diversification occurred post migration.

The route these early migrants took is also the subject of some dispute. However, the most likely route was via the landbridge which existed between the continents of America and Asia between 70,000 and 30,000 years ago. This grassy tundra-like wilderness, Beringia, would have supported some life, allowing nomadic people to feed themselves as they traveled from Asia to the Americas.

They may also have coasted along frozen coastline much as Eskimo Aluit people do to this day, allowing long distances to be covered in a relatively short time. It is likely that a combination of both were used in this population movement. From Beringia small family groups slowly traveled southward from Alaska through the ice-free corridor and exploited the lands south of the great ice sheets covering what is now Canada.

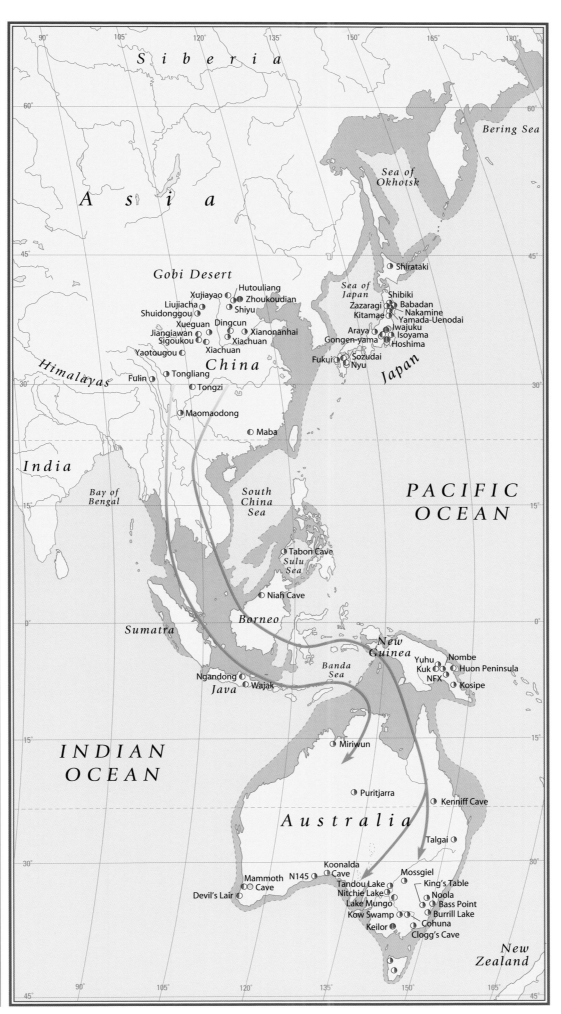

THE PEOPLING OF AUSTRALIA

It is estimated that the first people to arrive in what is now Australia arrived somewhere between 60,000 and 50,000 years ago. This movement of people was possible along two main routes, one originating in southern China and the other in south-east Asia. At periods of low sea levels the island chains of Sumatra, Java, Borneo, and the Philippines all became joined. The Australian landmass, however, was never joined to this group, leaving some 37–50 miles of open sea between the islands that comprised New Guinea, Australia, and Tasmania.

How this gap was crossed remains a mystery— excavations to date have shown no evidence of a sea-going technology. The major sites of Keilor and Lake Mungo are both over 30,000 years old and have revealed stone tools, cremation burials, and food remains.

By 10,000 years ago the dry hinterland of Australia had been settled and exploited, and the human population of the island had adapted to a desert environment.

LANDBRIDGE TO THE AMERICAS C. 18,000 YEARS AGO

- ⁓ Ancient coastline, c. 18,000 years ago
- ⁓ Modern coastline
- ▢ Ice cover, c. 18,000 years ago
- ➤ Probable migration routes

PEOPLING OF AUSTRALIA 50,000–10,000 BC

- ◐ 50,000–25,000 BC
- ◑ 25,000–10,000 BC
- ◕ 50,000–10,000 BC
- ○ Controversial evidence
- ➤ Colonization route
- ▨ Ancient coastline

7000 BC – 2000 BC SPREAD OF AGRICULTURE

SPREAD OF AGRICULTURE
Agriculture and domestication of animals reached southeastern Europe from the Near East around 6500 BC. In the following 2–3,000 years agriculture spread north and westward from the Balkans. As farming spread from the river valleys and nearby plains onto less productive soils, the clearing of forests followed by ploughing became an essential ingredient to the technology of farming. This required a plentiful supply of flint axes, whose makers became established across Europe. There was extensive trade, mostly along river routes, the

Loire, the Danube, and the Rhine being prime examples. As the population grew larger, societies began to undertake megalithic construction, the most famous being at Stonehenge in southern Britain and Carnac in western France. Gradually, dependency on stone tools declined with the mining of copper and later tin to produce bronze. The necessary specialization involved in this new metallurgy would suggest that society was becoming increasingly differentiated, with specialist tradesmen coexisting with farming societies. Grave finds containing bronze swords and

decorative items also suggest a growing social elite and the development of a warrior caste.

THE BEGINNINGS OF AGRICULTURE

Farming transformed the lives of our ancestors. With the change from nomadic or semi-nomadic lifestyles to settled farming communities, people began to exploit the available natural resources more efficiently, resulting in substantially improved crop yields. This, together with the domestication of animals, produced food surpluses that supported communities through the changing seasons.

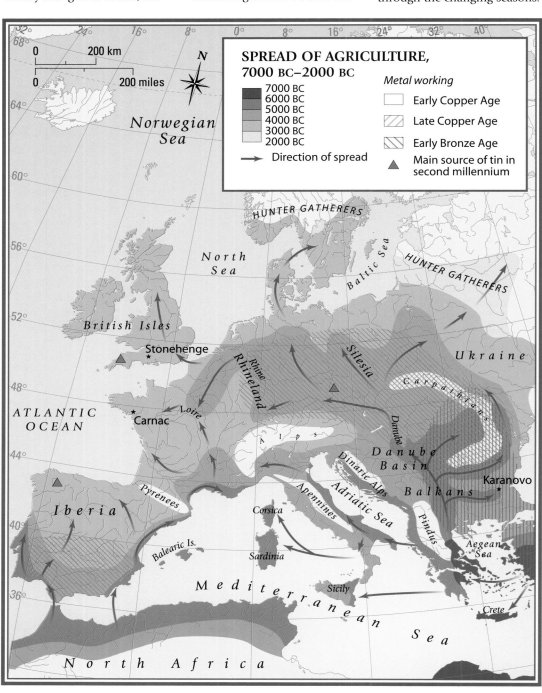

SPREAD OF AGRICULTURE, 7000 BC–2000 BC

7000 BC
6000 BC
5000 BC
4000 BC
3000 BC
2000 BC
→ Direction of spread

Metal working
☐ Early Copper Age
▨ Late Copper Age
▧ Early Bronze Age
▲ Main source of tin in second millennium

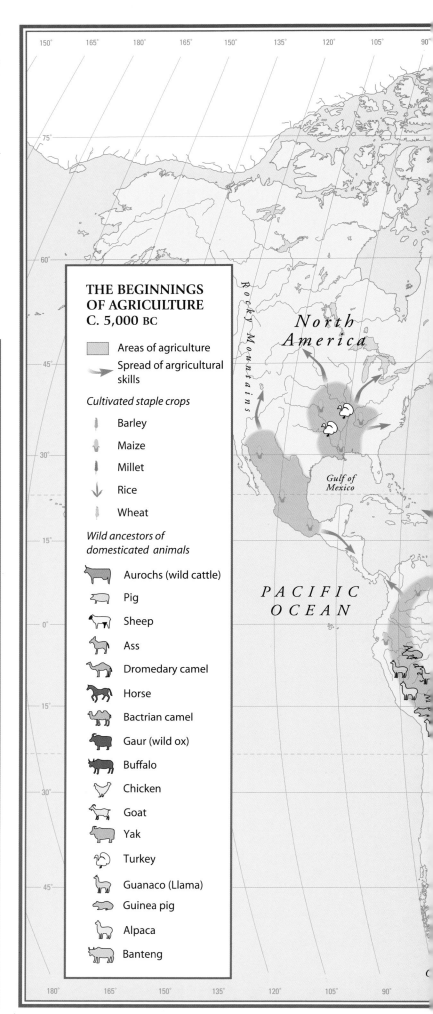

THE BEGINNINGS OF AGRICULTURE C. 5,000 BC

☐ Areas of agriculture
→ Spread of agricultural skills

Cultivated staple crops
Barley
Maize
Millet
Rice
Wheat

Wild ancestors of domesticated animals
Aurochs (wild cattle)
Pig
Sheep
Ass
Dromedary camel
Horse
Bactrian camel
Gaur (wild ox)
Buffalo
Chicken
Goat
Yak
Turkey
Guanaco (Llama)
Guinea pig
Alpaca
Banteng

THE BEGINNINGS OF AGRICULTURE

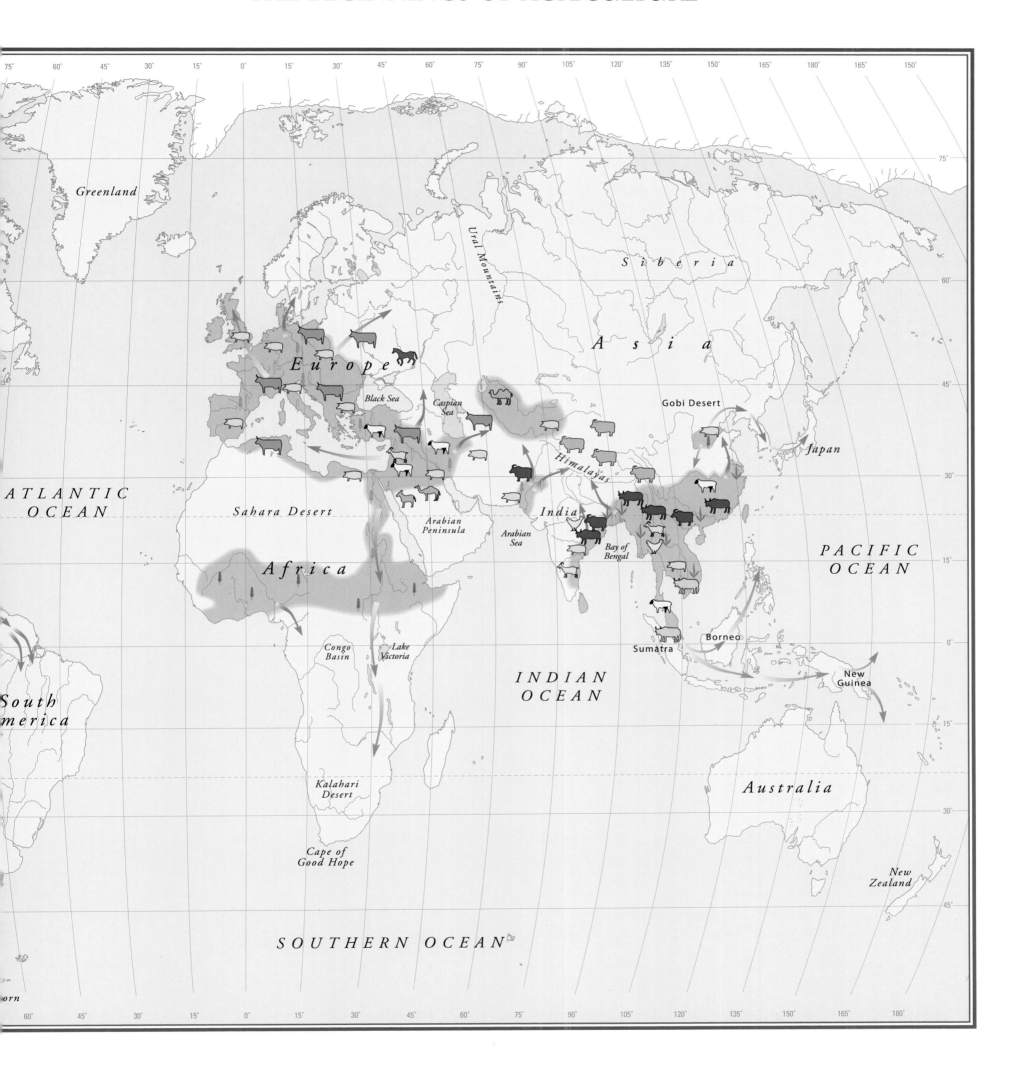

THE OLD KINGDOM

6000 BC – 2000 BC

THE OLD KINGDOM

The inhabitants of the Nile Valley had mastered the art of controlling seasonal flooding and irrigation. By the time of the Old Kingdom this settled way of life had created the world's most populated region.

The Old Kingdom includes the first four Pharaoh dynasties. These Pharaohs were responsible for building the Great Stepped Pyramid at Saqqara, the oldest stone building in the world, and later the Great Pyramids at Giza. Entirely dependent on the labor of its growing population, Egypt prospered, trading with tribes and states of Africa and the Near East.

CIVILIZATION OF THE INDUS VALLEY

Meanwhile to the east, the Harappa civilization of the Indus Valley thrived and developed. Covering some 5,000 square miles, this sophisticated culture paralleled Bronze-Age Egypt.

Just as Egypt relied on the annual flooding of the Nile, the Harappa civilization relied on the annual flooding of the Indus to bring down deposits of fertile silt, which allowed the growth of wheat, barley, and rice. This provided the basis for a wealthy manufacturing and trading society. However, unlike Egypt, the Indus civilization came to an end some time after 2000 BC when the Indus River changed its course, leaving villages infertile and trade disrupted.

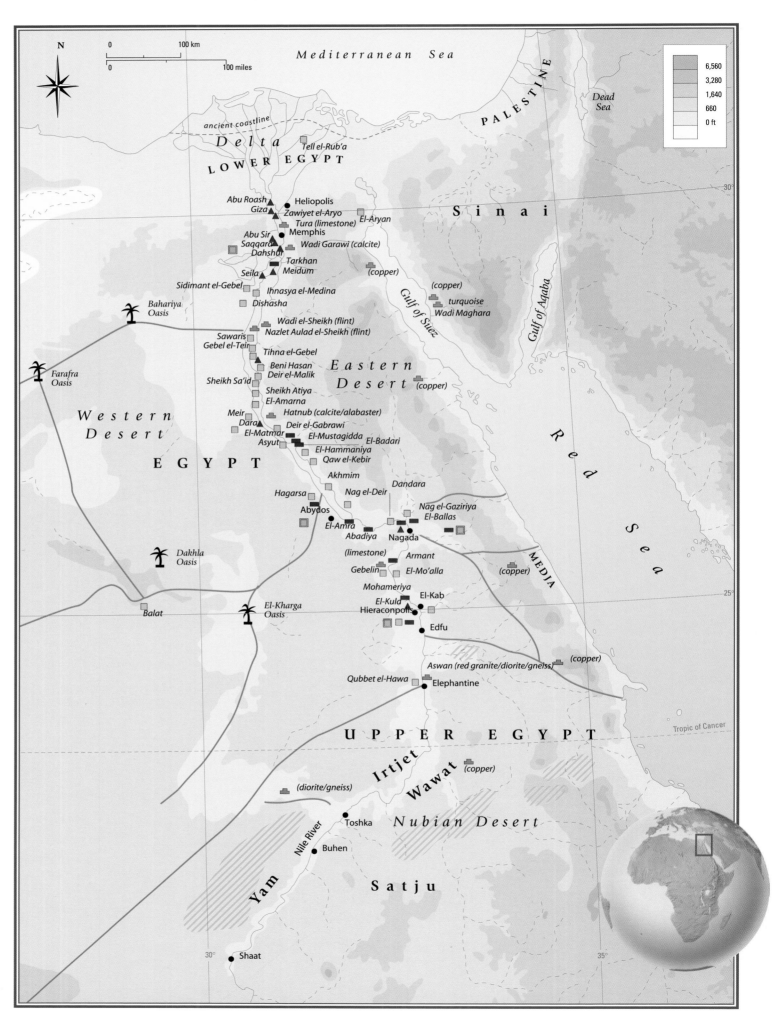

THE OLD KINGDOM

- 🔵 Town or city, c. 3250–2000 BC
- ▬ Cemetery
- ▢ Royal tomb, c. 3250–2650 BC
- ▫ Noble's tomb, c. 2500–2000 BC
- ▲ Pyramid, c. 2500–2000 BC
- ⚒ Mines/raw materials
- ▨ Gold
- — Desert routes

CIVILIZATION IN THE INDUS VALLEY

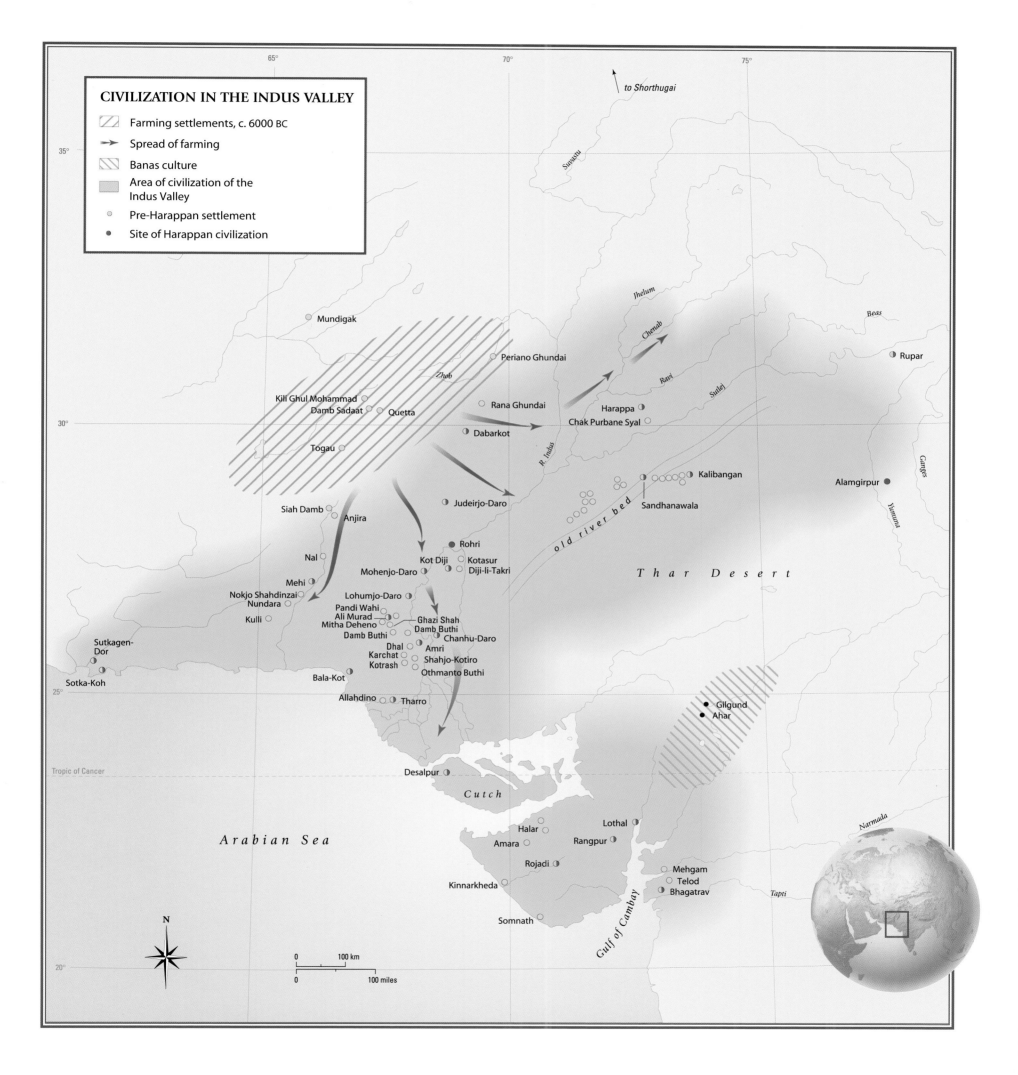

CIVILIZATION IN THE INDUS VALLEY

- Farming settlements, c. 6000 BC
- Spread of farming
- Banas culture
- Area of civilization of the Indus Valley
- ○ Pre-Harappan settlement
- ● Site of Harappan civilization

to Shorthugai

Mundigak

Swastu

Jhelum

Beas

Chenab

Periano Ghundai

Zhob

Kill Ghul Mohammad
Damb Sadaat
Quetta
Rana Ghundai
Harappa
Chak Purbane Syal

Ravi

Sutlej

Rupar

Togau
Dabarkot

R. Indus

Kalibangan

Alamgirpur

Ganges

Siah Damb
Anjira
Judeirjo-Daro
Sandhanawala

old river bed

Nal

Thar Desert

Rohri
Kot Diji
Kotasur
Mohenjo-Daro
Diji-li-Takri

Mehi
Nokjo Shahdinzai
Nundara
Lohumjo-Daro
Pandi Wahi
Ali Murad
Mitha Deheno
Ghazi Shah
Damb Buthi
Kulli
Damb Buthi
Dhal
Chanhu-Daro
Karchat
Amri
Kotrash
Shahjo-Kotiro
Othmanto Buthi

Sutkagen-Dor

Bala-Kot

Gilgund
Ahar

Yamuna

Sotka-Koh

Allahdino
Tharro

Tropic of Cancer

Narmada

Desalpur

C u t c h

Arabian Sea

Halar
Lothal
Amara
Rangpur

Rojadi

Mehgam
Telod
Bhagatrav

Tapti

Kinnarkheda

Gulf of Cambay

Somnath

N

0   100 km

0   100 miles

THE BABYLONIAN EMPIRE

THE BABYLONIAN EMPIRE

Originating in a relatively small state, Babylon would eventually extend its rule to cover the whole of the area we call Mesopotamia. Perhaps the most gifted leader of the ruling Amorite Dynasty was Hammurabi, c. 1792–1750 BC. His rule saw the flowering of cultural, intellectual, and military achievements, and these included the first Code of Laws in recorded history, written in the cuneiform script Akkadian. The success and wealth created by Babylon inevitably made the empire attractive to rivals within the region. In 1595 BC Babylon was sacked by the Hittites and later suffered invasions by the Mittani, Kassites, Hurrians, and others. By the end of the 15th Century BC the Assyrians had established dominance in the region.

THE HITTITE EMPIRE AND NEIGHBORING STATES

An Indo-European people, the Hittites originated beyond the Black Sea. They invaded Anatolia in the 2nd millennium BC and set up their capital in Hattusas. By 1590 BC their Empire extended to most of Anatolia, Syria, and parts of the Babylonian Empire. By 1322 BC the Hittite Empire reached its maximum extent, bringing it into conflict with the Egyptians. After 1200 BC the Hittite Empire collapsed under attack from the migrating "sea peoples".

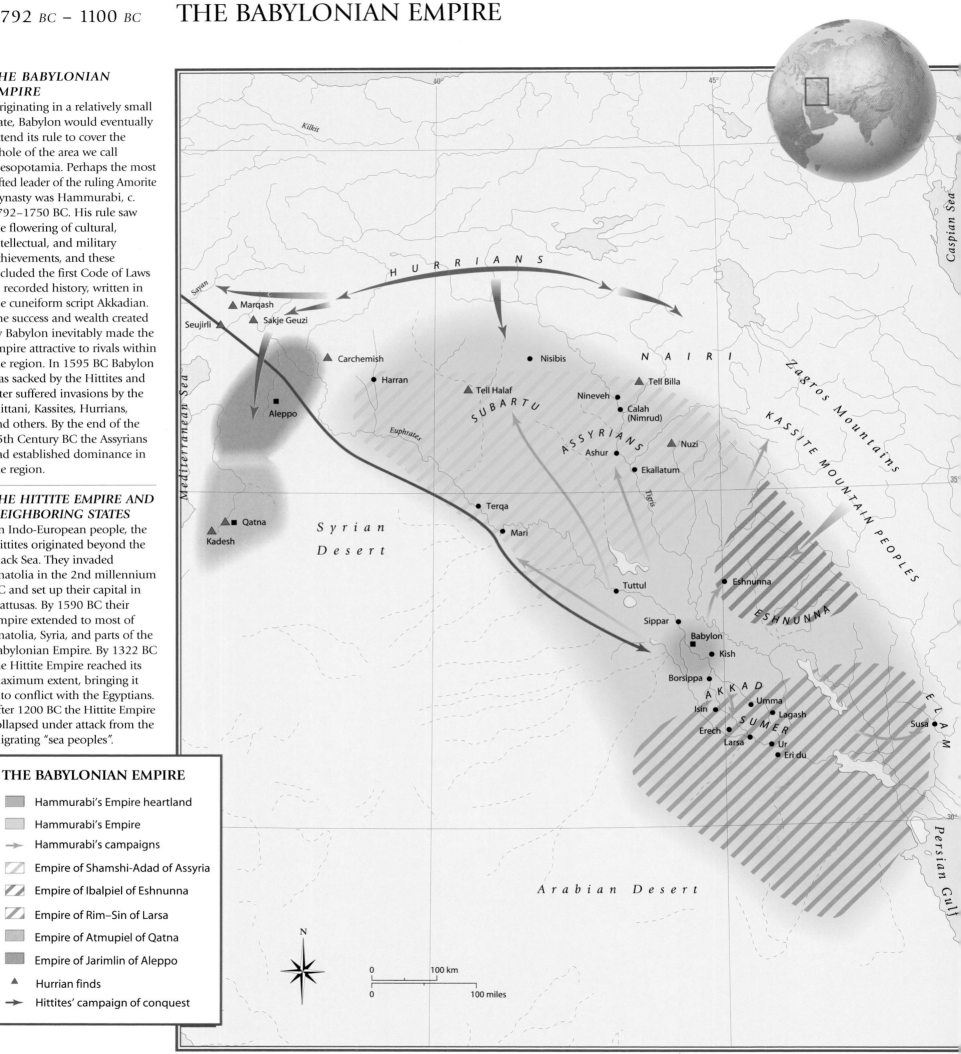

THE BABYLONIAN EMPIRE

- Hammurabi's Empire heartland
- Hammurabi's Empire
- → Hammurabi's campaigns
- Empire of Shamshi-Adad of Assyria
- Empire of Ibalpiel of Eshnunna
- Empire of Rim–Sin of Larsa
- Empire of Atmupiel of Qatna
- Empire of Jarimlin of Aleppo
- ▲ Hurrian finds
- → Hittites' campaign of conquest

THE HITTITE EMPIRE

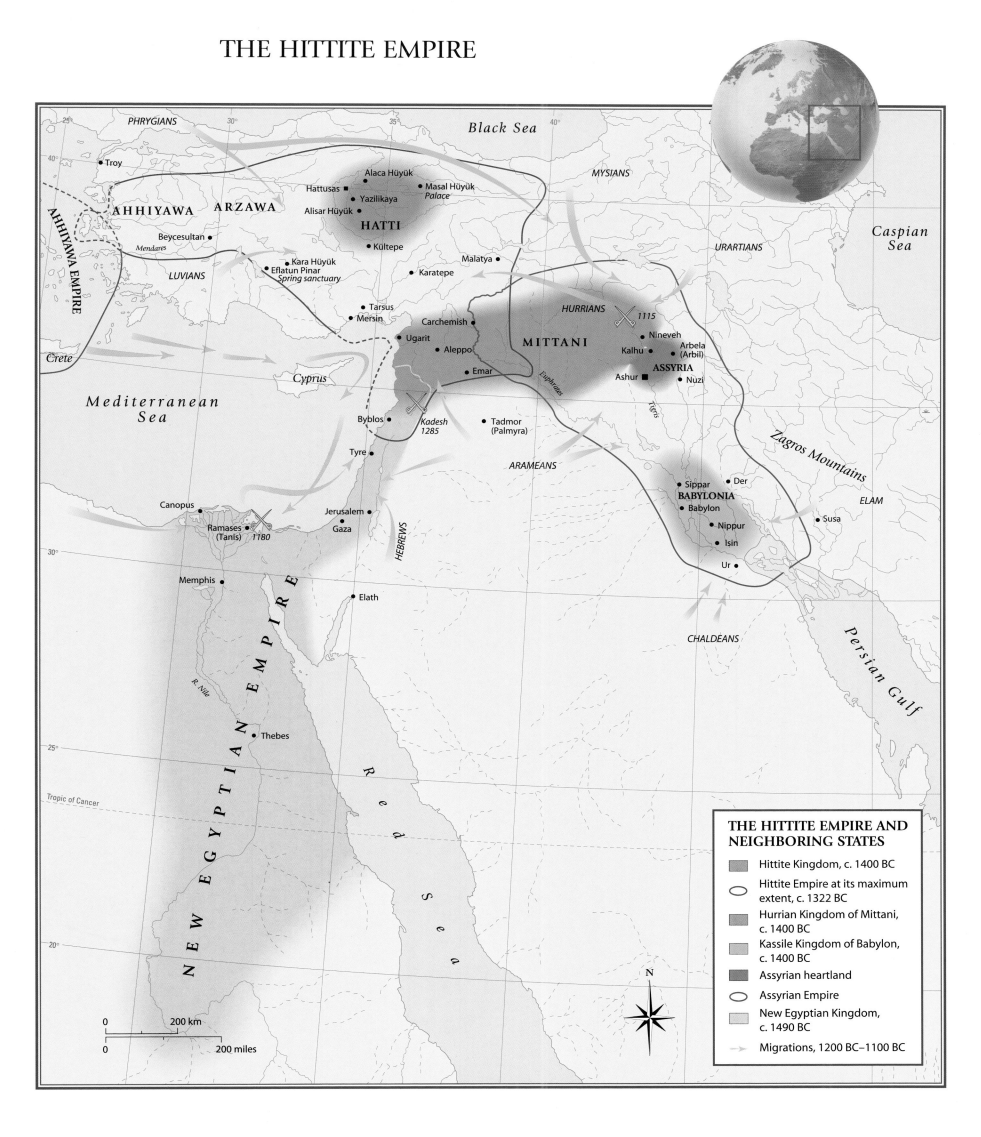

PHRYGIANS

Black Sea

MYSIANS

Caspian Sea

Troy

AHHIYAWA   ARZAWA

Alaca Hüyük

Hattusas   Masal Hüyük
Yazilikaya   *Palace*

Alisar Hüyük

HATTI

URARTIANS

AHHIYAWA EMPIRE

Beycesultan

Mendares

LUVIANS

Kültepe

Kara Hüyük
Eflatun Pinar
Spring sanctuary

Malatya

Karatepe

HURRIANS

1115

Crete

Tarsus
Mersin

Carchemish

Nineveh

MITTANI

Kalhu   Arbela (Arbil)

Ugarit
Aleppo

ASSYRIA

Ashur   Nuzi

Cyprus

Emar

Euphrates

Tigris

Mediterranean Sea

Byblos

Kadesh 1285

Tadmor (Palmyra)

Tyre

ARAMEANS

Zagros Mountains

BABYLONIA

Sippar   Der

ELAM

Canopus

Ramases (Tanis) 1180

Jerusalem

Gaza

HEBREWS

Babylon

Nippur

Susa

Memphis

Isin

Elath

Ur

CHALDEANS

R. Nile

Persian Gulf

NEW EGYPTIAN EMPIRE

Thebes

Tropic of Cancer

Red Sea

N

0   200 km

0   200 miles

THE HITTITE EMPIRE AND NEIGHBORING STATES

Hittite Kingdom, c. 1400 BC

Hittite Empire at its maximum extent, c. 1322 BC

Hurrian Kingdom of Mittani, c. 1400 BC

Kassile Kingdom of Babylon, c. 1400 BC

Assyrian heartland

Assyrian Empire

New Egyptian Kingdom, c. 1490 BC

Migrations, 1200 BC–1100 BC

THE WORLD 2500 BC; THE HUNTER GATHERER PEOPLES

THE WORLD IN 2500 BC
The great urban civilizations emerged based on the great river valleys of the Nile, Euphrates, Tigris, Indus, and the Huang Ho.

Elite and literate classes developed who were able to use their administrative, written, military, and religious skills to organize and rule their societies. This resulted in the emergence of formidable states, some of which controlled populations numbering millions.

THE HUNTER-GATHERER PEOPLES
3000 BC TO AD 2000
In 15,000 BC the human population of the world is estimated to have been in the region of ten million individuals, all of whom existed by hunting and gathering. By AD 1500 the human population had climbed to some 350 million, of whom hunter-gatherers had shrunk to three and half million. By the end of the 20th century the human population had grown enormously to six and a half billion, and by this time hunter-gatherers numbered only a few hundred thousand out of this vast total.

THE WORLD
2500 BC

- ■ Important sites
- Transition from hunting and gathering to agriculture
- Agricultural area
- Urban area
- Urban hinterland

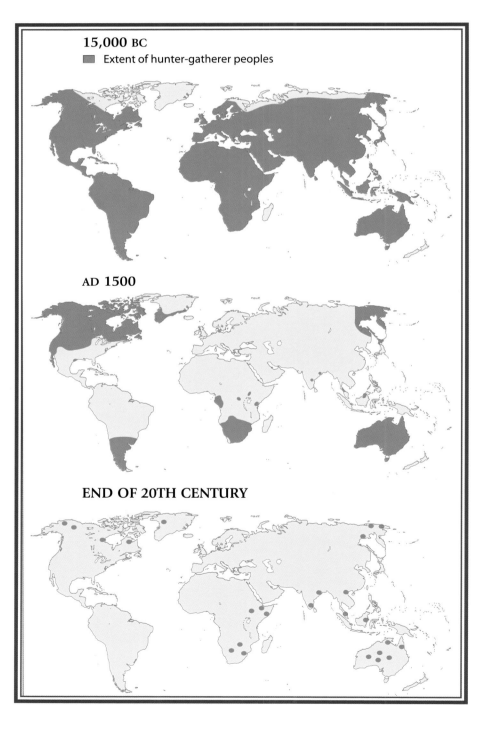

15,000 BC
■ Extent of hunter-gatherer peoples

AD 1500

END OF 20TH CENTURY

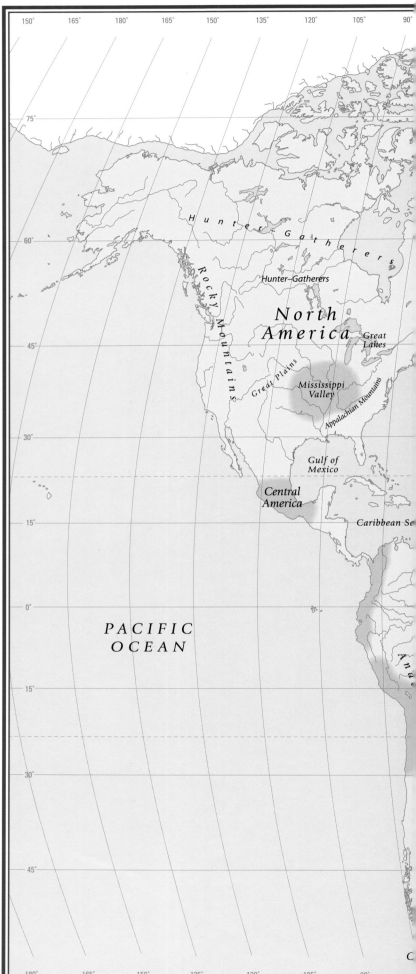

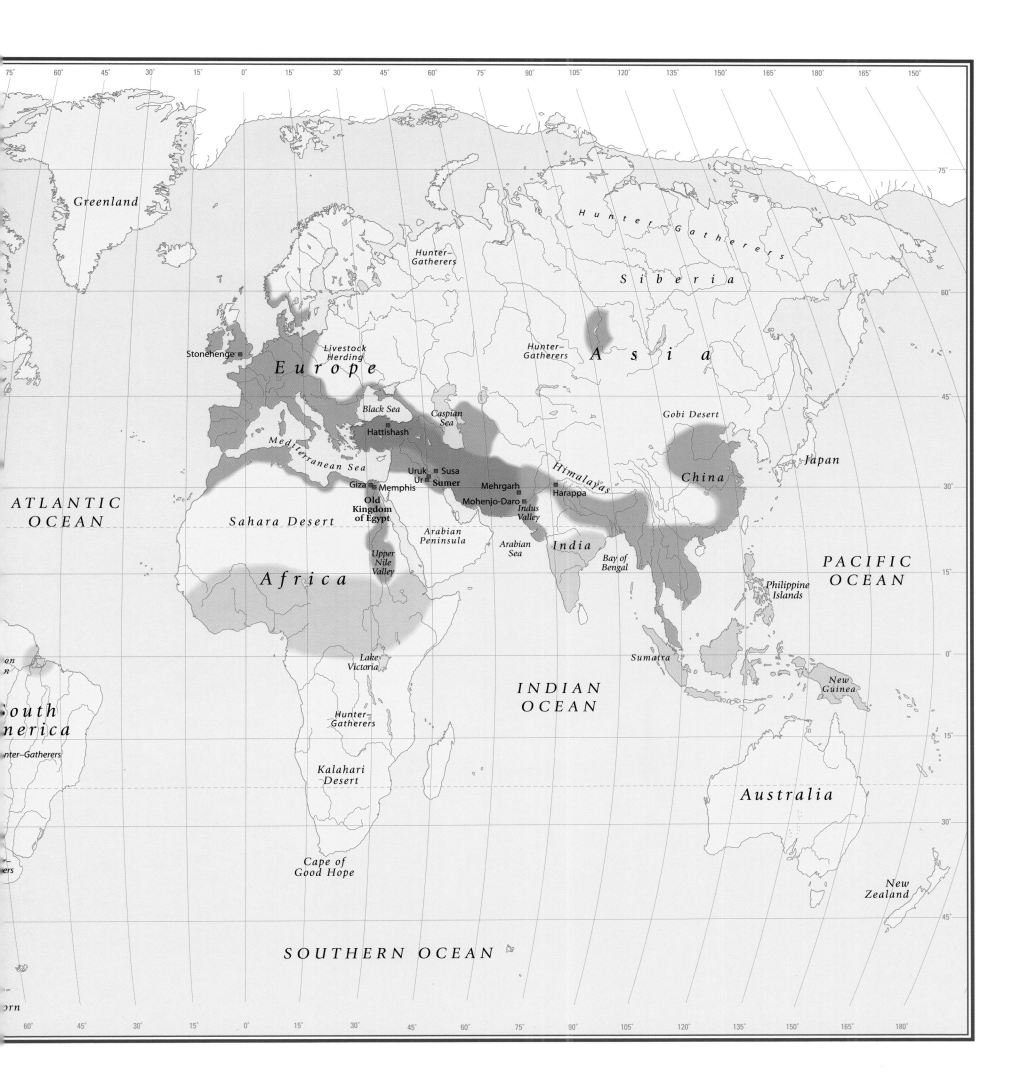

Greenland

Hunter–Gatherers

Siberia

Hunter–Gatherers

A s i a

Livestock Herding

Stonehenge

Europe

Black Sea

Caspian Sea

Hattishash

Mediterranean Sea

Gobi Desert

Japan

Himalayas

China

Uruk ■ Susa
Ur ■ **Sumer**

Giza ■ Memphis
Old Kingdom of Egypt

Mehrgarh

Mohenjo-Daro ■

Harappa ■

Indus Valley

ATLANTIC OCEAN

Sahara Desert

Arabian Peninsula

Arabian Sea

India

Bay of Bengal

PACIFIC OCEAN

Africa

Upper Nile Valley

Philippine Islands

Lake Victoria

Hunter–Gatherers

INDIAN OCEAN

Sumatra

New Guinea

Kalahari Desert

Australia

South America

Hunter–Gatherers

Cape of Good Hope

New Zealand

SOUTHERN OCEAN

INDO-EUROPEAN MIGRATION

6000 BC – 900 BC

INDO-EUROPEAN LANGUAGES 5000–900 BC
The recently deciphered Hittite, along with ancient Greek and Sanskrit, all show characteristics of a common route language we call Proto-Indo-European. By 2000 BC this ancient language had evolved into sub-families such as Tocharian, Slavic, Germanic, Albanian, Greek, and others. Historians still debate the location of the Indo-European homeland; archaeological studies dating from the 1960s, based on a specific style of grave goods, suggest the Indo-Europeans were a nomadic or semi-nomadic group of peoples stretching from an area north of the Caucasus and reaching toward central Asia.

INDO-EUROPEAN MIGRATIONS
The Indo-Europeans migrated from their homeland, heading westward into Europe and southward into Anatolia and the Middle East, establishing separate societies and cultures. A few common words, however, provide evidence of a once united heritage. For instance, the word "father" in English is known as "Vater" in German, "Pater" in Latin and "Pacer" in Tocharian.

DEVELOPMENT OF INDO-EUROPEAN LANGUAGES
(After Tomas Gamkrelidze and Vyacheslav Ivanov, 1985)

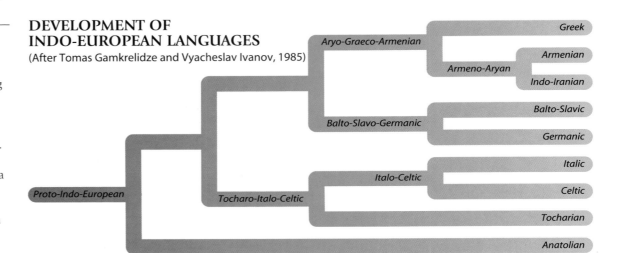

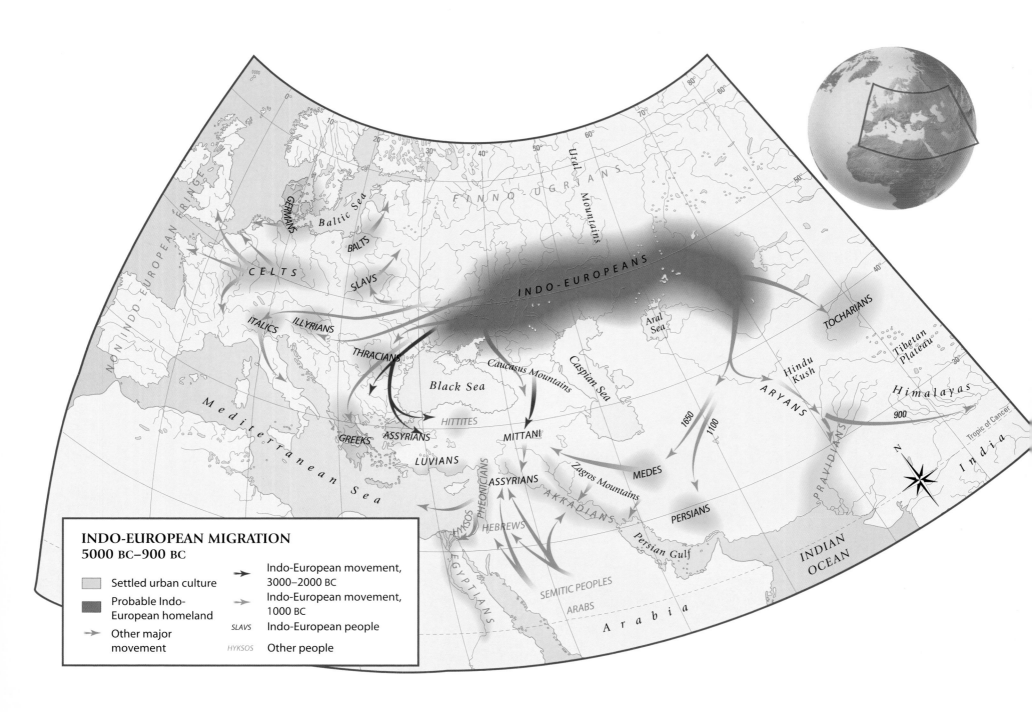

INDO-EUROPEAN MIGRATION 5000 BC–900 BC

- Settled urban culture
- Probable Indo-European homeland
- Other major movement
- Indo-European movement, 3000–2000 BC
- Indo-European movement, 1000 BC
- SLAVS Indo-European people
- HYKSOS Other people

SHANG CHINA; CHOU CHINA

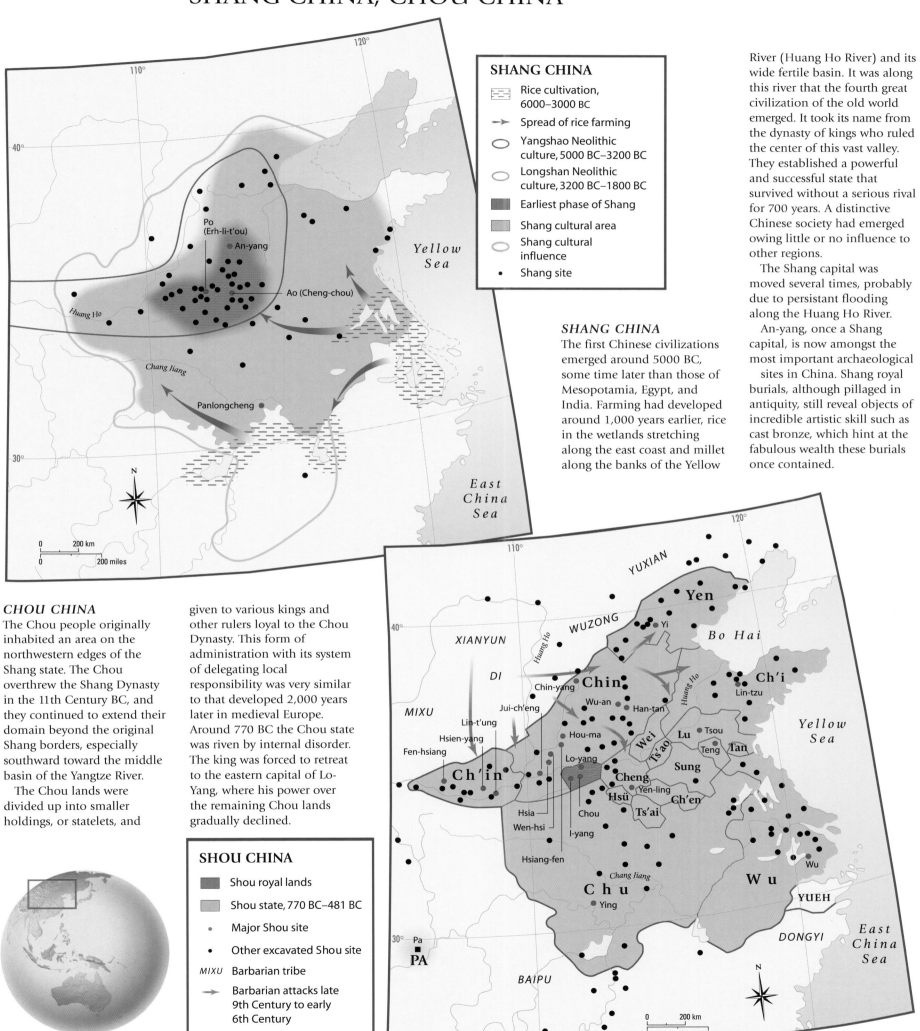

SHANG CHINA

- Rice cultivation, 6000–3000 BC
- → Spread of rice farming
- Yangshao Neolithic culture, 5000 BC–3200 BC
- Longshan Neolithic culture, 3200 BC–1800 BC
- Earliest phase of Shang
- Shang cultural area
- Shang cultural influence
- • Shang site

River (Huang Ho River) and its wide fertile basin. It was along this river that the fourth great civilization of the old world emerged. It took its name from the dynasty of kings who ruled the center of this vast valley. They established a powerful and successful state that survived without a serious rival for 700 years. A distinctive Chinese society had emerged owing little or no influence to other regions.

The Shang capital was moved several times, probably due to persistant flooding along the Huang Ho River.

An-yang, once a Shang capital, is now amongst the most important archaeological sites in China. Shang royal burials, although pillaged in antiquity, still reveal objects of incredible artistic skill such as cast bronze, which hint at the fabulous wealth these burials once contained.

SHANG CHINA

The first Chinese civilizations emerged around 5000 BC, some time later than those of Mesopotamia, Egypt, and India. Farming had developed around 1,000 years earlier, rice in the wetlands stretching along the east coast and millet along the banks of the Yellow

CHOU CHINA

The Chou people originally inhabited an area on the northwestern edges of the Shang state. The Chou overthrew the Shang Dynasty in the 11th Century BC, and they continued to extend their domain beyond the original Shang borders, especially southward toward the middle basin of the Yangtze River.

The Chou lands were divided up into smaller holdings, or statelets, and given to various kings and other rulers loyal to the Chou Dynasty. This form of administration with its system of delegating local responsibility was very similar to that developed 2,000 years later in medieval Europe. Around 770 BC the Chou state was riven by internal disorder. The king was forced to retreat to the eastern capital of Lo-Yang, where his power over the remaining Chou lands gradually declined.

SHOU CHINA

- Shou royal lands
- Shou state, 770 BC–481 BC
- • Major Shou site
- • Other excavated Shou site
- *MIXU* Barbarian tribe
- → Barbarian attacks late 9th Century to early 6th Century

THE MIDDLE EAST

1250 BC – 900 BC

THE MIDDLE EAST 900 BC
The urban civilizations of the world still only covered a fraction of its surface. The most intense area of urban civilized activity remained the Near East and the Nile Valley of Africa. In this region the development in the craft of metallurgy and other specialization was intense.

Typical of the emerging states, the Hittites ruled from their fortified citadel at Hattusash in central Anatolia, a growing state around 900 BC. Their campaigns southward toward the rich cities of the Levant inevitably brought them into conflict with the interests of the regional superpower of Egypt.

THE WORLD IN 1250 BC
As populations increased, new cities were founded and expanded, and this led to an increased rivalry for territory between the old and the new states.

The more successful states became increasingly militaristic, and the development of weapons and their deployment is pronounced in the archaeological finds from this period. Egyptian civilization reached a peak during the period of the New Kingdom, 1560–1085 BC, where supreme power rested on the monarch —on his abilities and decisions rested the future of the kingdom. This was typical of the state control of the period.

THE WORLD 1250 BC

- ■ Important sites
- New Kingdom of Egypt
- Hittites
- Mitanni
- Elam
- Shang China
- Mycenaean civilization
- Transition from hunting and gathering to agriculture
- Other urbanized regions

Major Bronze-using Regions
- Andronova steppe cultures
- Bronze Age Europe
- Mainland Southeast Asia

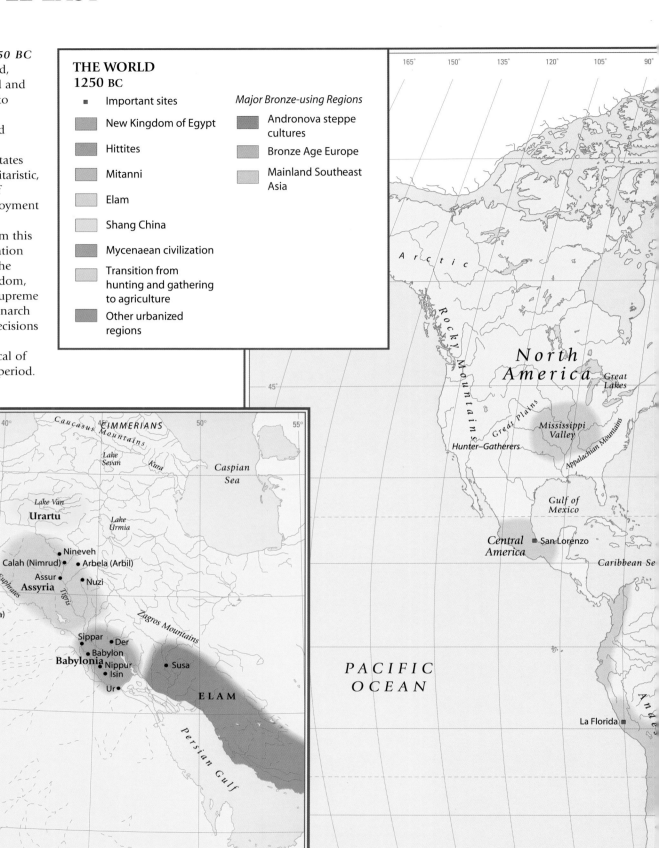

MIDDLE EAST c. 900 BC

THE WORLD 1250 BC

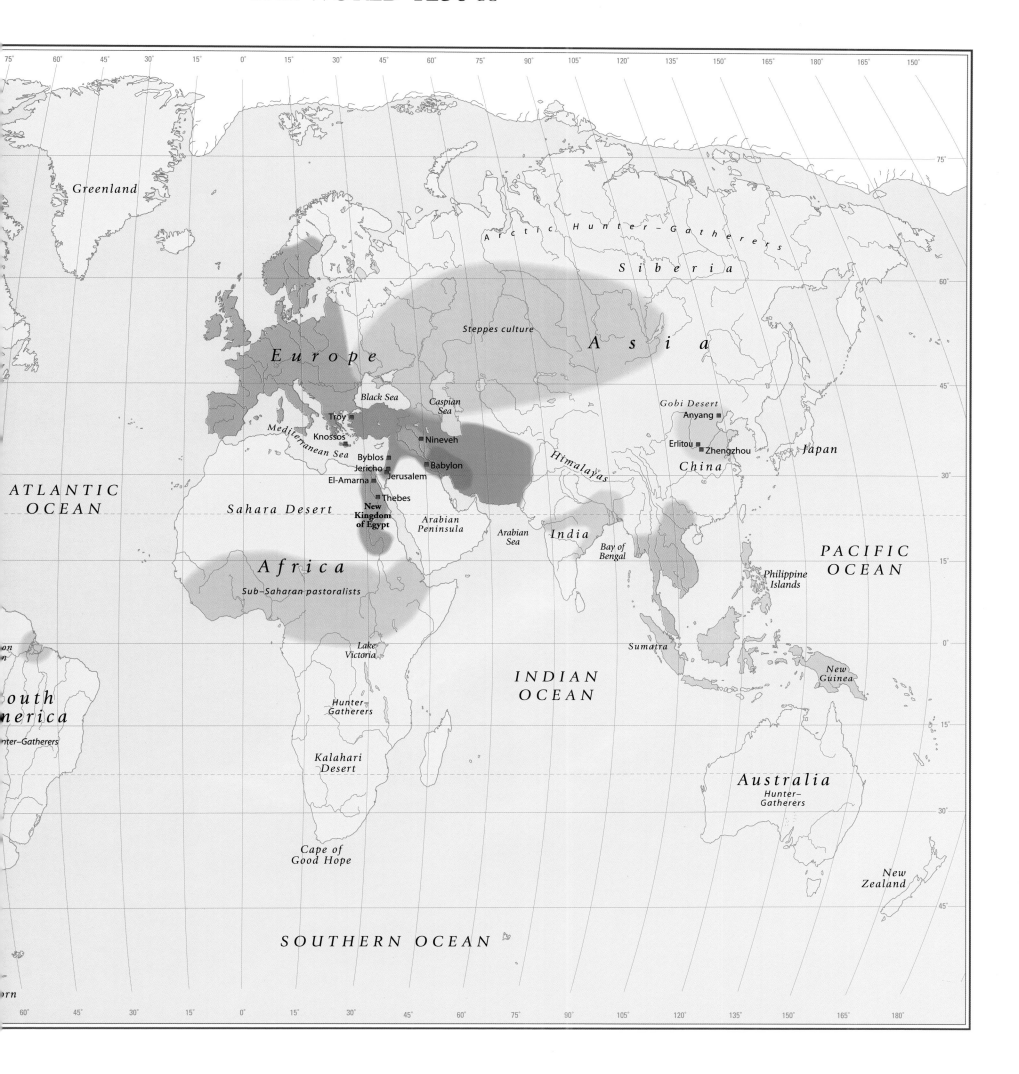

Greenland

ATLANTIC
OCEAN

Europe

Arctic Hunter-Gatherers

Siberia

Steppes culture

Asia

Black Sea

Caspian
Sea

Gobi Desert

Anyang

Troy

Mediterranean Sea

Knossos

Nineveh

Byblos

Jericho

Babylon

El-Amarna

Jerusalem

Thebes

New
Kingdom
of Egypt

Sahara Desert

Arabian
Peninsula

Arabian
Sea

India

Erlitou

Zhengzhou

Japan

China

Himalayas

Bay of
Bengal

Philippine
Islands

PACIFIC
OCEAN

Africa

Sub-Saharan pastoralists

Lake
Victoria

Sumatra

INDIAN
OCEAN

New
Guinea

on

outh
merica

nter-Gatherers

Hunter-
Gatherers

Kalahari
Desert

Australia
Hunter-
Gatherers

Cape of
Good Hope

New
Zealand

SOUTHERN OCEAN

rn

2000 BC – 750 BC EGYPT: THE MIDDLE KINGDOM

EGYPT: THE MIDDLE KINGDOM

The founders of the Middle Kingdom originated in the city of Thebes in Upper Egypt. They were responsible for a revival in Egypt's fortunes, reestablishing central control by military force and organising a new administrative system that collected taxes more efficiently. More land was brought into cultivation, especially around the Faiyum Depression east of the River Nile.

This period witnessed the unification of Upper and Lower Egypt. Many military and commercial expeditions were undertaken, especially southward to Nubia, to which the Egyptians were drawn by the richness of natural resources and, of course, the presence of gold. The power base of Egypt also moved south, as exemplified by the number of new building projects—palaces, temples, and tombs.

Senusret III captured all of Nubia, making it an Egyptian province. One kingdom then extended from the Nile delta in the north to Nubia (Cush) in the south.

The Middle Kingdom's power waned after a series of weak rulers and especially after the arrival of a new people from western Asia, the Hyksos. A capable military people, the Hyksos overwhelmed the ill-led Egyptians, seizing Avaris as their base and then expanding to conquer Memphis before founding the 17th Dynasty.

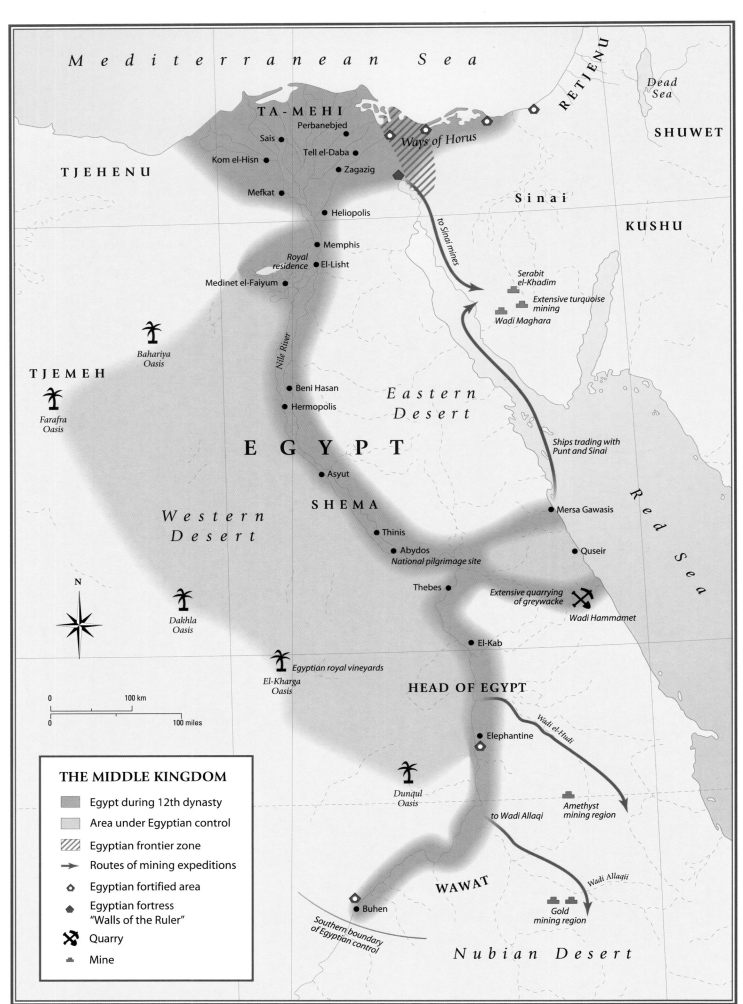

THE MIDDLE KINGDOM

- ■ Egypt during 12th dynasty
- ■ Area under Egyptian control
- ▨ Egyptian frontier zone
- → Routes of mining expeditions
- ◇ Egyptian fortified area
- ⬠ Egyptian fortress "Walls of the Ruler"
- ✖ Quarry
- ▬ Mine

EGYPT: THE NEW KINGDOM

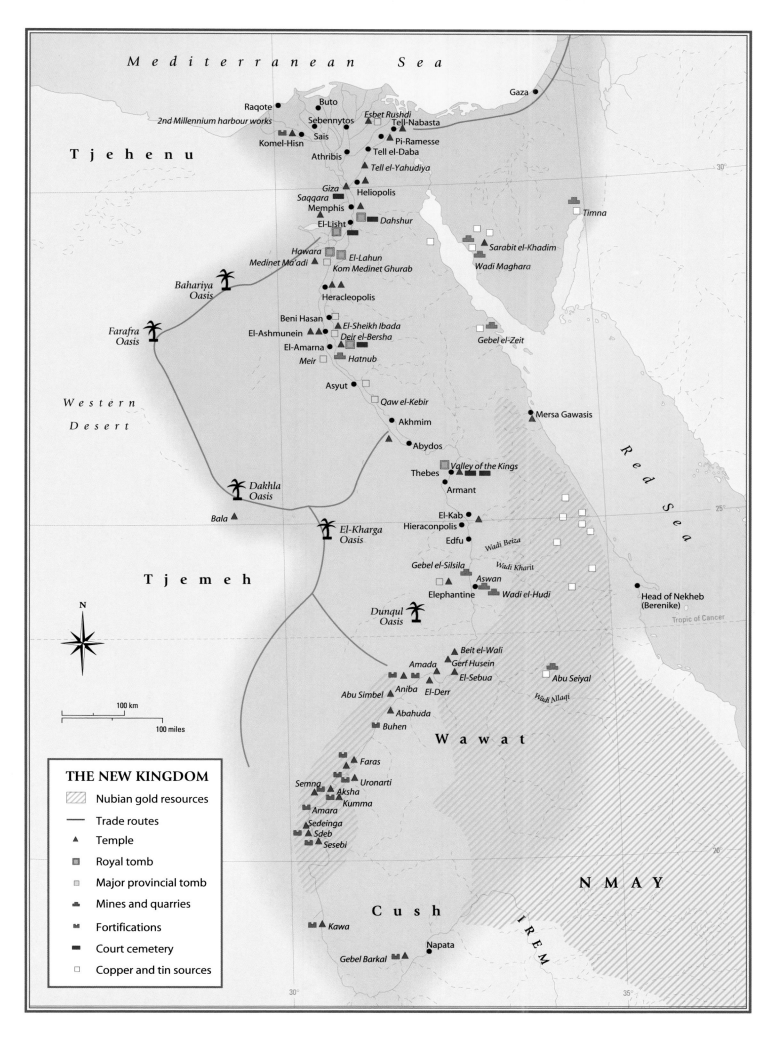

Mediterranean Sea

Gaza

Raqote
Buto
2nd Millennium harbour works
Sebennytos
Esbet Rushdi
Tell-Nabasta
Komel-Hisn
Sais
Pi-Ramesse
Athribis
Tell el-Daba

T j e h e n u

Tell el-Yahudiya

Giza
Heliopolis
Saqqara
Memphis
El-Lisht
Dahshur

Timna

Hawara
El-Lahun
Medinet Ma'adi
Kom Medinet Ghurab
Sarabit el-Khadim
Wadi Maghara

Bahariya
Oasis

Heracleopolis

Farafra
Oasis

Beni Hasan
El-Sheikh Ibada
El-Ashmunein
Deir el-Bersha
El-Amarna
Meir
Hatnub

Gebel el-Zeit

**W e s t e r n
D e s e r t**

Asyut

Qaw el-Kebir

Akhmim

Mersa Gawasis

Abydos

Dakhla
Oasis

Thebes
Valley of the Kings
Armant

Bala

El-Kharga
Oasis

El-Kab
Hieraconpolis
Edfu
Wadi Beiza

T j e m e h

Gebel el-Silsila
Wadi Kharit
Aswan
Elephantine
Wadi el-Hudi

Dunqul
Oasis

Head of Nekheb
(Berenike)

Tropic of Cancer

N

Beit el-Wali
Amada
Gerf Husein
El-Sebua
Abu Simbel
Aniba
El-Derr
Abu Seiyal
Wadi Allaqi
Abahuda
Buhen

W a w a t

100 km

100 miles

Faras
Semna
Uronarti
Aksha
Kumma
Amara
Sedeinga
Sdeb
Sesebi

THE NEW KINGDOM

- ▨ Nubian gold resources
- — Trade routes
- ▲ Temple
- ◼ Royal tomb
- ◻ Major provincial tomb
- ⛏ Mines and quarries
- ⬒ Fortifications
- ▬ Court cemetery
- ◻ Copper and tin sources

C u s h

Kawa

Napata

Gebel Barkal

I R E M

N M A Y

Red Sea

THE NEW KINGDOM
Ahmose I united the Egyptians against their foreign rulers, the Hyksos, who were all driven out of their capital, Avaris, toward Palestine and Lebanon. With this achievement he founded the 18th Dynasty in Egypt. The Egyptian rulers that followed lead a renewed and reinvigorated Egypt and reconquered Nubia up to the Third Cataract. The Egyptian Empire was also extended to include Palestine, Lebanon, and Syria.

The 19th Dynasty began with the reign of Horemheb, who strengthened the kingdom by suppressing corruption at all levels and by the introduction of a national tax. This period also witnessed the strengthening of the Egyptian army and witnessed a return to the building of great temples, tombs, and statues.

The New Kingdom Egyptianized Nubia with the building of many temple projects and the settlement of soldiers, scribes, priests, and craftsmen. Egypt in return relied on Nubia's numerous products: grain, cattle, ivory, timber, slaves, and above all, gold. Whatever Egypt's future held it would need the support of Nubia.

1000 BC – 663 BC   SOLOMON'S EMPIRE

SOLOMON'S EMPIRE
The triumph of Solomon's succession marked the end of the old conservative religious order. The Jews had now become predominantly a settled agricultural and trading people rather than nomadic shepherds.

Solomon ruthlessly removed any potential rivals, ensuring his unthreatened passage to power. He improved and consolidated the administrative system started by David, giving us the first reliable Hebrew written records. King Solomon's administrative ability was the foundation of his reputation for "wisdom," and his reign was a golden age for the Jewish people.

His achievements required large-scale organization of labor, and his success owed much to his understanding of the divisive tribal tendencies in Jewish society. Solomon managed to maintain a form of national unity, but this unity evaporated with his death in 931 BC.

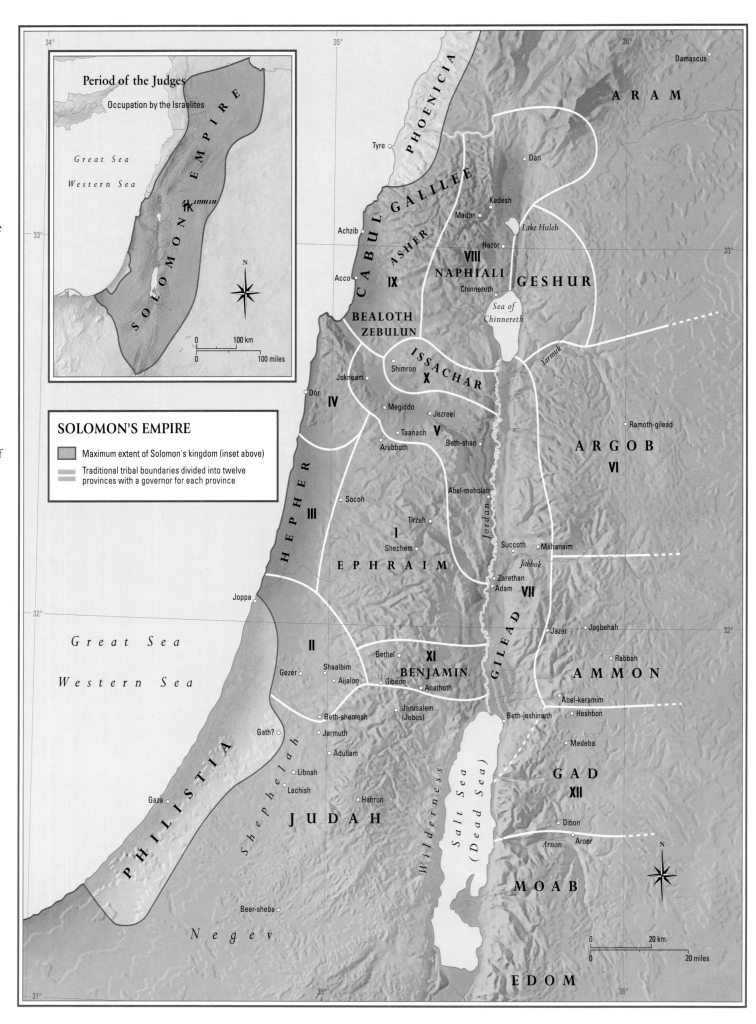

Period of the Judges
Occupation by the Israelites

SOLOMON EMPIRE

Great Sea Western Sea

N

| 0 | 100 km |
| 0 | 100 miles |

SOLOMON'S EMPIRE

▨ Maximum extent of Solomon's kingdom (inset above)

▨ Traditional tribal boundaries divided into twelve provinces with a governor for each province

Damascus

ARAM

PHOENICIA

Tyre

Dan

CABUL   GALILEE

Achzib

ASHER

Kedesh

Madon

Lake Huleh

Acco

IX

Hazor

VIII

NAPHIALI

GESHUR

Chinnereth

Sea of Chinnereth

BEALOTH
ZEBULUN

ISSACHAR

Shimron

X

Jokneam

Dor

IV

Megiddo

Jezreel

Taanach

V

Arubboth

Beth-shan

Ramoth-gilead

ARGOB

VI

Abel-meholah

HEPHER

III

Socoh

Tirzah

I

Shechem

Jordan

Succoth

Mahanaim

EPHRAIM

Jabbok

Zarethan
Adam

VII

Joppa

GILEAD

Jazer

Jogbehah

Great Sea

Western Sea

II

Bethel

XI

BENJAMIN

Gibeon

Anathoth

AMMON

Rabbah

Gezer

Shaalbim

Aijalon

Jerusalem
(Jebus)

Abel-keramim

Heshbon

Beth-jeshimoth

Beth-shemesh

Medeba

Gath?

Jarmuth

Adullam

GAD

XII

Shephelah

Libnah

Wilderness

Salt Sea (Dead Sea)

Dibon

Gaza

Lachish

Hebron

Arnon

Aroer

JUDAH

Beer-sheba

MOAB

N

Negev

| 0 | 20 km |
| 0 | 20 miles |

EDOM

PHILISTIA

NUBIA ASCENDENT;
THE STRUGGLE FOR EGYPT

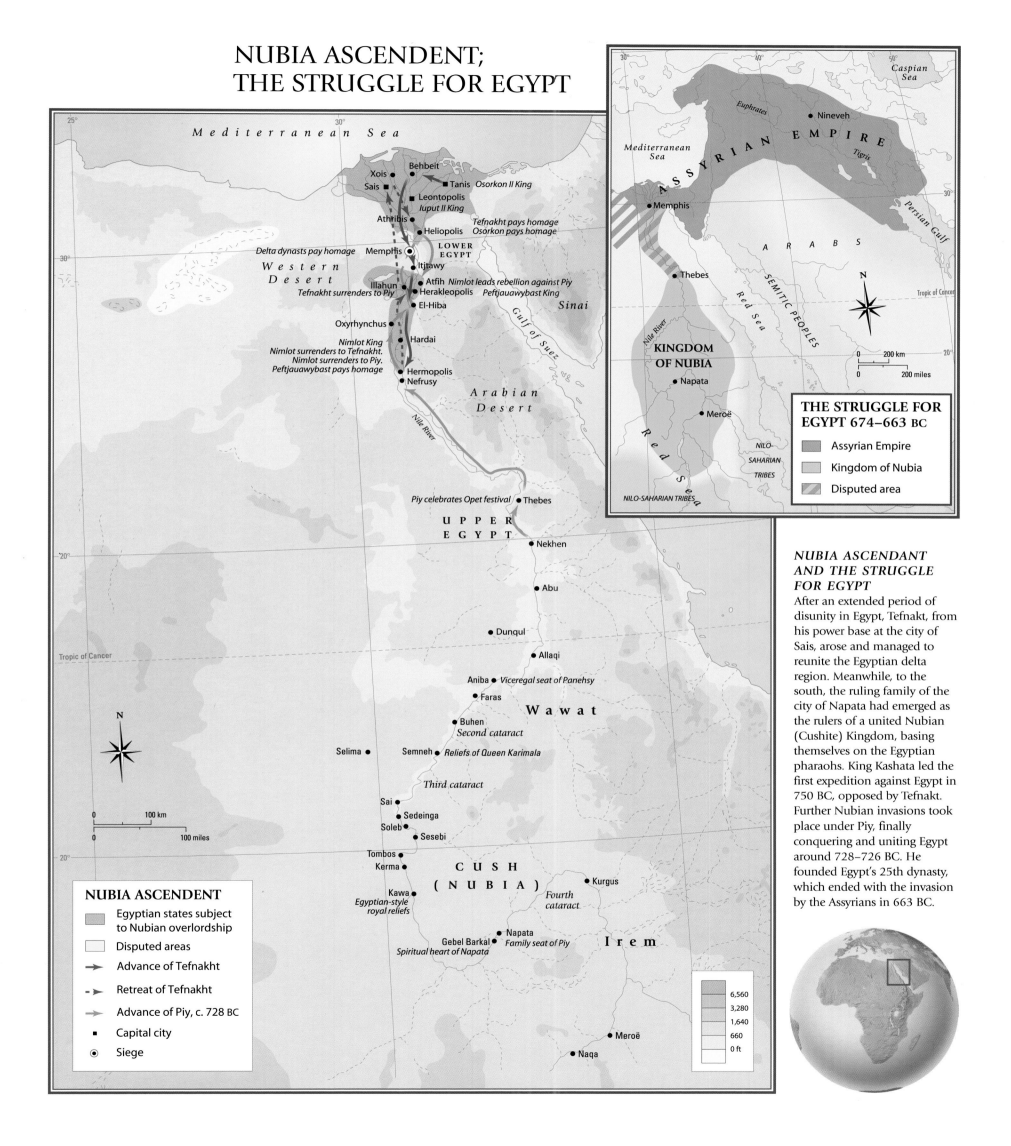

Mediterranean Sea

Xois • Behbeit
Sais ■ Tanis *Osorkon II King*
Leontopolis
Iuput II King
Athribis •
• Heliopolis *Tefnakht pays homage*
Osorkon pays homage

Delta dynasts pay homage Memphis ◉ **LOWER EGYPT**
Itjtawy
Illahun • Atfih *Nimlot leads rebellion against Piy*
Tefnakht surrenders to Piy • Herakleopolis *Peftjauawybast King*
• El-Hiba

Oxyrhynchus •
• Hardai
Nimlot King
Nimlot surrenders to Tefnakht.
Nimlot surrenders to Piy. • Hermopolis
Peftjauawybast pays homage • Nefrusy

Western Desert

Arabian Desert

Gulf of Suez

Sinai

Nile River

Piy celebrates Opet festival • Thebes
UPPER EGYPT
• Nekhen
• Abu
• Dunqul
• Allaqi
Aniba • *Viceregal seat of Panehsy*
• Faras
Wawat
• Buhen
Second cataract
Selima • • Semneh *Reliefs of Queen Karimala*
Third cataract
Sai •
• Sedeinga
Soleb •
• Sesebi
Tombos •
Kerma • **CUSH (NUBIA)**
Kawa • *Fourth cataract* • Kurgus
Egyptian-style royal reliefs
• Napata
Gebel Barkal • *Family seat of Piy*
Spiritual heart of Napata **Irem**

• Meroë
• Naqa

NUBIA ASCENDENT
- Egyptian states subject to Nubian overlordship
- Disputed areas
- → Advance of Tefnakht
- ⇢ Retreat of Tefnakht
- → Advance of Piy, c. 728 BC
- ■ Capital city
- ◉ Siege

THE STRUGGLE FOR EGYPT 674–663 BC
- Assyrian Empire
- Kingdom of Nubia
- Disputed area

Caspian Sea
• Nineveh
Euphrates *Tigris*
ASSYRIAN EMPIRE
Mediterranean Sea
• Memphis
ARABS
Red Sea
SEMITIC PEOPLES
Persian Gulf
• Thebes
Tropic of Cancer
KINGDOM OF NUBIA
• Napata
• Meroë
NILO-SAHARIAN TRIBES

NUBIA ASCENDANT AND THE STRUGGLE FOR EGYPT
After an extended period of disunity in Egypt, Tefnakt, from his power base at the city of Sais, arose and managed to reunite the Egyptian delta region. Meanwhile, to the south, the ruling family of the city of Napata had emerged as the rulers of a united Nubian (Cushite) Kingdom, basing themselves on the Egyptian pharaohs. King Kashata led the first expedition against Egypt in 750 BC, opposed by Tefnakt. Further Nubian invasions took place under Piy, finally conquering and uniting Egypt around 728–726 BC. He founded Egypt's 25th dynasty, which ended with the invasion by the Assyrians in 663 BC.

43

550 – 330 *BC*   # THE PERSIAN EMPIRE

THE PERSIAN EMPIRE

In 539 BC King Cyrus of Persia (555–529 BC) received the surrender of Babylon without having to fight. This was the climax of the campaign in which Persian armies had swept across the eastern frontiers of the Babylonian Empire from the Persian Gulf to the Black Sea, before striking southward into Mesopotamia. This expansion was added to, and consolidated by, his successors Cambyses II and Darius I. Though the Persians were decisively defeated by the Greeks at the Battle of Marathon in 490 BC their Empire survived for another 200 years, until it was finally destroyed by Alexander the Great in 331 BC.

EURASIA 750 BC (OVERLEAF)

The shifting pattern of allegiances within western Asia was created by the incursions of nomadic tribes like the Medes, Hebrews, and Phrygians, and their attempts to create their own states and to seize power in others they had invaded. By 750 BC the Assyrians had ruthlessly created the world's first Empire, which was controlled by their large and efficient professional army. They had utilized their wealth to create the fiercest and best-trained armed force in the world. Any resistance was ruthlessly repressed. In India, the city state civilization along the Indus Valley came to an end, possibly as a result of Sanskrit-speaking Aryan invaders. In China, the Zhou Dynasty collapsed when its former fiefdoms rose up against its central authority. As a result, China was divided into several kingdoms.

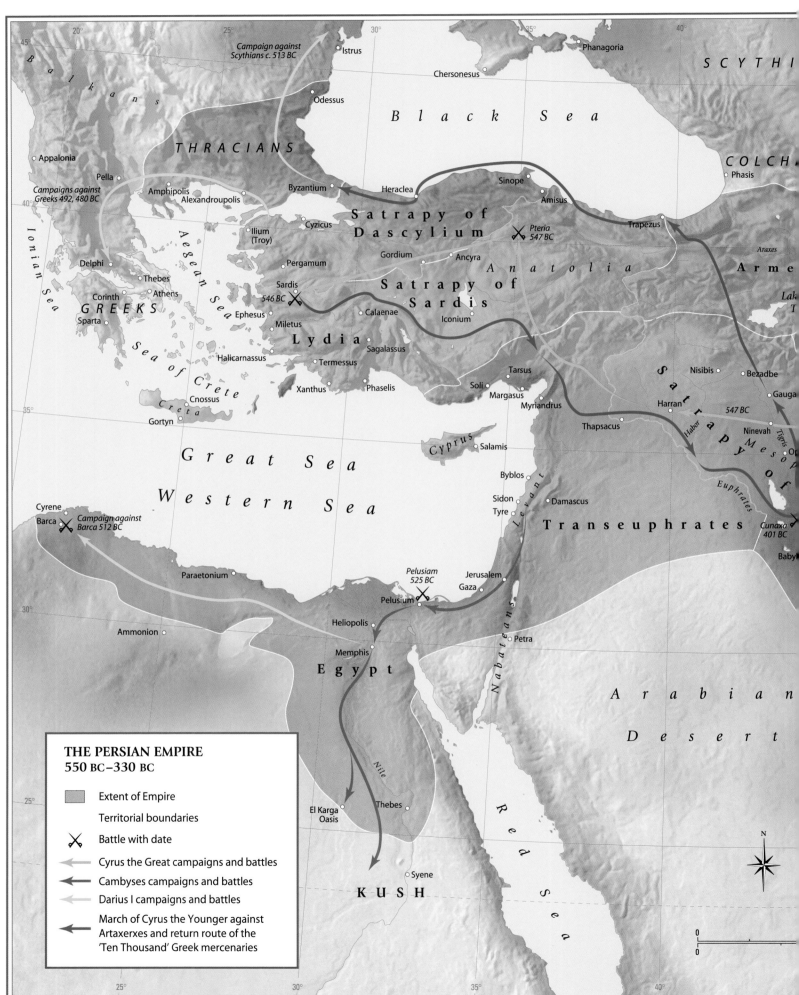

THE PERSIAN EMPIRE
550 BC–330 BC

▨	Extent of Empire
	Territorial boundaries
✕	Battle with date
→	Cyrus the Great campaigns and battles
→	Cambyses campaigns and battles
→	Darius I campaigns and battles
→	March of Cyrus the Younger against Artaxerxes and return route of the 'Ten Thousand' Greek mercenaries

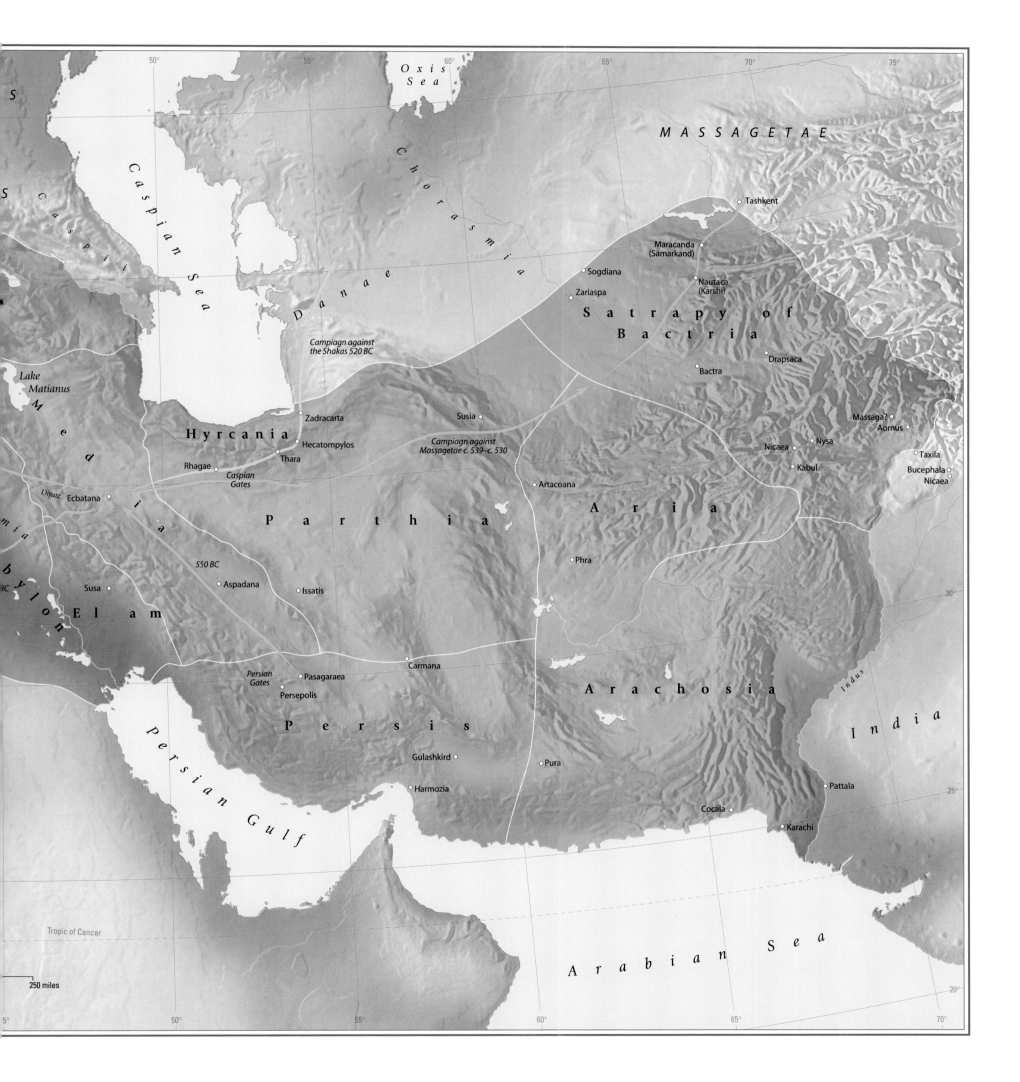

Oxus
Sea

MASSAGETAE

Tashkent

Chorasmia

Maracanda
(Samarkand)

Sogdiana

Nautaca
(Karshi)

Zariaspa

Satrapy of
Bactria

Drapsaca

Campiagn against
the Shakas 520 BC

Danae

Bactra

Caspian Sea

Lake
Matianus

Zadracarta

Susia

Massaga?
Aornus

Hyrcania

Campiagn against
Massagetae c. 539–c. 530

Nicaea

Nysa

Hecatompylos

Taxila

Thara

Kabul

Rhagae

Bucephala
Nicaea

Caspian
Gates

Artacoana

Aria

Diyaz
Ecbatana

Parthia

550 BC

Phra

bylon

Susa

Aspadana

Issatis

El am

Arachosia

Carmana

Indus

Persian
Gates

Pasagaraea

India

Persepolis

Persis

Gulashkird

Pura

Harmozia

Pattala

Persian Gulf

Cocala

Karachi

Tropic of Cancer

Arabian Sea

250 miles

45

EURASIA

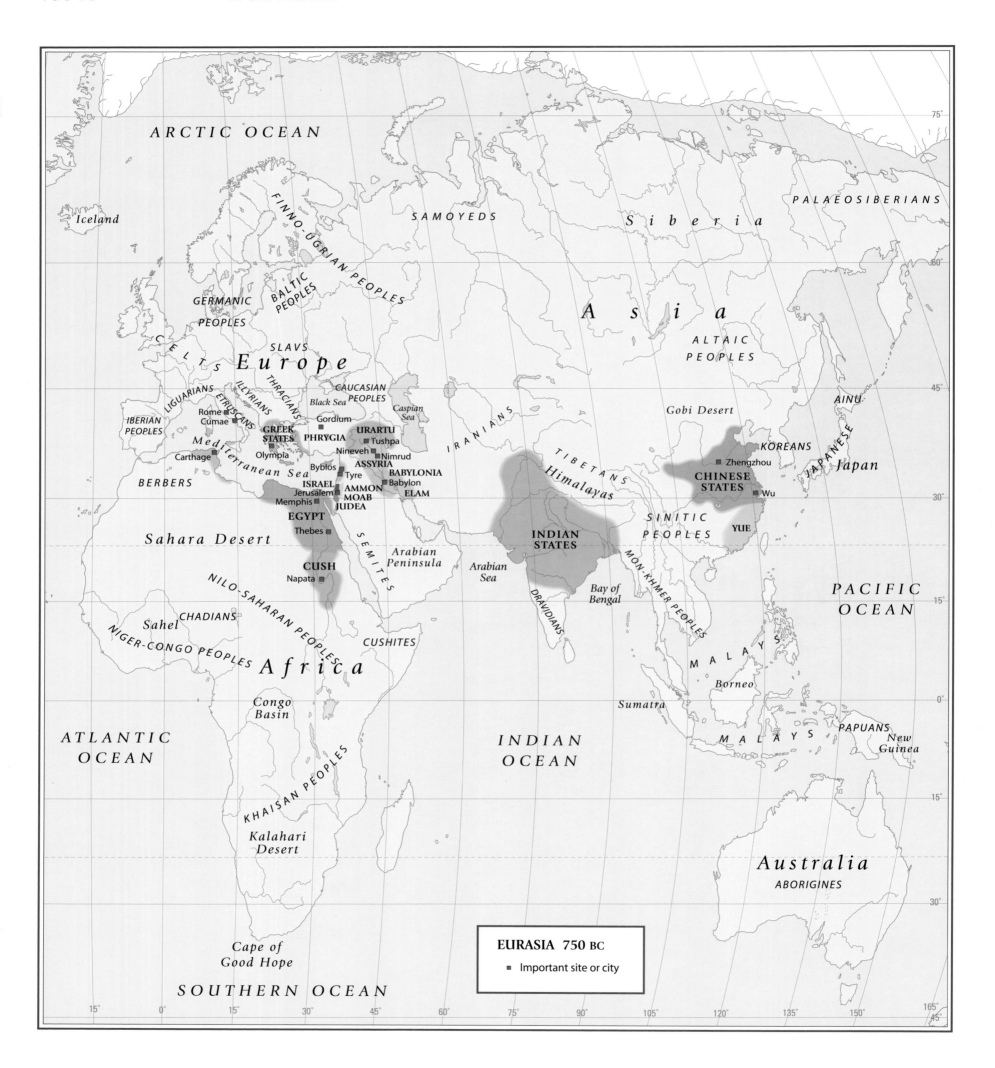

ARCTIC OCEAN

Iceland

PALAEOSIBERIANS

SAMOYEDS

Siberia

FINNO-UGRIAN PEOPLES

GERMANIC
PEOPLES

BALTIC
PEOPLES

SLAVS

Asia

ALTAIC
PEOPLES

CELTS

Europe

AINU

THRACIANS

CAUCASIAN
PEOPLES

Black Sea

Caspian
Sea

IRANIANS

Gobi Desert

KOREANS

JAPANESE

Japan

LIGURIANS

ILLYRIANS

IBERIAN
PEOPLES

Rome
Cumae

ETRUSCANS

GREEK
STATES

PHRYGIA

Gordium

URARTU

Tushpa

TIBETANS

Himalayas

Zhengzhou

CHINESE
STATES

Wu

Mediterranean Sea

Olympia

Nineveh
Nimrud

Carthage

Byblos

ASSYRIA

Tyre

BABYLONIA

Babylon

SINITIC
PEOPLES

YUE

BERBERS

ISRAEL

AMMON

ELAM

Jerusalem

MOAB

Memphis

JUDEA

EGYPT

Sahara Desert

Thebes

SEMITES

Arabian
Peninsula

Arabian
Sea

INDIAN
STATES

MON-KHMER PEOPLES

PACIFIC
OCEAN

CUSH

Napata

DRAVIDIANS

Bay of
Bengal

NILO-SAHARAN PEOPLES

CHADIANS

Sahel

CUSHITES

MALAYS

Borneo

NIGER-CONGO PEOPLES

Africa

Sumatra

MALAYS

PAPUANS

New
Guinea

ATLANTIC
OCEAN

Congo
Basin

INDIAN
OCEAN

KHAISAN PEOPLES

Kalahari
Desert

Australia

ABORIGINES

Cape of
Good Hope

SOUTHERN OCEAN

EURASIA 750 BC

■ Important site or city

PART 2

THE CLASSICAL WORLD

*T*HE CLASSICAL WORLD DEVELOPED a series of civilizations across continents. Mesopotamia witnessed several empires before it was superseded by the Persian Empire, which spread to India, Egypt, and Anatolia. The Greek world is well known for the growth of Minoan Crete and the Mycenaean civilization, both of which disintegrated around 1275 bc, possibly brought down by the migrating Sea Peoples. The growth of city-state Greece brought conflict with the Persian Empire. An internecine Peloponnesian War between Athenian and Spartan alliances so damaged Greece that it fell easy prey to Alexander the Great's imperial dream, and then to Rome. The latter state grew after throwing off Etruscan dominance and defeating the Carthaginians in three Punic Wars. The Roman Empire pushed eastward acquiring Palestine and its recalcitrant population, which rebelled twice; the first Zealot revolt was iconized by mass suicide at Masada. Rome received trade along the Silk Road, but when this was blocked by the Sasanians, Zoroastrian Persia responded by forging commercial bonds with the Indian Mauryan Empire and Han China. India also witnessed the Gupta Empire, which presided over classical Hindu civilization. Eventually, the Roman Empire divided into two, with administrative capitals at Rome and Byzantium, the western part succumbing to invading Germanic tribes.

1500 BC – 1250 BC   MYCENAEAN GREECE

MYCENAEAN GREECE
The Mycenaean civilization was responsible for some considerable achievements, as demonstrated by the immense architecture of the period and the detailed skill of its craftsmen.

The period between 1450 and 1200 BC witnessed the greatest period of expansion of the Mycenaean culture, especially in mainland Greece. There were a number of palace-based states at this time, Mycenae being the most powerful.

The rulers of the more

powerful of these states enjoyed diplomatic and trade relationships with other major states in the region, notably Egypt and the states of western Asia Minor.

At the apex of Mycenaean development massive city walls were constructed around the more important settlements or palaces. The widespread distribution of other undefended settlements suggests that this defense was not due to an atmosphere of distrust and constant warfare, but sprang more out of a

desire to emphasize the importance of certain centers like Tiryns and the treasures held within them. Like the Cretan palaces, Mycenaean buildings were richly decorated with frescos and included bathrooms with sophisticated drainage systems. Much of this would come to a sudden and catastrophic end with the collapse of Mycenae around 1200 BC.

TIRYNS CITADEL
— Old citadel, 1400 BC
1. Main gateway
2. Inner gateway to palace
3. Greater propælum
4. Lesser propælum
5. Court to chief Megaron
6. Chief Megaron
7. Court to lesser Megaron
8. Lesser Megaron

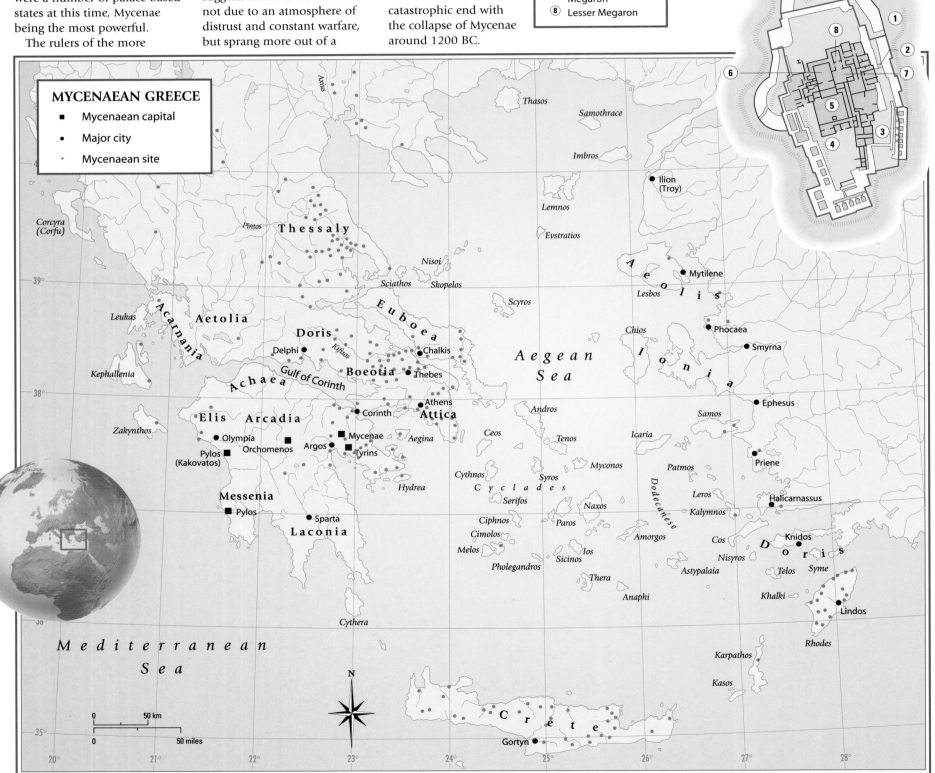

MINOAN CRETE

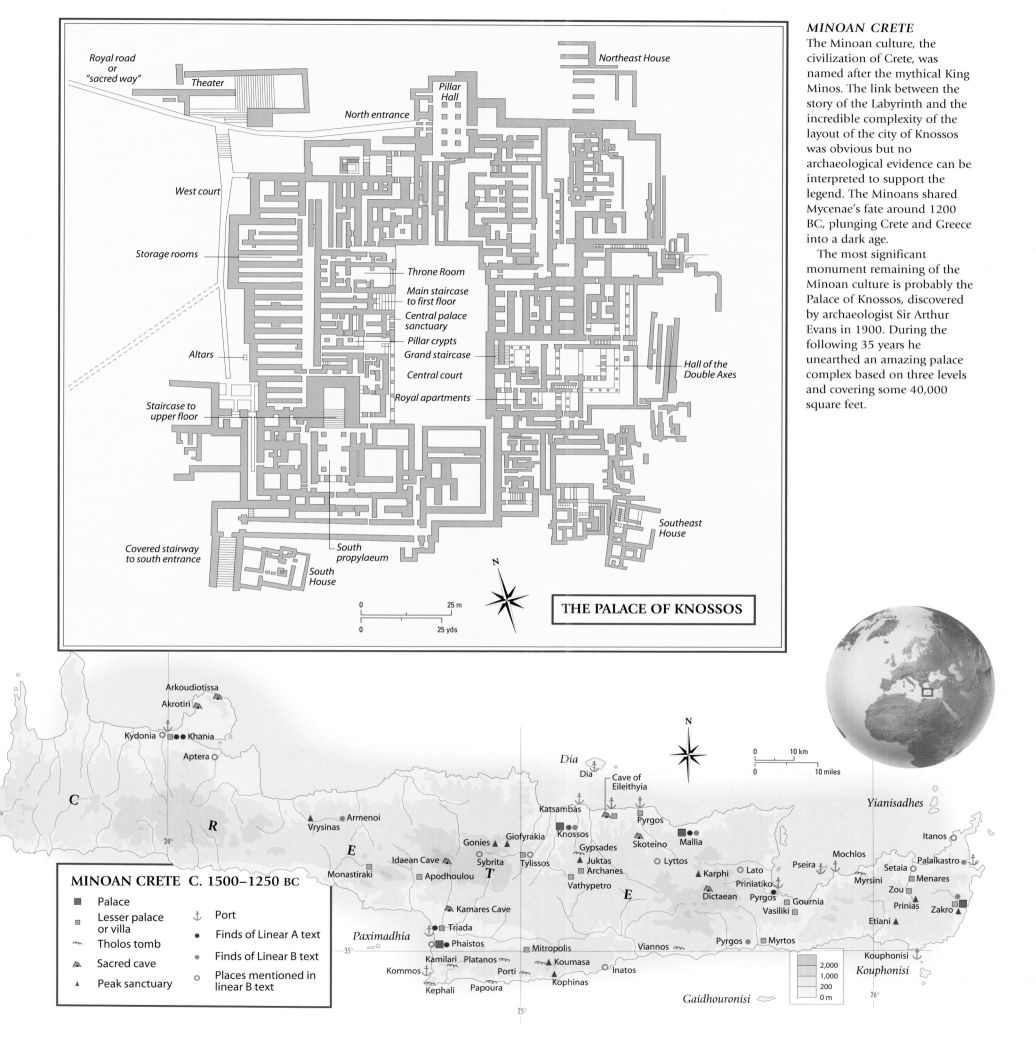

Royal road
or
"sacred way"

Theater

Northeast House

Pillar
Hall

North entrance

West court

Storage rooms

Throne Room

Main staircase
to first floor

Central palace
sanctuary

Pillar crypts

Grand staircase

Central court

Royal apartments

Altars

Hall of the
Double Axes

Staircase to
upper floor

Southeast
House

Covered stairway
to south entrance

South
propylaeum

South
House

N

0   25 m

0   25 yds

THE PALACE OF KNOSSOS

MINOAN CRETE

The Minoan culture, the civilization of Crete, was named after the mythical King Minos. The link between the story of the Labyrinth and the incredible complexity of the layout of the city of Knossos was obvious but no archaeological evidence can be interpreted to support the legend. The Minoans shared Mycenae's fate around 1200 BC, plunging Crete and Greece into a dark age.

The most significant monument remaining of the Minoan culture is probably the Palace of Knossos, discovered by archaeologist Sir Arthur Evans in 1900. During the following 35 years he unearthed an amazing palace complex based on three levels and covering some 40,000 square feet.

Arkoudiotissa

Akrotiri

Kydonia   Khania

Aptera

C

R

E

T

E

Vrysinas   Armenoi

Gonies   Giofyrakia

Idaean Cave   Sybrita   Tylissos

Monastiraki

Apodhoulou

Juktas
Archanes

Vathypetro

Kamares Cave

Triada

Kamilari   Platanos
Kommos   Porti

Kephali   Papoura

Phaistos

Mitropolis

Koumasa

Kophinas

Inatos

Dia
Dia

Cave of
Eileithyia

Katsambas

Knossos   Pyrgos

Gypsades   Skoteino   Mallia

Lyttos

Karphi   Lato
Priniatiko
Dictaean   Pyrgos   Gournia

Vasiliki

Pyrgos   Myrtos

Viannos

Yianisadhes

Itanos

Mochlos
Pseira   Palaikastro
Setaia
Myrsini   Menares
Zou
Prinias   Zakro
Etiani

Kouphonisi

Kouphonisi

Paximadhia

Gaidhouronisi

N

0   10 km

0   10 miles

MINOAN CRETE c. 1500–1250 BC

- ■ Palace
- ◾ Lesser palace or villa
- ⌢ Tholos tomb
- ▲ Sacred cave
- ▲ Peak sanctuary
- ⚓ Port
- ● Finds of Linear A text
- ● Finds of Linear B text
- ○ Places mentioned in linear B text

2,000
1,000
200
0 m

1200 BC – 400 BC   EARLY GREECE

EARLY GREECE

At the end of the Bronze Age, around 1200–1000 BC, waves of militarily-superior invaders, known as the Dorians, moved into Greece and the Aegean. These invaders had mounted warriors whose iron weapons were superior to the bronze weapons of the indigenous population. The northwestern Greeks settled in Aetolia and some moved to Achaea, while others dispersed along the north coast of the Aegean. The Dorians first settled in Thessaly before moving to the Pelopennese and then by sea to Crete, Rhodes and the southwest part of Asia minor. The Ionians survived the Dorian migrations and spread themselves through the central part of the Aegean, as well as settling parts of eastern Asia minor and areas to the north of the Aegean.

The Aeolians migrated eastward across the Aegean, also settling parts of western Asia Minor. Historians have debated the timing and nature of the Dorian invasions. However, there is no doubting that large-scale population movements occurred, and in this process many Bronze Age sites were destroyed, setting in motion 200 years of instability after which the distribution of Greek-speaking peoples was reflected by its most important dialects.

THE PHOENICIANS AND GREEKS COLONIZE THE MEDITERRANEAN

The Phoenicians were a grouping of city kingdoms on the east Mediterranean coast. Sometime around 1100 BC the Phoenicians developed their maritime technology, enabling them to extend their trade throughout the entire Mediterranean basin and occasionally beyond it into the Atlantic Ocean. The Phoenicians also founded many colonies, including Cathage in north Africa and Malaca in what is now southern Spain. Greek trade and colonization occurred at the same time as the Phoenician, and in the Greek case population pressures may have been an influence. The growth of Near Eastern empires prevented Greek colonization heading eastward, so the Greeks concentrated principally on the north coast of the Mediterranean and the Black Sea, though there were important colonies at Cyrene in north Africa, Naucratis, and the island of Cyprus.

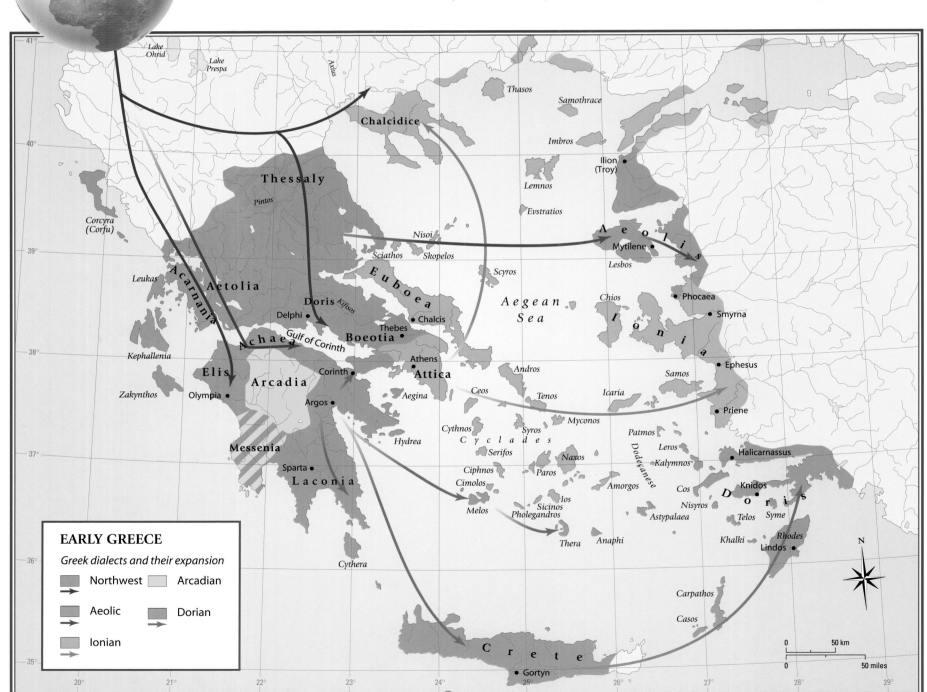

EARLY GREECE

Greek dialects and their expansion

- Northwest
- Aeolic
- Ionian
- Arcadian
- Dorian

EARLY ATTICA; GREEKS COLONISE THE MEDITERRANEAN

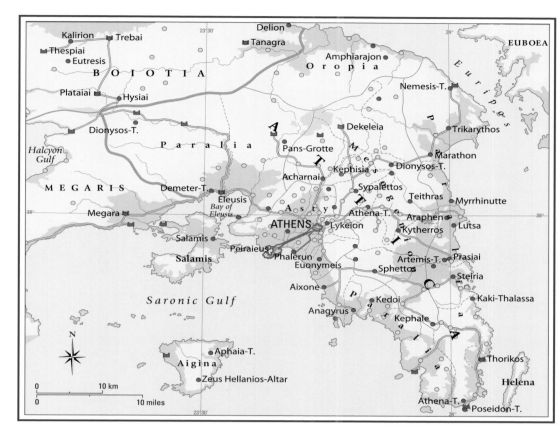

EARLY ATTICA
4th and 5th Centuries

- ○ Settlement
- ● Sacred site
- ▣ Fortress and sacred site
- ▣ Fortresses of the 4th Century BC
- — National border
- — District boundary
- ⋯ Frontiers of the Trittyen
- — Main highways (assumed)
- — the 'Long Walls'

Map labels: Kalirion, Trebai, Delion, Tanagra, EUBOEA, Thespiai, Eutresis, Amphiarajon, Oropia, Euripos, BOIOTIA, Nemesis-T., Plataiai, Hysiai, Dekeleia, Trikarythos, Dionysos-T., Paralia, Pans-Grotte, Marathon, Halcyon Gulf, Kephisia, Dionysos-T., Acharnai, Demeter-T., Sypalettos, Teithras, Myrrhinutte, MEGARIS, Eleusis, Bay of Eleusis, Asty, Athena-T., Araphen, Lutsa, Megara, Salamis, ATHENS, Lykeion, Kytherros, Peiraieus, Phalerun, Artemis-T., Prasiai, Salamis, Euonymeis, Sphettos, Steiria, Aixone, Kaki-Thalassa, Saronic Gulf, Kedoi, Kephale, Anagyrus, Aphaia-T., Thorikos, Aigina, Helena, Zeus Hellanios-Altar, Athena-T., Poseidon-T.

0   10 km
0   10 miles

EARLY ATTICA
During the 8th and 9th Centuries BC, Athens probably absorbed the other independent cities of Attica.
  Although this new Greek entity did not have rich agricultural land it did enjoy some geographical advantages. It was well supplied with good harbors for trade and military expeditions and, to the north and east, was protected by mountains from invasion. Athens, with its fleet and imperial ambitions, became a powerhouse of ancient Greece.

THE PHOENICIANS AND GREEKS COLONISE THE MEDITERRANEAN 9TH–6TH CENTURY BC

- ▪ Phoenicia, c. 750 BC
- Phoenician settlement, from the 9th Century BC
- ▪ Greece, c. 750 BC
- Greek settlement, 8th–6th Century BC
- ▪ Principal Phoenician colonizing cities
- ▪ Principal Greek colonizing cities
- ● Greek or Phoenician colony

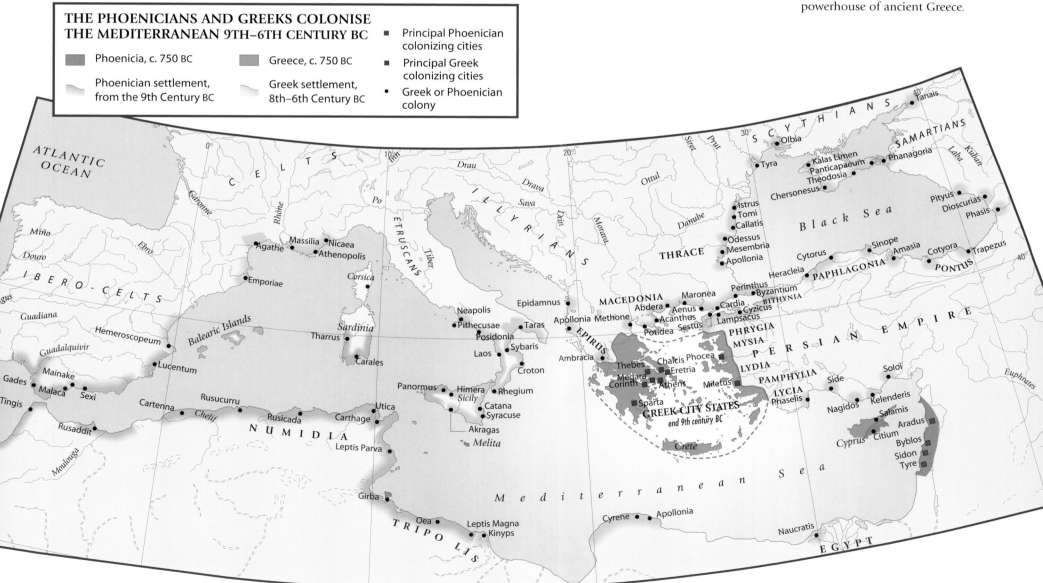

ETRUSCAN EXPANSION

ETRUSCAN EXPANSION

According to Herodotus, the Etruscans originated in Lydia in south western Asia Minor, and after migration they settled in what would become Italy. They settled a region known as Etruria, almost equivalent to modern Tuscany. Here the Etruscans founded a state based on the League of Twelve Cities, from which the Etruscan elite could dominate, control, and develop the region. They slowly extended their power by a process of conquest and colonization into the Po Valley and southward beyond Rome and to Campania. Etruscan expansion, though impressive, was never really fully coordinated, with each city to some degree deciding its own fate. However, both Rome and the Greek cities of the area were so alarmed at this growth in Etruscan power that they decided to join forces to fight against it. Between 535 BC and 396 BC various wars were fought between the Etruscans and Greco-Roman alliances, and by 283 BC Rome had conquered Etruria. The area became increasingly Latinized, though many Etruscan forms survived in architecture and frescos.

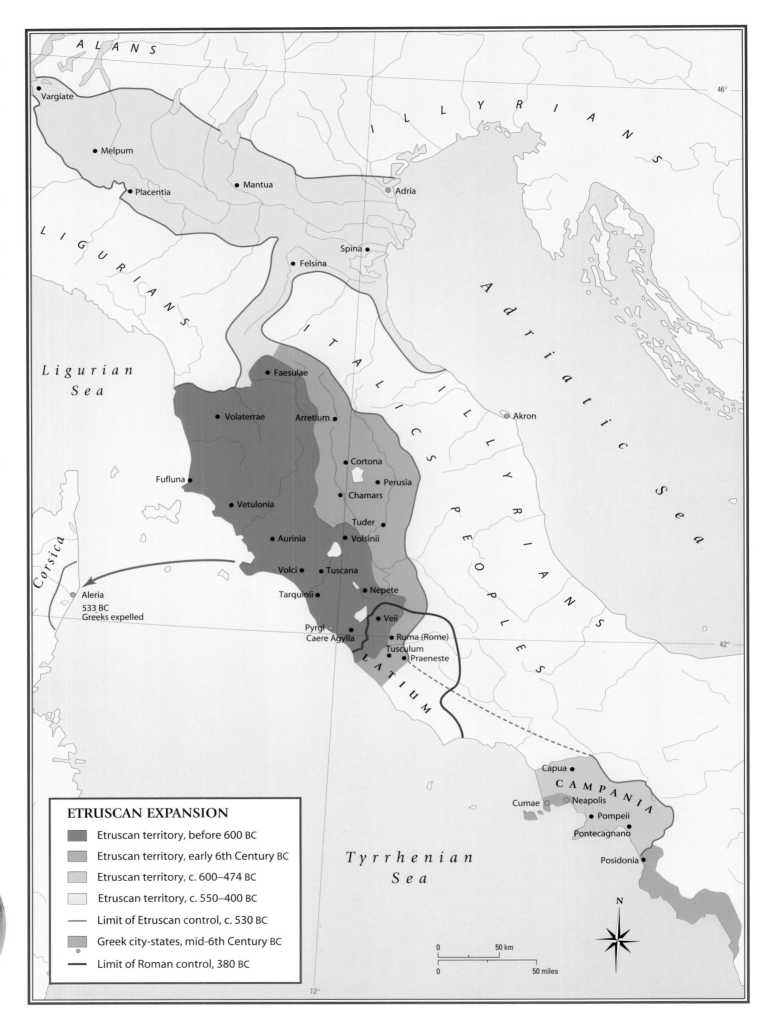

ETRUSCAN EXPANSION

- Etruscan territory, before 600 BC
- Etruscan territory, early 6th Century BC
- Etruscan territory, c. 600–474 BC
- Etruscan territory, c. 550–400 BC
- — Limit of Etruscan control, c. 530 BC
- Greek city-states, mid-6th Century BC
- — Limit of Roman control, 380 BC

THE RISE OF MACEDONIA

THE RISE OF MACEDONIA

- Core area of Macedonian control, early 4th Century BC
- Added to Macedonia by 359 BC
- Added to or subdued by Macedonia by 336 BC
- Added to or subdued by Macedonia after 336 BC
- Probable extent of the Corinthian League from 337 BC
- Other Greek states

THE RISE OF MACEDONIA Philip II, on his return from Thebes to Macedonia where he had been held hostage, immediately set about re-organizing the Macedonian state, concentrating particularly on his army. He organized his army into units of cavalry, javelin throwers, and archers, whose job on the battlefield was to support a phalanx of infantry armed with shields and pikes. In 357 BC Philip captured the Athenian colony of Amphipolis and seized the gold mines of Pangaeus—the latter went some way to financing his future military operations. By 348 BC Philip had conquered Thrace and Chalcidice, and two years later Philip intervened in a war between Thebes and Phocis. His victory in this war allowed him to replace Phocis in the Amphictyonic League, a form of Greek religious organization. This membership gave Macedonia the right to participate in Greek political issues and made Philip the senior military commander of all league forces. Athens grew increasingly concerned at the growth of Macedonia's power. The subsequent alliance between Athens and Thebes was destroyed by Philip's Macedonian army at Chaeronea in 338 BC, which left Philip the master of Greece. While preparing an invasion of Persia, Philip was murdered and was immediately succeeded by his son Alexander, who ruthlessly executed all those accused of his father's murder and any possible rivals or factions that could in any way threaten his position. With Alexander now in command, Macedonia was once again poised for further conquests.

THE EMPIRE OF ALEXANDER THE GREAT

THE EMPIRE OF ALEXANDER THE GREAT
Alexander inherited from his father, Philip II of Macedonia, both a large and capable army and a plan to conquer Persia. After ruthlessly consolidating his position in Greece, in the spring of 334 BC, he crossed the Hellespont with 35,000 men. He attacked and destroyed a united army of Persians and Greek mercenaries at the River Granicus, defeating it with little loss to his own forces. Alexander would go on to take the Greek language and civilization to the limits of the known world. Eventually Alexander was forced to return home by his rebellious army, which was camped on the banks of the Indus River. He agreed to return to the west but died on the return journey in 323 BC.

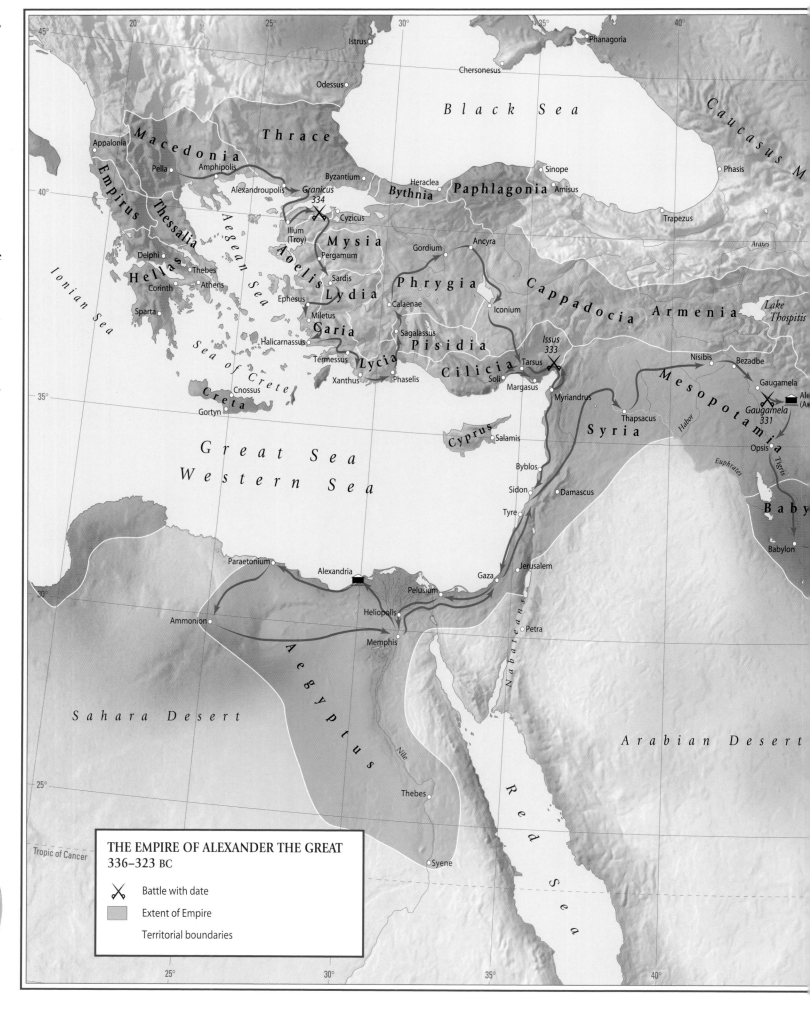

THE EMPIRE OF ALEXANDER THE GREAT
336–323 BC

✗ Battle with date

▨ Extent of Empire

Territorial boundaries

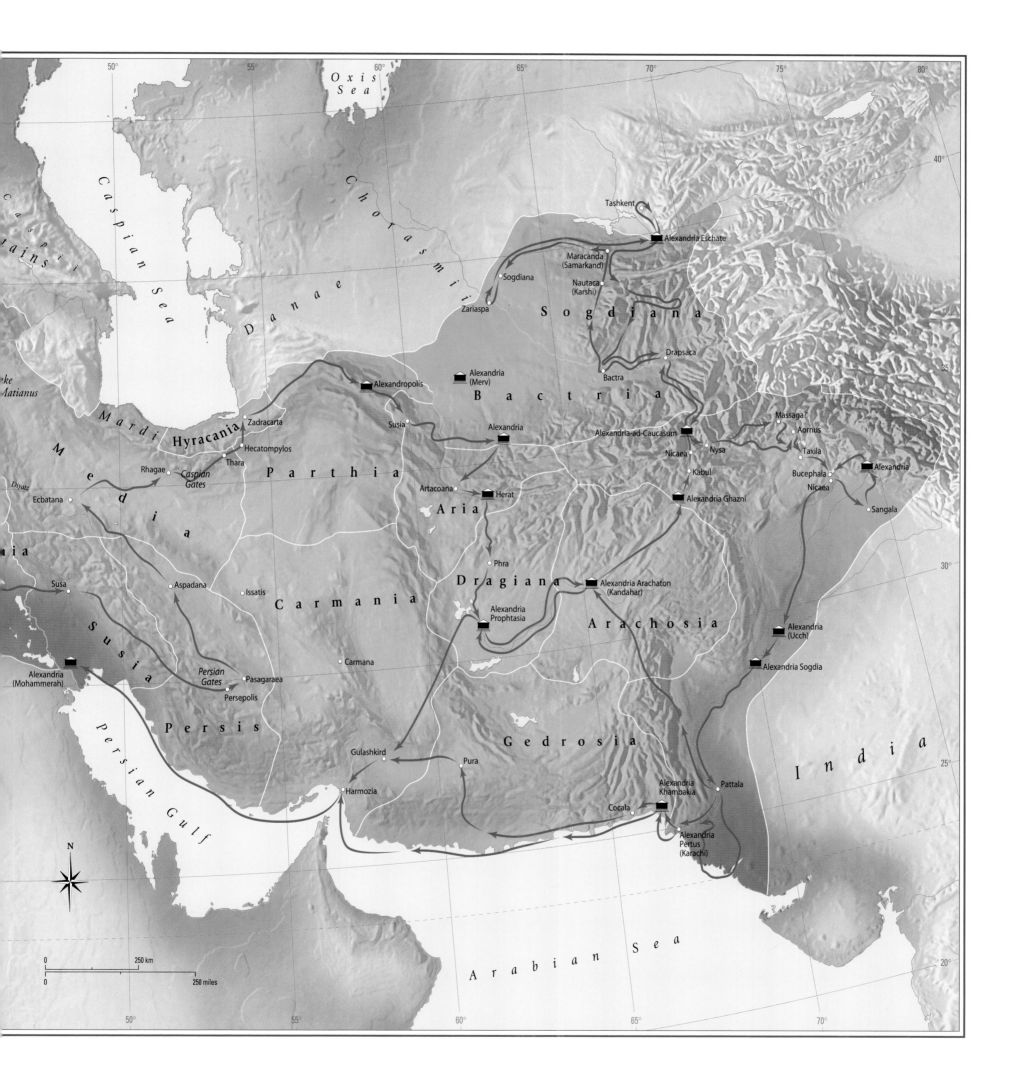

Oxis
Sea

Caspian Sea

Chorasmii

Caspii

ke
Matianus

Tashkent

Alexandria Eschate

Maracanda
(Samarkand)

Sogdiana

Nautaca
(Karshi)

Sogdiana

Danae

Zariaspa

Drapsaca

Bactra

Mardi

Hyracania

Zadracarta

Alexandropolis

Alexandria
(Merv)

Bactria

Susia

Alexandria

Alexandria-ad-Caucasum

Massaga?

Aornus

Nysa

Nicaea

Taxila

Hecatompylos

Susia

Parthia

Kabul

Bucephala

Alexandria

Diyatz

Rhagae

Thara

Caspian
Gates

Nicaea

Medi

Artacoana

Herat

Aria

Sangala

Ecbatana

a

Phra

Alexandria Ghazni

Susa

Aspadana

Issatis

Dragiana

Alexandria Arachaton
(Kandahar)

Carmania

Arachosia

Alexandria
(Ucch?)

Susia

Alexandria Prophtasia

Alexandria Sogdia

Carmana

Alexandria
(Mohammerah)

Persian
Gates

Pasagaraea

Persepolis

Persis

Gedrosia

India

Persian Gulf

Gulashkird

Pura

Alexandria
Khambakia

Pattala

Cocala

Harmozia

Alexandria
Pertus
(Karachi)

N

Arabian Sea

250 km

0

250 miles

0

THE HALLSTATT CULTURE; THE CELTS

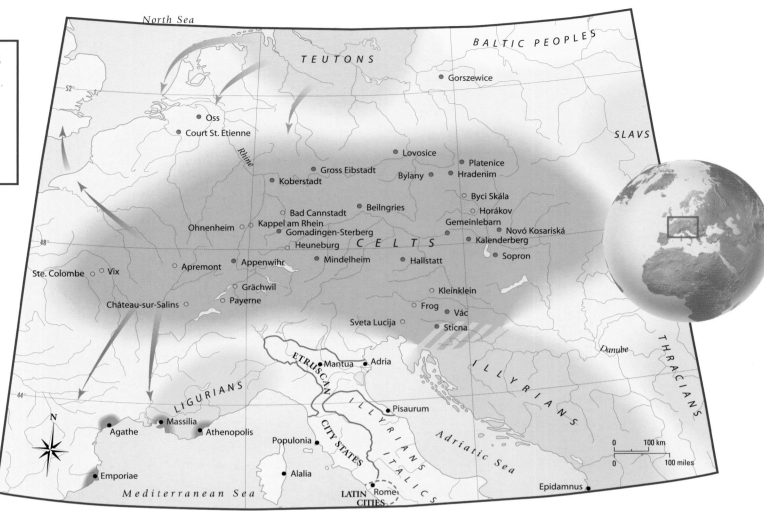

THE HALLSTATT CULTURE

SLAVS	People
→	Teutonic expansion
→	Celtic expansion
•	Early Hallstatt site
◦	Late Hallstatt site

THE HALLSTATT CULTURE

The period of Hallstatt Culture dates from 750 BC. It is named after the Celtic burial ground that was excavated in Austria and it marks the beginning of the slow spread of Celtic civilization and Iron Age technology throughout south central Europe, France, Spain, and parts of the Balkans. Archaeological finds also suggest that these Celts began to settle the British Isles. Hallstatt Celtic society seems to have been made up of tribes or clans, which were themselves subdivided into family groups. Society was made up of chiefs, warriors, druids (religious leaders), craftsmen, farmers, servants, and finally slaves.

THE CELTS

The Celtic La Tene culture was given its name after an archaeological site on Lake Neuchatel in Switzerland and existed from about 450 BC. Between the 8th and 3rd centuries BC, Celtic tribes left their home territory and migrated westward, southwest into Iberia, southeast through the Balkans, and southward across the Alps into Italy. Here they came into violent contact with the Etruscans and the Romans. Despite this expansion the Celts lacked any kind of political unity. Ultimately they would be caught between the expanding power of Rome and the Germanic tribes in the north.

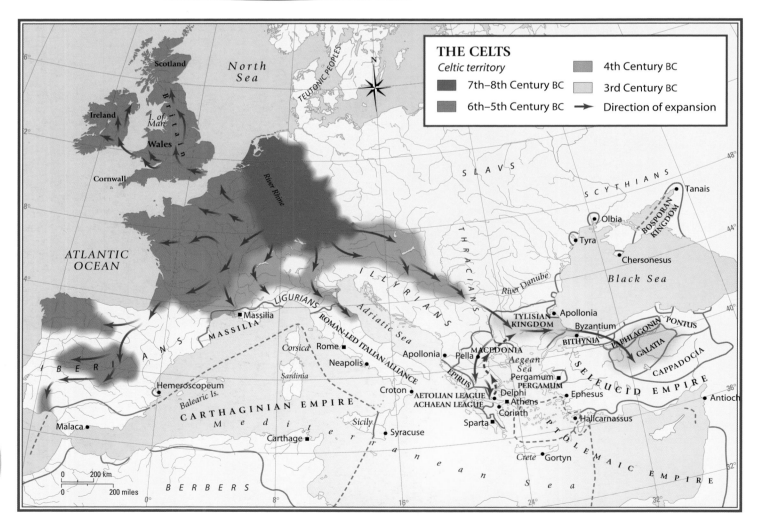

THE CELTS

Celtic territory

■	7th–8th Century BC
■	6th–5th Century BC
■	4th Century BC
■	3rd Century BC
→	Direction of expansion

THE RISE OF ROME

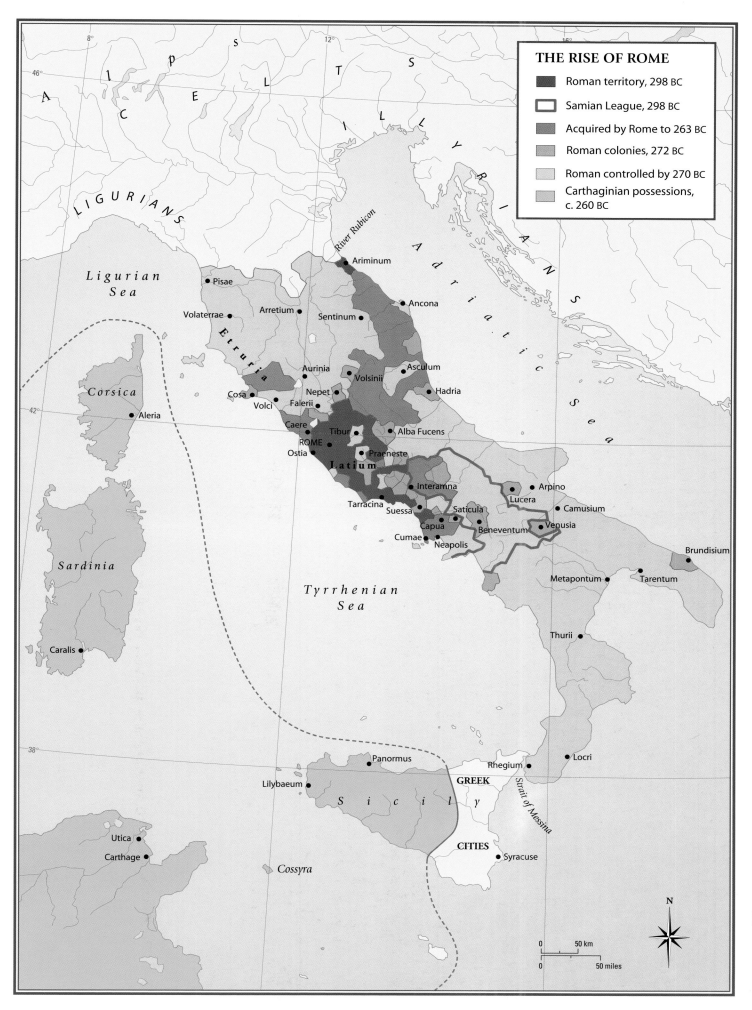

THE RISE OF ROME

Roman territory, 298 BC

Samian League, 298 BC

Acquired by Rome to 263 BC

Roman colonies, 272 BC

Roman controlled by 270 BC

Carthaginian possessions, c. 260 BC

A L P S

C E L T S

I L L Y R I A N S

LIGURIANS

Ligurian Sea

Pisae

Volaterrae

Arretium

Sentinum

Ancona

Etruria

Aurinia

Volsinii

Asculum

Hadria

Cosa

Nepet

Volci

Falerii

Caere

Tibur

Alba Fucens

ROME

Ostia

Latium

Praeneste

Interamna

Arpino

Lucera

Tarracina

Suessa

Saticula

Camusium

Capua

Beneventum

Venusia

Cumae

Neapolis

Brundisium

Corsica

Aleria

Sardinia

Caralis

Tyrrhenian Sea

Adriatic Sea

River Rubicon

Ariminum

Metapontum

Tarentum

Thurii

Panormus

Rhegium

Locri

Lilybaeum

GREEK

Sicily

CITIES

Syracuse

Utica

Carthage

Cossyra

Strait of Messina

N

0   50 km

0   50 miles

THE RISE OF ROME

After its foundation in 753 BC, Rome remained in the Etruscan sphere of influence for almost 250 years. Rome commanded a strategic crossing point of the River Tiber: to the north lay the powerful Etruscan cities and to the south the numerous Greek settlements. For 200 years the Romans slowly extended their power over one tribe after another. Eventually in 510 BC the last Etruscan king was overthrown and Rome became a republic. However, its position remained insecure and an Etruscan bid to retake the city had to be beaten off. Other Latin cities joined with Rome and independence was finally won from the Etruscans at the battle of Arica in 506 BC.

Rapidly growing in importance, Rome was now able to expand its power southward. The Romans took on their one-time allies, the Samnites, defeating them completely by 290 BC. By 266 BC Roman control extended north to the River Rubicon, and Roman citizenship was granted throughout this region.

PUNIC WARS

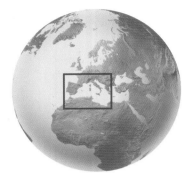

PUNIC WARS

After Rome had consolidated its position on the Italian peninsula, it became involved in a series of three wars against the Empire of Carthage.

The first Punic war (after Poeni in Latin), 264–241 BC, was fought largely at sea, which favored the Carthaginians, a maritime trading power who commanded a large and capable navy. The Romans were successful when fighting on land in Sicily but it would take them a further eight years to beat the Cathaginians at sea. Rome constructed a large fleet of warships and mastered the necessary naval skills to eventually defeat the Carthaginians near the Aegates islands in 241 BC. By 238 BC the Carthaginians had been driven from Sicily, Corsica, and Sardina. The second Punic war began in 218 BC; it was an attempt by Carthage to destroy Roman power and restore control of the vital sea routes

THE PUNIC WARS
264–146 BC

Second War: 218–201 BC

▨	Carthaginian gains by 218 BC
▤	Roman gains by 201 BC
→	Scipio's campaign 218–210 BC
→	Roman campaign against Macedonia 216–211 BC
→	Movements of Carthaginian fleet 215–209 BC
→	Hannibal's campaign 216–203 BC
→	Hasdrupal's campaign 208–207 BC
→	Mago's campaign 205–203 BC
✕	Site of battle with date

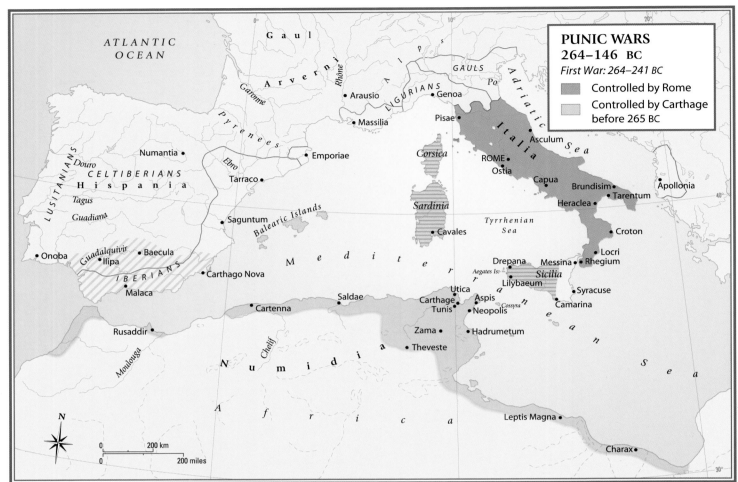

PUNIC WARS
264–146 BC
First War: 264–241 BC
- ▨ Controlled by Rome
- ▨ Controlled by Carthage before 265 BC

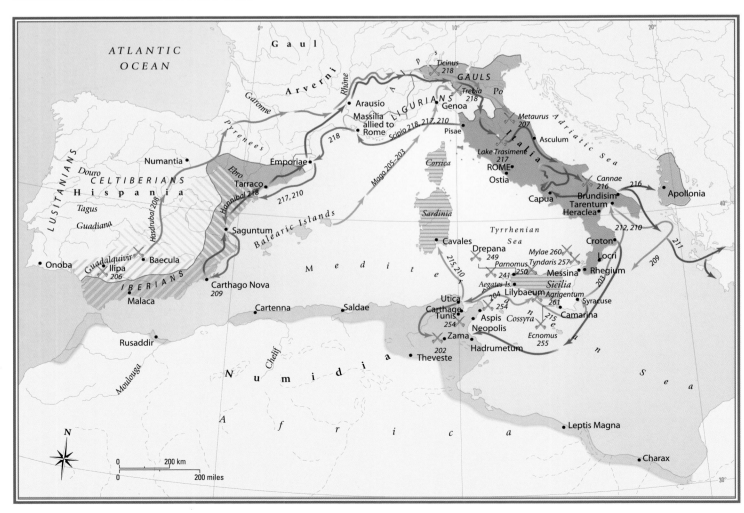

ROME; THE ROMAN EMPIRE

back to Carthage. The famous Carthaginian General, Hannibal, marched an army from Spain across what is now southern France, through the Alps and down into the Roman heartlands. There he fought a tactically-successful war for 16 years. It was, however, ultimately strategically unsuccessful, as Rome was never completely defeated. The Roman army, under Scipio, in turn invaded Carthage itself and at the

Battle of Zama in 202 BC Carthaginian forces were utterly defeated. As a result Carthage lost substantial territories and was forced to pay indemnities. It also had to surrender its navy to Roman control.

Fifty years later Carthage had partly recovered and was beginning again to develop as a major regional commercial power. Fearing the consequences if this was left unchecked, Rome once again went to war with Carthage in 149 BC. For two years the city of Carthage resisted the Roman siege but was eventually overwhelmed. In 146 BC the victorious Romans decided to make sure that its rival would never be a threat again; the city was destroyed, the surrounding farmlands

ploughed up and sown with salt and its population sold into slavery. Rome annexed Carthage's north African territories, confirming its complete domination of the western Mediterranean.

THE ROMAN EMPIRE 55 BC

After the victories over Carthage, Rome continued to expand through military conquest. Under the leadership of military dictators —Sulla (138–78 BC), Pompey (106–48 BC), and Caesar (100–44 BC)—Rome had moved from Republic to Empire. By 55 BC Rome controlled the entire Mediterranean coastline and large parts of western Asia minor. Julius Caesar had finally conquered Gaul and with Egypt now an ally of Rome, the city had become the capital of an undisputed superpower.

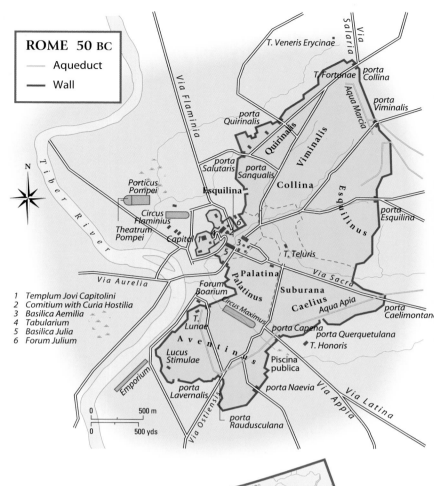

THE FIRST JEWISH REVOLT; THE ROMAN EMPIRE

THE FIRST JEWISH REVOLT

The Jewish–Roman War of AD 66–70 began with a series of disturbances near the Roman administrative headquarters at Caesarea, then spread throughout the province. The war was a severe test of the Roman occupation of Palestine.

In the Roman view complete defeat of the rebels was necessary to maintain order in a vast and diverse Empire; this they would do despite the suicidal commitment of the Jewish Zealots.

THE ROMAN EMPIRE

The power of the Roman Empire was at its zenith under the early emperors. Their vast

and populous Empire extended over southern and western Europe, Asia Minor, parts of the Near East, and also included the coasts of north Africa and much of Egypt.

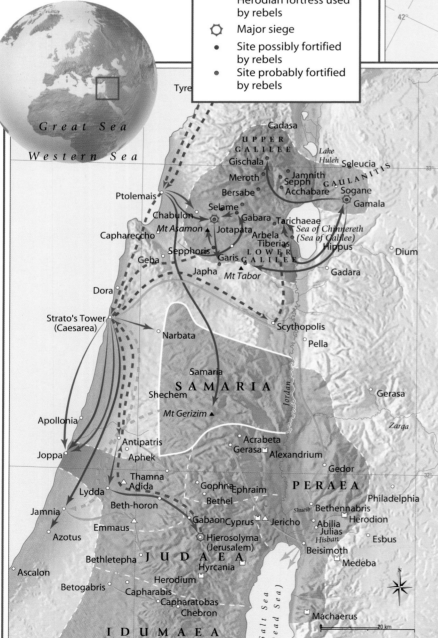

THE FIRST JEWISH REVOLT AD 66–68

- ◄- - Non-hostile troop movements
- ◄━━ Cestius Gallus AD 66
- ◄━━ AD 67
- ◄━━ AD 68
- � Primarily Jewish population
- ▨ Primarily Samaritan population
- ▭ Rebel military district
- △ Major Roman camp
- ⌂ Hasmonaean or Herodian fortress used by rebels
- ⬡ Major siege
- • Site possibly fortified by rebels
- ● Site probably fortified by rebels

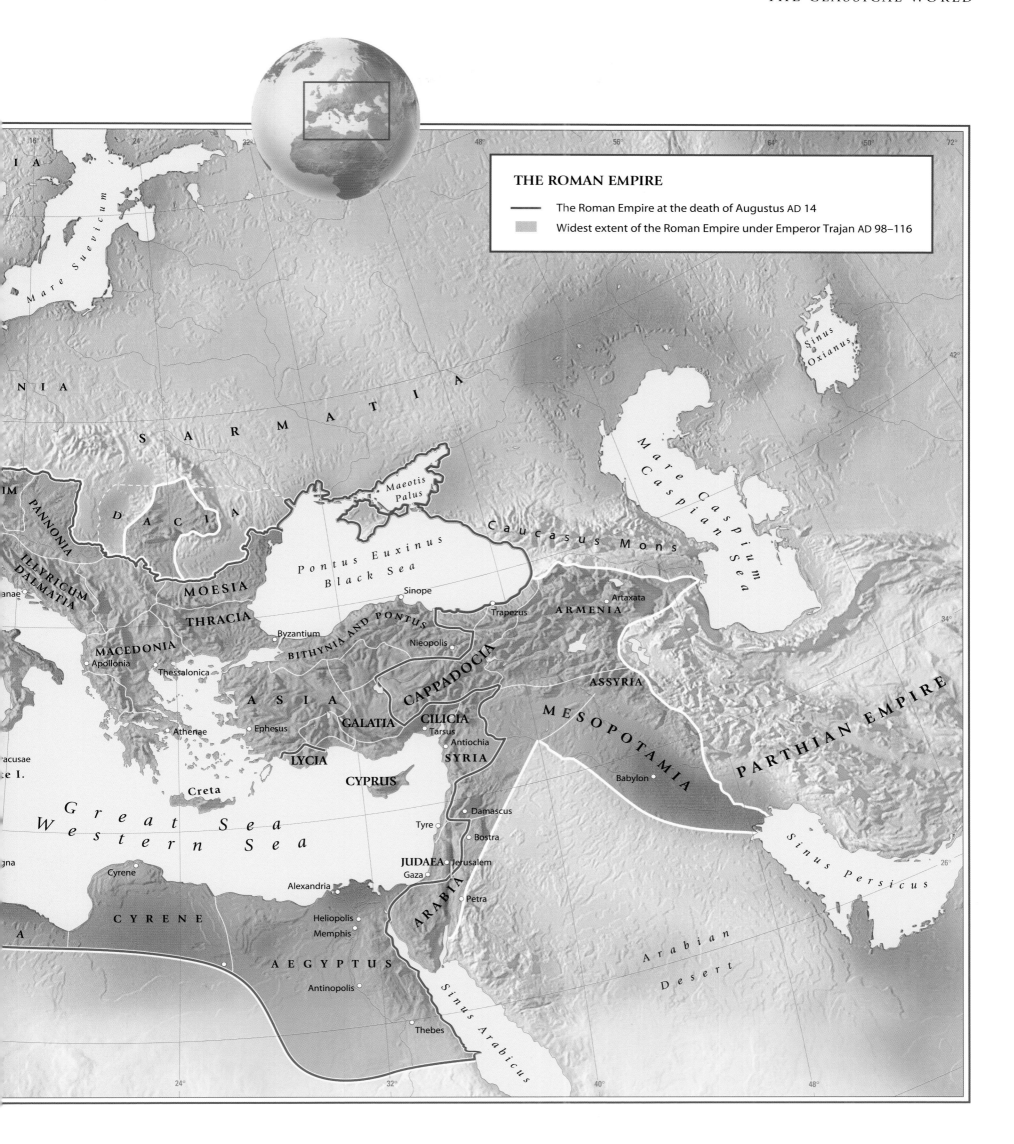

THE ROMAN EMPIRE

—— The Roman Empire at the death of Augustus AD 14

▨ Widest extent of the Roman Empire under Emperor Trajan AD 98–116

Mare Suevicum

NIA

IM

SARMATIA

PANNONIA

ILLYRICUM

DALMATIA

DACIA

anae

MOESIA

THRACIA

MACEDONIA

Apollonia

Thessalonica

Maeotis Palus

Pontus Euxinus
Black Sea

Byzantium

BITHYNIA AND PONTUS

Sinope

Trapezus

Caucasus Mons

ARMENIA

Artaxata

Mare Caspium
Caspian Sea

Sinus Oxianus

ASIA

GALATIA

Nicopolis

CAPPADOCIA

ASSYRIA

PARTHIAN EMPIRE

Athenae

Ephesus

CILICIA

Tarsus

Antiochia

SYRIA

MESOPOTAMIA

racusae
e I.

LYCIA

CYPRUS

Creta

Babylon

Great
Western
Sea
Sea

Damascus

Tyre

Bostra

Sinus Persicus

gna

Cyrene

Alexandria

JUDAEA

Gaza

Jerusalem

Petra

ARABIA

Arabian
Desert

CYRENE

Heliopolis

Memphis

A

AEGYPTUS

Antinopolis

Sinus Arabicus

Thebes

FEUDING STATES OF CHINA; EXPANSION OF THE CH'IN

350 BC – AD 100

THE FEUDING STATES
Around 480 BC the Chou dynasty lost control over China. As power from the center disintegrated, successor states formed and fought each other in their various bids for power. Seven major states contested for power, but slowly the Ch'in established control over the west and by 221 BC they had overcome their rivals. Its ruler, Qin Shi Huang, proclaimed himself First Emperor of all China.

HAN EMPIRE
The short-lived Ch'in dynasty was replaced by the Han in 206 BC, but many of the Ch'in's innovations survived. The Han ruled for 200 years until AD 9 when, for a brief interlude, the usurpation of Wang Mang held sway, before the later Han dynasty assumed power again in AD 25. Their state reached further westward, southward and eastward into Manchuria and Korea (Lo-Yang). In 220 the last Han Emperor abdicated; China was divided into the Three Kingdoms and would remain divided for 369 years.

FEUDING STATES OF CHINA c. 350 BC
- ⇢ Major line of expansion

THE EXPANSION OF THE CH'IN
Qin Shi Huang became the first ruler of China to call himself Emperor in 221 BC. During his eight-year reign he established a new imperial system of rule, replacing the old feudal hierarchy with a centralized bureaucratic administration that would last for two thousand years. The Great Wall was also begun in 221 BC and eventually stretched from Kansu to the sea, a distance of 2250 km.

EXPANSION OF THE CH'IN 316–209 BC
- Original Ch'in territory
- Expansion to 221 BC
- Other states conquered, with date
- Other areas conquered after unification
- → Nomadic invasions, 315–201 BC
- ⊔⊓ Wall

THE HAN EMPIRE; THE SILK ROAD

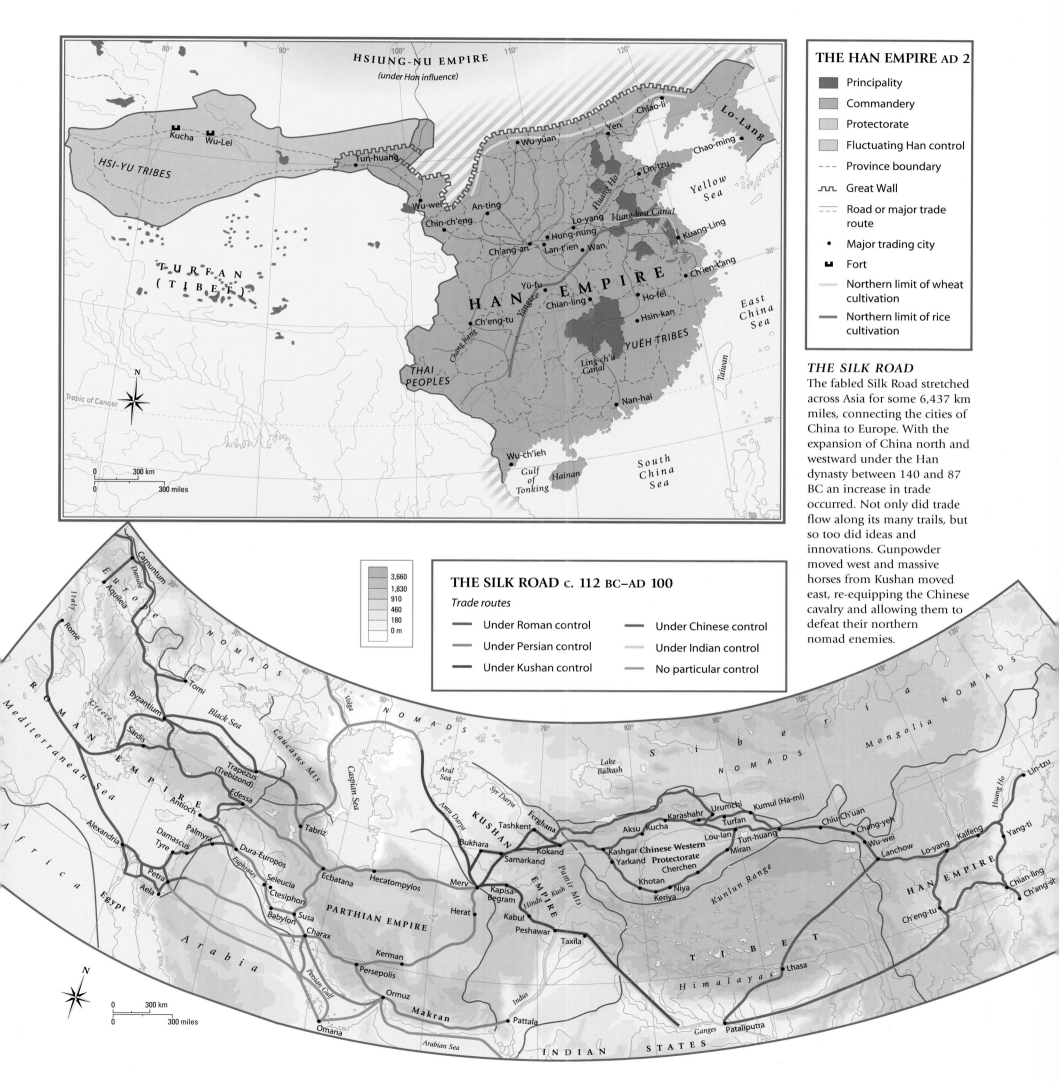

THE HAN EMPIRE AD 2
- Principality
- Commandery
- Protectorate
- Fluctuating Han control
- – – – Province boundary
- Great Wall
- Road or major trade route
- • Major trading city
- Fort
- Northern limit of wheat cultivation
- Northern limit of rice cultivation

THE SILK ROAD
The fabled Silk Road stretched across Asia for some 6,437 km miles, connecting the cities of China to Europe. With the expansion of China north and westward under the Han dynasty between 140 and 87 BC an increase in trade occurred. Not only did trade flow along its many trails, but so too did ideas and innovations. Gunpowder moved west and massive horses from Kushan moved east, re-equipping the Chinese cavalry and allowing them to defeat their northern nomad enemies.

THE SILK ROAD c. 112 BC–AD 100
Trade routes
- Under Roman control
- Under Persian control
- Under Kushan control
- Under Chinese control
- Under Indian control
- No particular control

THE MAURYAN EMPIRE

THE MAURYAN EMPIRE
The Mauryan Empire was founded by Chandragupta, who initially seized control of the Kingdom of Magadha. From there he built an empire that covered all of northern India. After the death of Alexander the Great Chandragupta seized Arachosia from its Macedonian conquerors. He later defeated Alexander's successor, Selucis, extending his domain to include most of modern Afghanistan and Pakistan.

The Empire reached its greatest extent under the rule of Asoka. He covered his empire with rock and pillar edicts intended to inform the population of his thoughts and actions. However, the empire did not last long after Asoka's death. Divided between his sons its power declined, inviting invasion and rebellion.

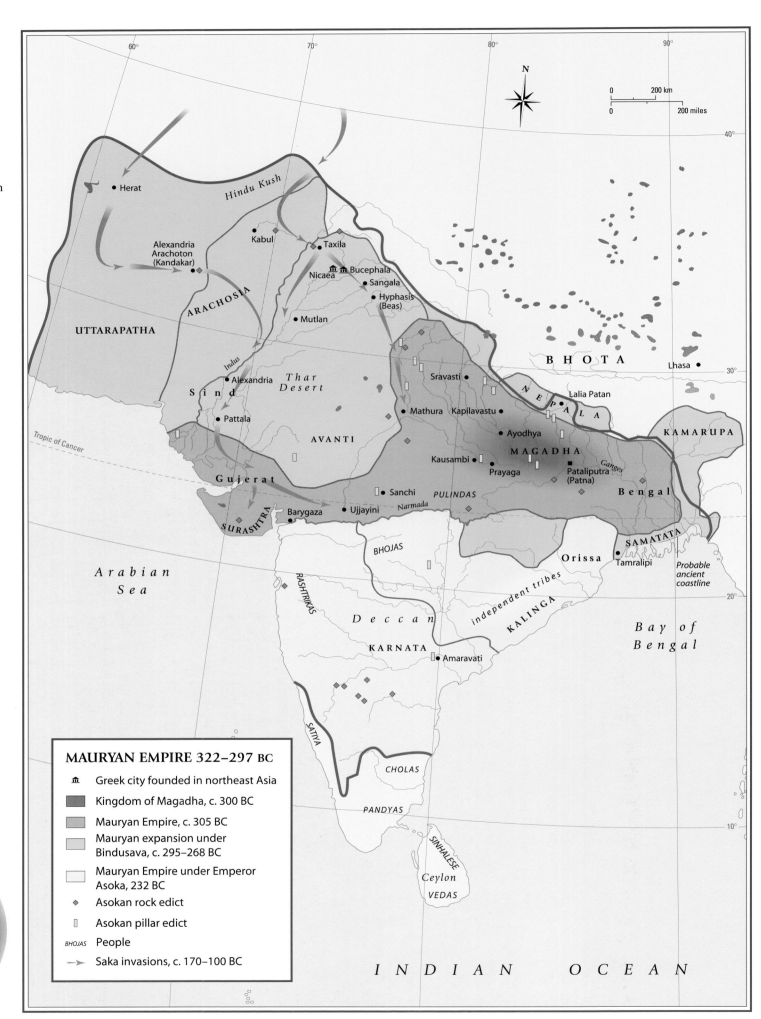

MAURYAN EMPIRE 322–297 BC

🏛 Greek city founded in northeast Asia

◼ Kingdom of Magadha, c. 300 BC

◼ Mauryan Empire, c. 305 BC

☐ Mauryan expansion under Bindusava, c. 295–268 BC

☐ Mauryan Empire under Emperor Asoka, 232 BC

◆ Asokan rock edict

▯ Asokan pillar edict

BHOJAS People

➜ Saka invasions, c. 170–100 BC

THE GUPTA EMPIRE

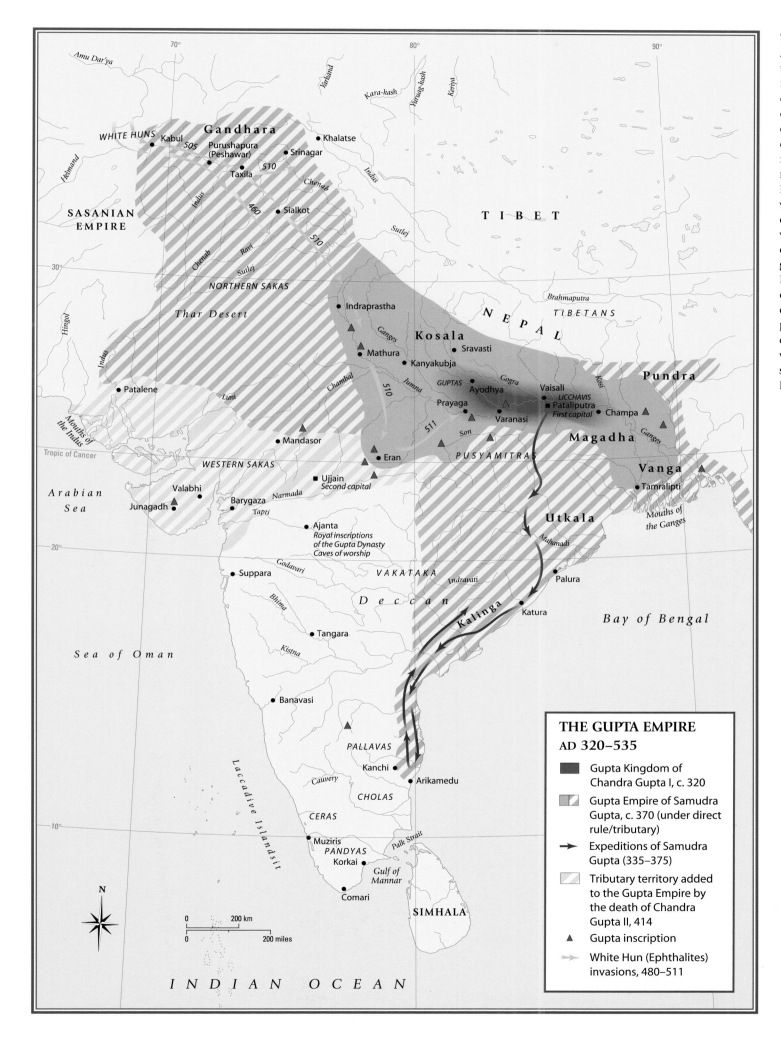

THE GUPTA EMPIRE
THE GUPTA EMPIRE
After centuries of disunity, a unified India began to emerge in the Ganges Valley, centered on Patna. Here the dynasty of the Guptas became established, and by a combination of careful marriages and military power, reunited most of northern India. Once again the region was well protected from external threat and entered what some describe as its classical age. It was a period of growth for the status of the Hindu faith and many aspects of Indian life became established. During the Gupta period the preeminent status of the Hindu Brahmin priest was established and the caste system was integrated into India's social system.

THE WORLD AD 500

THE WORLD IN 500

Massive migrations in Europe had effectively ended the western half of the Roman Empire, which had been replaced by several Germanic States. However, the East Roman Empire survived with its capital at Constantinople. To the east, the Sassanians survived attacks by the nomadic Hephthalites, or white Huns, managing to remain almost intact. In India, the Guptas had gradually extended their authority and, by the year 500, covered most of northern India. Locally, rulers were allowed to remain on their thrones as long as they paid tribute and acknowledged their vassal status to their Gupta overlords.

China, after a period of disunity, was briefly united by the Jin dynasty in 280. However, nomad assaults succeeded in destroying Chang'an in 316. The Jin dynasty moved southward to a new capital at Nanjing where they managed to remain in control of southern China; the north of the country was dominated by successive waves of steppe nomads.

In the Americas, the Mayan civilization constructed sophisticated cities, such as Uaxactun and Tikal, largely built from stone. The Mayan city states maintained an independence where each city traded or fought with each other as opportunity dictated.

Despite this division the Maya developed the only fully literate society in pre-Columbian America.

THE WORLD AD 500

- ■ Major cities

- —— Extent of Ostrogoth Empire under Ermanaric, 370

- —— Extent of Hun Empire under Attila, 450

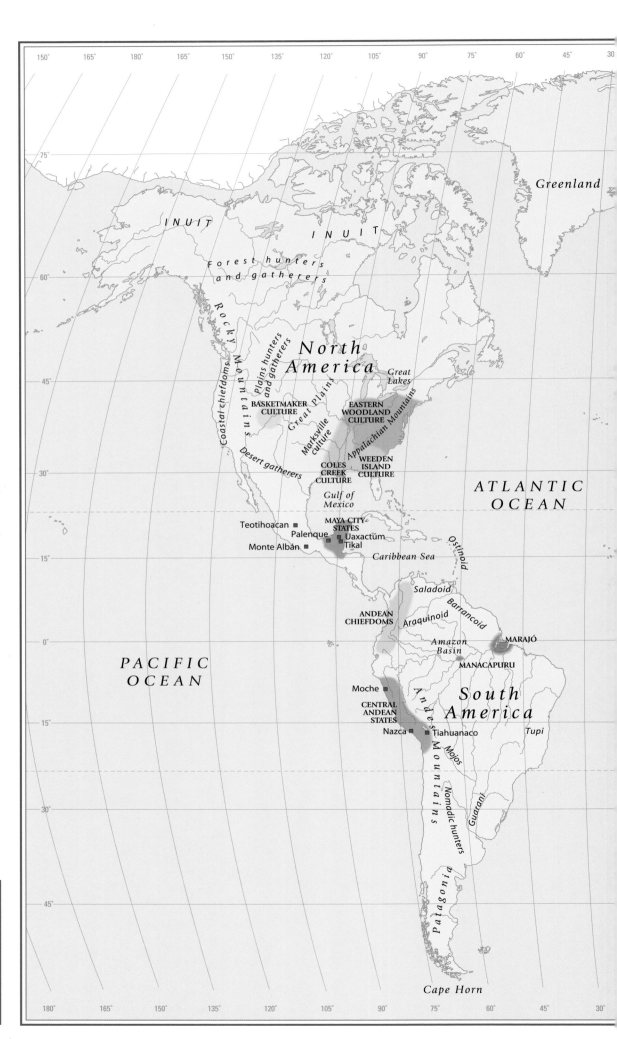

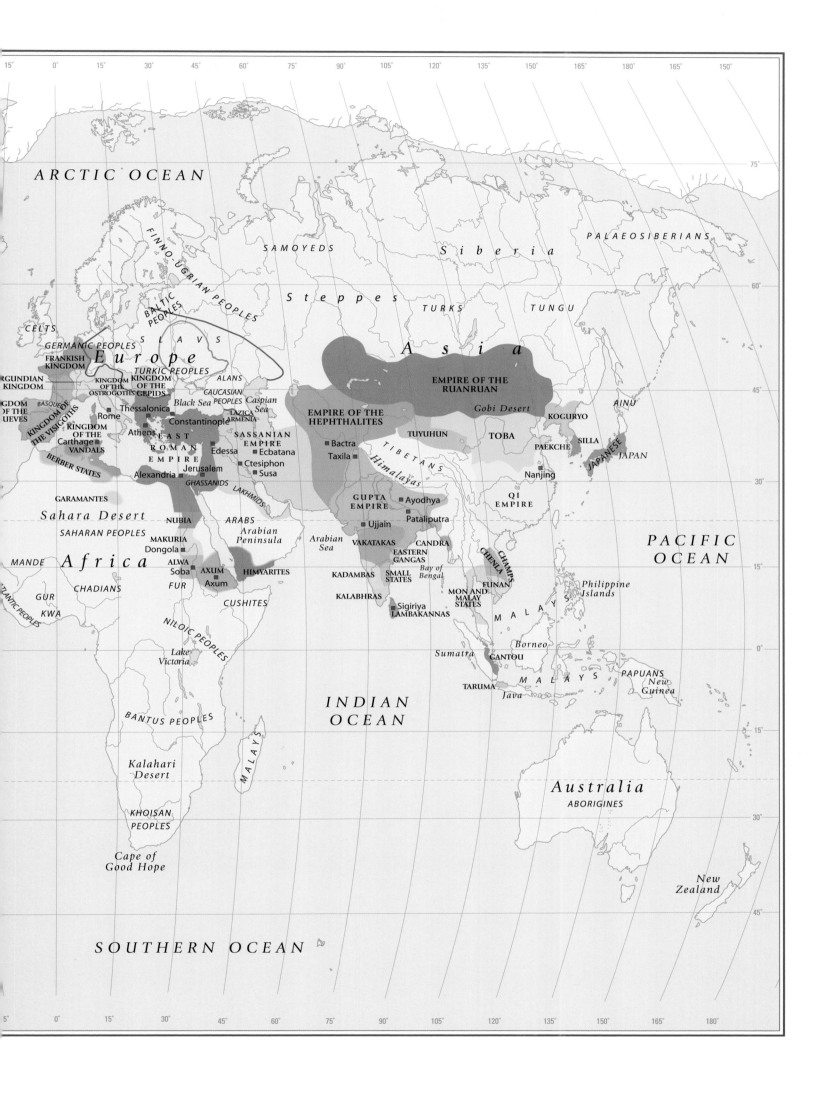

ARCTIC OCEAN

SAMOYEDS

S i b e r i a

PALAEOSIBERIANS

FINNO-UGRIAN PEOPLES

S t e p p e s

TURKS

TUNGU

BALTIC PEOPLES

CELTS

GERMANIC PEOPLES

S L A V S

A s i a

EMPIRE OF THE
RUANRUAN

Gobi Desert

AINU

FRANKISH
KINGDOM

Europe

BURGUNDIAN
KINGDOM

TURKIC PEOPLES

KINGDOM
OF THE
OSTROGOTHS

KINGDOM
OF THE
GEPIDS

ALANS

CAUCASIAN
PEOPLES

KINGDOM
OF THE
SUEVES

BASQUE

KINGDOM
OF THE
VISIGOTHS

Thessalonica

Rome

Black Sea

LAZICA

ARMENIA

Caspian
Sea

EMPIRE OF THE
HEPHTHALITES

TUYUHUN

TOBA

KOGURYO

PAEKCHE

SILLA

Constantinople

EAST
ROMAN
EMPIRE

Athens

Carthage

KINGDOM OF THE
VANDALS

SASSANIAN
EMPIRE

Edessa

Bactra

Taxila

T I B E T A N S

Himalayas

JAPANESE

JAPAN

Nanjing

Ecbatana

BERBER STATES

Alexandria

Jerusalem

Ctesiphon

Susa

QI
EMPIRE

GHASSANIDS

LAKHMIDS

GARAMANTES

Sahara Desert

SAHARAN PEOPLES

NUBIA

ARABS

Arabian
Peninsula

GUPTA
EMPIRE

Ayodhya

Pataliputra

Ujjain

Arabian
Sea

VAKATAKAS

CANDRA

EASTERN
GANGAS

CHENLA

CHAMPS

PACIFIC
OCEAN

MANDE

Africa

MAKURIA

Dongola

ALWA

Soba

AXUM

Axum

FUR

HIMYARITES

KADAMBAS

SMALL
STATES

Bay of
Bengal

FUNAN

Philippine
Islands

CHADIANS

GUR

KWA

ATLANTIC PEOPLES

CUSHITES

KALABHRAS

Sigiriya

LAMBAKANNAS

MON AND
MALAY
STATES

M A L A Y S

NILOIC PEOPLES

Lake
Victoria

Borneo

Sumatra

CANTOU

M A L A Y S

PAPUANS

New
Guinea

INDIAN
OCEAN

BANTUS PEOPLES

TARUMA

Java

MALAYS

Kalahari
Desert

Australia

ABORIGINES

KHOISAN
PEOPLES

Cape of
Good Hope

New
Zealand

SOUTHERN OCEAN

THE EMPIRE DIVIDED

THE EMPIRE DIVIDED

It is with the overthrow of Emperor Romulus Augustus in 476, at the hands of the Germanic chieftain Odoacer, that the Western Roman Empire is said to have come to an end. However, a date for the fall of the empire is hard to pinpoint with any great accuracy, as the strength of the empire differed from region to region. In the heart of Italy, consuls continued to be elected and the rhythm of life was largely unaffected. In other parts of the empire, however, Rome's influence was terminated in a more a decisive manner, and invasions by the Visigoths in the north and the violent collapse of Roman culture in Britain are just two examples of indigenous peoples throwing off Roman control. The decline experienced in the West during the 5th century was largely spared the East, which had much greater riches at its disposal. Indeed, during the 6th Century the Eastern Roman Empire under Emperor Justinian I reconquered the Italian peninsula from the Ostrogoths and also retook North Africa, southern Hispania, and parts of Illyria. But less than a century later the Emperor Heraclius made sweeping reforms to the empire in the east, the most significant of which was to make Greek its official language. From that point on Latin influence declined and the empire metamorphosed into what historians now refer to as the Byzantine Empire.

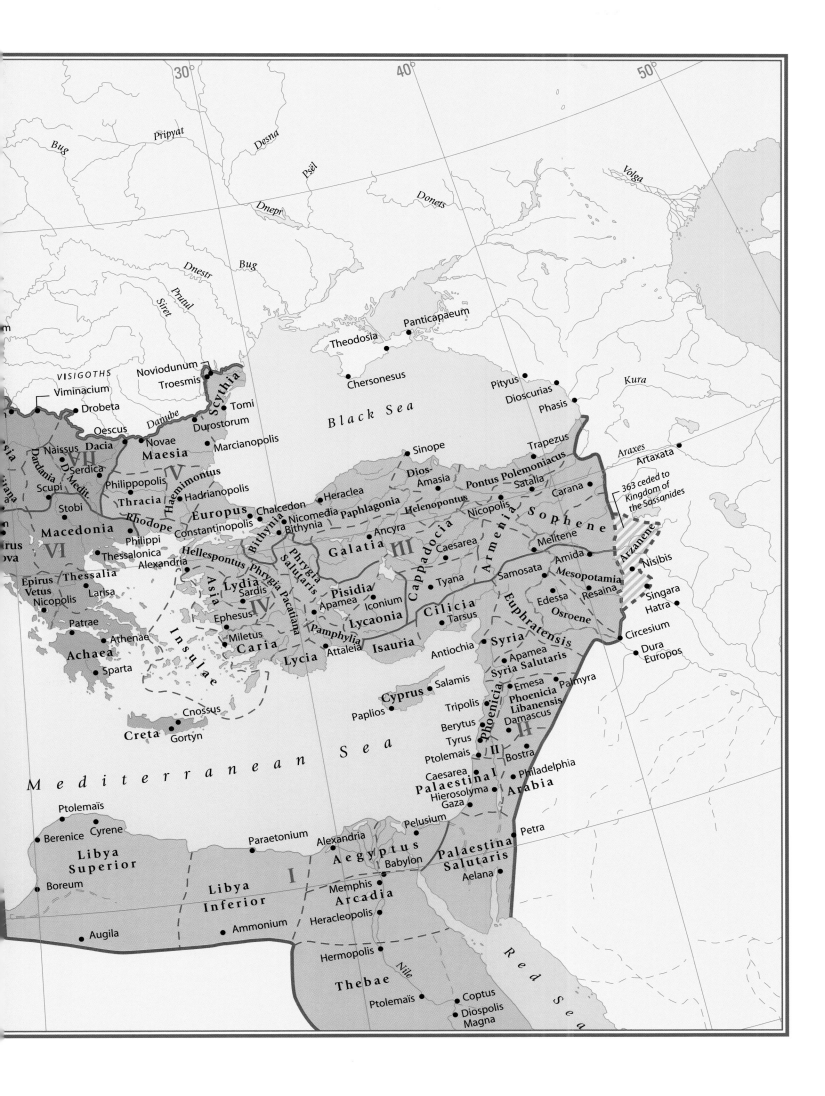

ENEMY AT THE GATES

ENEMY AT THE GATES

In 376 the Visigoths, driven by fear of nomad Huns moving westward, crossed the River Danube seeking the protection of the Roman Empire.

The eastern Emperor Valens decided to drive them back. In 378, during a disastrous battle at Adrianople, he was defeated and killed by the Visigoths. His successor, Theodosius I, made peace in 382, allowing the Visigoths to settle within the Empire. In 395 a Visigothic ruler, Alaric, emerged; he sought new concessions from the East Roman Empire. By 402 he raided Italy; on his second raid in 410, he sacked Rome. Meanwhile, in 406, the western Germanic tribes crossed the Rhine frontier. The defense of the province of Britain was

abandoned in 410 subject to attack by seaborne Germanic invaders. By 412, though, Italy remained in Roman hands, while large parts of Gaul and Spain were occupied by Germanic tribes. Rome granted "Federate" status to many of the incomers, in the hope of creating new allies, but the tribes began to develop power centers of their own, which did not fit with that of Rome. In 429 the Vandals crossed from Spain intent on conquering Roman provinces in North Africa. By 439 Carthage had fallen, the west was in tatters and Rome stood on the edge of breakdown.

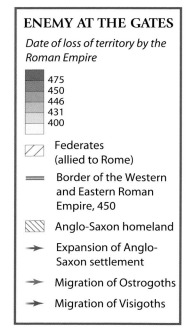

ENEMY AT THE GATES

Date of loss of territory by the Roman Empire

- 475
- 450
- 446
- 431
- 400

- Federates (allied to Rome)
- Border of the Western and Eastern Roman Empire, 450
- Anglo-Saxon homeland
- Expansion of Anglo-Saxon settlement
- Migration of Ostrogoths
- Migration of Visigoths

GERMANIC KINGDOMS

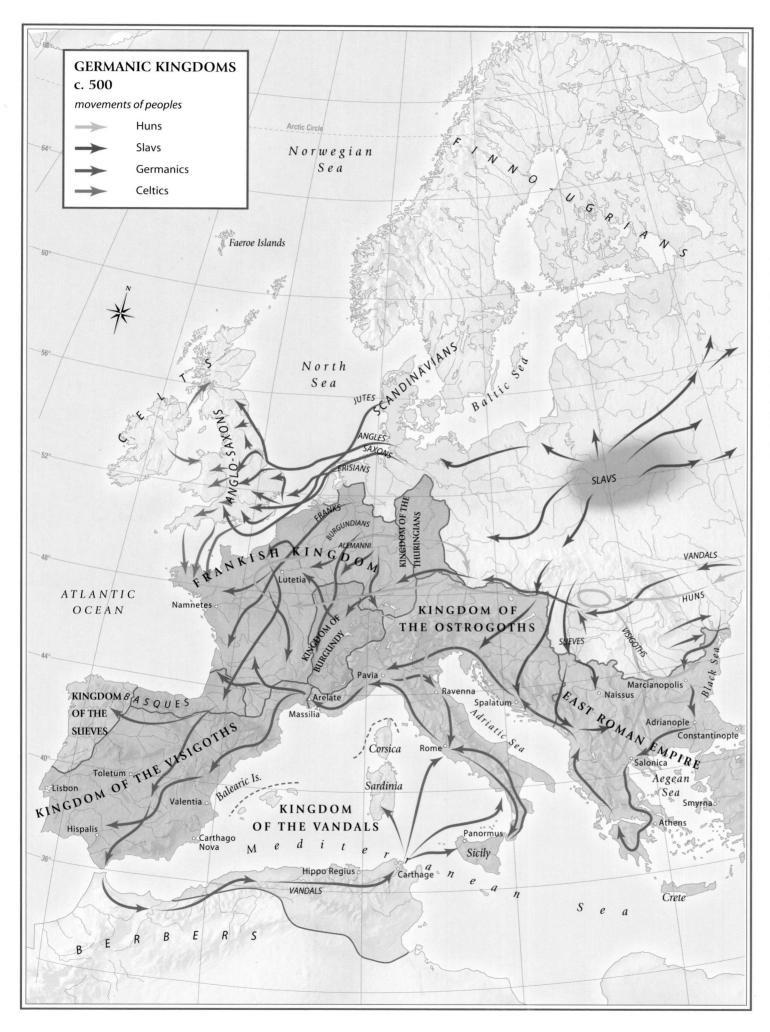

GERMANIC KINGDOMS
c. 500

movements of peoples

→ Huns
→ Slavs
→ Germanics
→ Celtics

Arctic Circle

Norwegian Sea

FINNO-UGRIANS

Faeroe Islands

C E L T S

North Sea

SCANDINAVIANS

JUTES

Baltic Sea

ANGLES
SAXONS
ANGLO-SAXONS
FRISIANS

SLAVS

FRANKS
BURGUNDIANS
ALEMANNI

KINGDOM OF THE THURINGIANS

FRANKISH KINGDOM

VANDALS

ATLANTIC OCEAN

Lutetia

Namnetes

KINGDOM OF BURGUNDY

KINGDOM OF THE OSTROGOTHS

HUNS

SUEVES

VISIGOTHS

Pavia

Ravenna
Spalatum

Marcianopolis
Naissus

Black Sea

Arelate
Massilia

EAST ROMAN EMPIRE

Adrianople
Constantinople

KINGDOM OF THE SUEVES

BASQUES

Adriatic Sea

Corsica

Rome

Salonica

Toletum

KINGDOM OF THE VISIGOTHS

Balearic Is.

Sardinia

Aegean Sea

Lisbon

Valentia

KINGDOM OF THE VANDALS

Smyrna

Hispalis

Carthago Nova

Panormus
Sicily

Athens

Mediterranean

Hippo Regius
Carthage

VANDALS

Sea

Crete

B E R B E R S

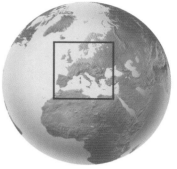

GERMANIC KINGDOMS
By the 470s Germanic
Kingdoms ruled what had
been the West Roman Empire.
The last Emperor, Romulus
Augustus, abdicated into
comfortable retirement
under the gaze of the new
Ostrogothic ruling elite. In
many areas the old country
ruling class remained, as
did the Christian religion.
Although these people were
subject to new masters, they
were needed by the new ruling
authorities to administer and
to collect taxes.

THE EMPIRE OF THE EAST

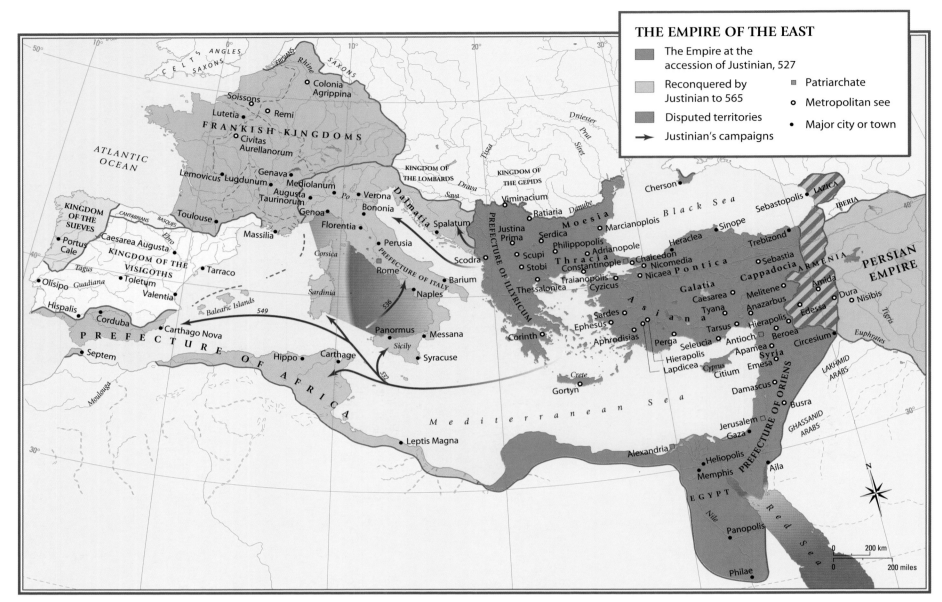

THE EMPIRE OF THE EAST

- The Empire at the accession of Justinian, 527
- Reconquered by Justinian to 565
- Disputed territories
- → Justinian's campaigns
- ■ Patriarchate
- ○ Metropolitan see
- ● Major city or town

THE EMPIRE OF THE EAST

Justinian I became Emperor of the Byzantine Empire in 527. He was inspired by the ideal of restoring Roman rule to its old borders. To achieve his aims he rooted out corruption and established a codification of laws—the *Codex Justinianus*.

Justinian instigated a series of campaigns that, by his death in 565, had re-established Roman rule over Italy, parts of Spain, and North Africa. In the east the Persians were held at bay, though the Danube frontier remained a problem.

The Muslims were defeated in France at Poitiers in 732 and most Mediterranean islands were retaken, but they were able to hold on to areas of Spain, developing there a distinct culture until the completion of the reconquest in 1492.

PART 3

DIVIDED REGIONS

AFTER THE FALL OF the Western Roman Empire a number of cultures developed in a completely haphazard fashion. Many of these grew outside known history, and modern archaeologists are still attempting to understand them. Meanwhile, in the east, the Byzantine world had confronted Islam, which had spread from Persia as far as Spain. The Crusaders had been invited to stem the Muslim onslaught and they savaged Islam, but the subsequent Crusader states were in turn destroyed by Saladin. Eventually a whole new wave of Muslim invaders, the Ottomans, were to sweep into Europe and conquer the Near East and North Africa. Elsewhere, American civilizations grew in Central and Southern America, while Native American cultures and settlements were established in northern America. The Scandinavians showed their power and innovation in colonizing voyages across the Atlantic to Labrador and Greenland, as well as making raids into Britain, France, Spain, and the Mediterranean, seriously damaging the already declining Carolingian Empire. Chinese unity had disintegrated, but Chinese cultural influences had spread to Japan, which had unified itself by the sword. Several civilizations grew up in Africa, particularly around the gold trade in Ghana and Mali, while other states developed in the Horn of Africa. In Eastern Europe Kievan Russia and the Slav principalities were overrun by Tartar conquests, and the Grand Duchy of Moscow became a center for Tatar tax collection.

300 BC – AD 1500 THE MAYA

THE MAYA

For hundreds of years the Maya were an important force in Central America. There were many city-states and each was ruled by a king who was engaged in perpetual warfare to acquire prisoners to sacrifice to Mayan gods. The Mayans were technically and scientifically able—they developed secular and sacred calendars and used a form of hieroglyphic writing. The 10th century saw the invasion of the Toltecs.

From their capital in Tula, about 60 miles northwest of present-day Mexico City, they spread throughout the entire region, but in spite of this, remnants of Mayan culture lingered on until it was eventually wiped out by the Spanish Conquistadors.

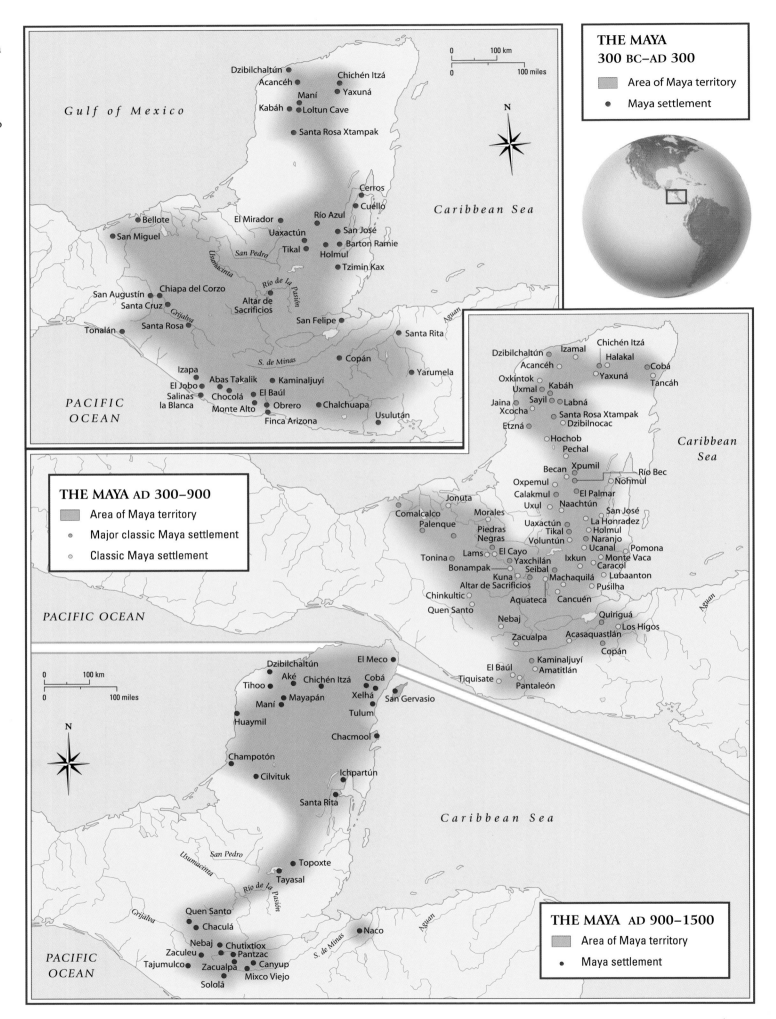

THE MAYA
300 BC–AD 300
- Area of Maya territory
- Maya settlement

THE MAYA AD 300–900
- Area of Maya territory
- Major classic Maya settlement
- Classic Maya settlement

THE MAYA AD 900–1500
- Area of Maya territory
- Maya settlement

THE TOLTEC STATES; THE CENTRAL AREA OF TEOTIHUACÁN

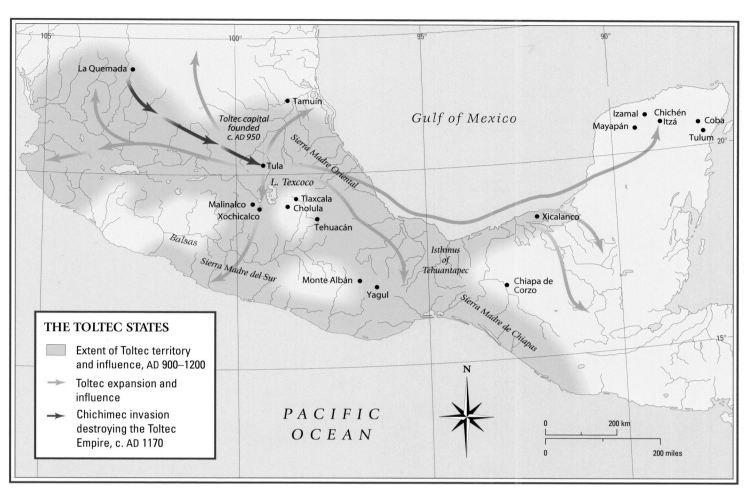

THE TOLTEC STATES

Extent of Toltec territory and influence, AD 900–1200

Toltec expansion and influence

Chichimec invasion destroying the Toltec Empire, c. AD 1170

TOLTEC STATES

The Toltecs were a multiethnic group made up of people from many parts of what is now modern Mexico. Among them were the Tolteca-Chichimeca from whose language, Nahuatl, the word Toltecatl comes—this has been simplified to Toltec in English. In the chronology of central Mexico, the Toltec period lasted between ad 900 and 1200. The Toltec heartland, based on the city of Tula, lies to the north of the Basin of Mexico and is located further north than any other ancient Mesoamerican city. Tula incorporated many innovations of earlier traditions, such as pyramids, ball courts, and its grid plan. Toltec influence can be seen in neighboring and later civilizations, not only in building styles but also in traditions. These are exemplified by the legendary hero called Quetzalcoatl or Kukulcan. This feathered servant was the fabled founder of the Toltec civilization and a great cultural hero of the Maya.

The eventual fall of Tula is thought to have been caused by a variety of problems: poor farming techniques, internal social dislocation and persistent threats from external enemies.

TEOTIHUACÁN

At its height, Teotihuacán was the largest city in the Americas, reaching its peak between AD 150 and 450. The name Teotihuacán is also used to refer to the civilization and culture of this city, which was comparable in power and influence to that of Ancient Rome. At its greatest extent it included much of central Mexico. The city was located approximately 25 miles northeast of present-day Mexico City and covered a total surface area of 17 square miles. The stepped pyramids that were quite prominent in Maya and Aztec architecture came from Teotihuacán.

THE CENTRAL AREA OF TEOTIHUACÁN

Ceremonial center

Other buildings

VIKINGS IN THE NORTH; ATLANTIC ROUTES OF THE VIKINGS; VIKING HEARTLAND

VIKINGS IN THE NORTH

Norse sailors, from their settlements in Iceland, discovered Greenland in ad 985 and established a colony there in 986. In 952, Bjarni Herjolfsson was blown off course while heading for Greenland. He sighted land in what is probably modern Labrador and sailed along its coast before turning back for Greenland. Fifteen years later Leif Eriksson sailed from Greenland and discovered a land he called Helluland. Sailing further south he discovered lands he called Markland and Vinland, the exact locations of which are unclear. However, the remains of a Norse settlement were discovered at L'Anse aux Meadows in Newfoundland. This may have been Vinland, the first recorded European settlement in the Americas at around AD 1000.

ATLANTIC ROUTES OF THE VIKINGS

Viking expansion in the North Atlantic was driven by the search for new land to settle rather than raiding and conquest, as had been their main motive along the coasts of western Europe. The Vikings had already settled the Faroe Islands in the late 820s and had reached Iceland in the 860s. Greenland was discovered by an off-course, storm-driven seafarer around 930, but its grim appearance excited little interest. In 983 Eric the Red, exiled from Iceland, discovered the ice-free Eastern Fjords. News of this discovery attracted further settlers from Iceland.

VIKINGS IN THE NORTH

AD 985–c. 1020

- Norse settlement
- → Bjarni Herjolfsson 985
- → Leif Eriksson c. 1000
- ⇢ Conjectural Norse voyages

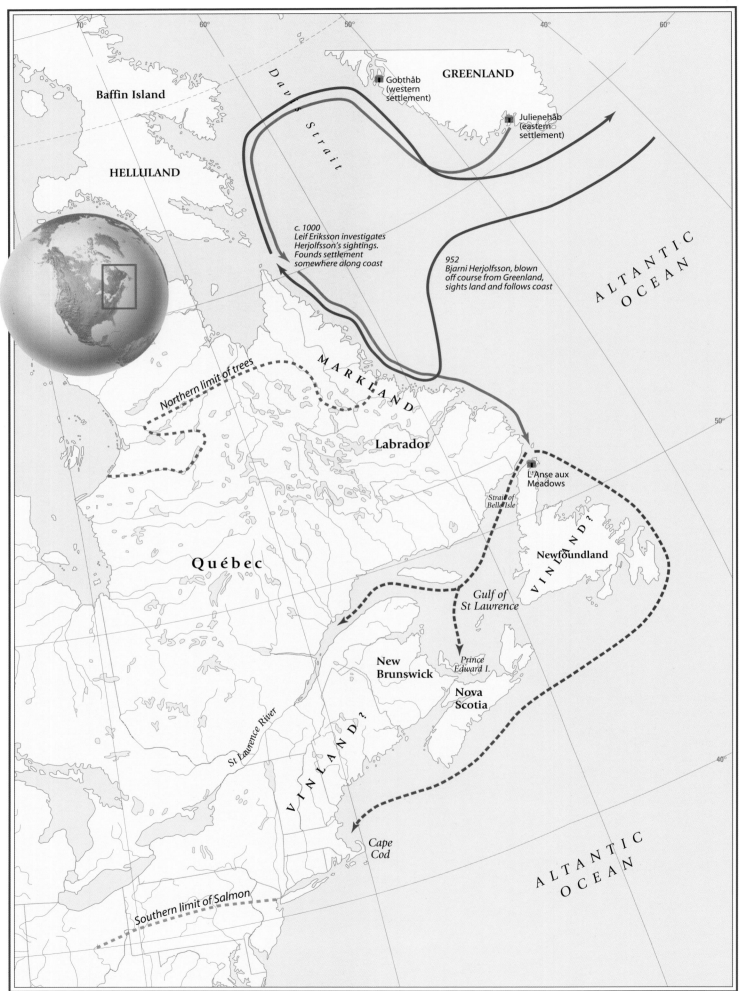

GREENLAND

Baffin Island

Gobthåb (western settlement)

Julienehåb (eastern settlement)

Davis Strait

HELLULAND

c. 1000 Leif Eriksson investigates Herjolfsson's sightings. Founds settlement somewhere along coast

952 Bjarni Herjolfsson, blown off course from Greenland, sights land and follows coast

ATLANTIC OCEAN

Northern limit of trees

MARKLAND

Labrador

L'Anse aux Meadows

Strait of Belle Isle

VINLAND ?

Newfoundland

Québec

Gulf of St Lawrence

New Brunswick

Prince Edward I.

Nova Scotia

St Lawrence River

VINLAND ?

Cape Cod

ATLANTIC OCEAN

Southern limit of Salmon

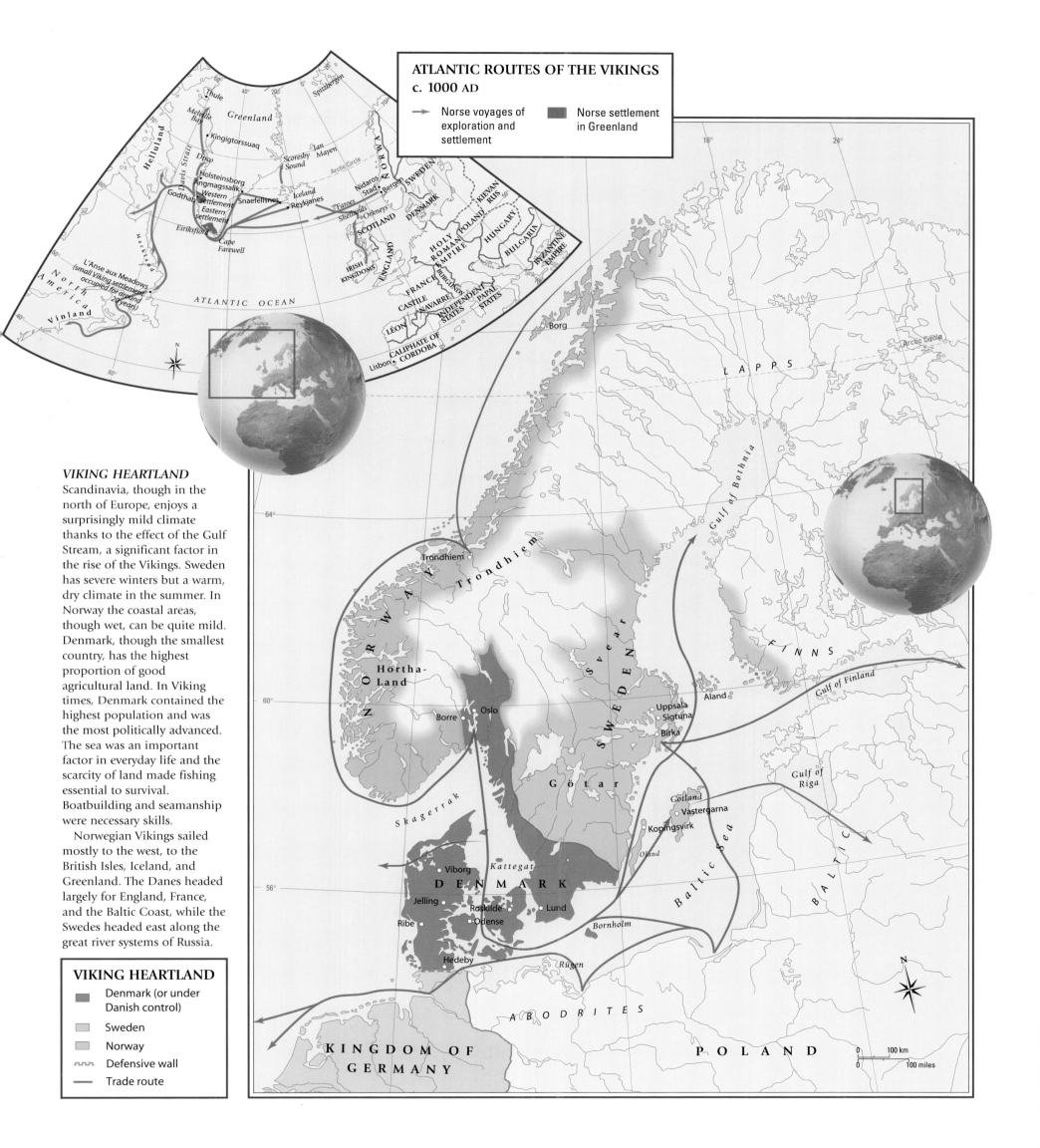

ATLANTIC ROUTES OF THE VIKINGS
c. 1000 AD

→ Norse voyages of exploration and settlement

■ Norse settlement in Greenland

Thule
Greenland
Melville Bay
Kingigtorssuaq
Helluland
Disco
Scoresby Sound
Jan Mayen
Spitzbergen
Holsteinsborg
Angmagssalik
Godthab
Western settlement
Snaefellsnes
Iceland
Eastern settlement
Reykjanes
Faroes
Nidaros
Stad
Bergen
NORWAY
SWEDEN
Shetlands
Orkneys
Eiriksfjord
SCOTLAND
DENMARK
KIEVAN RUS
Cape Farewell
ENGLAND
IRISH KINGDOMS
HOLY ROMAN EMPIRE
POLAND
HUNGARY
FRANCE
BURGUNDY
BULGARIA
Markland
BYZANTINE EMPIRE
L'Anse aux Meadows (small Viking settlement occupied for around 20 years)
CASTILE
NAVARRE
INDEPENDENT STATES
PAPAL STATES
North America
LÉON
ATLANTIC OCEAN
Vinland
Lisbon
CALIPHATE OF CORDOBA
Arctic Circle

VIKING HEARTLAND

Scandinavia, though in the north of Europe, enjoys a surprisingly mild climate thanks to the effect of the Gulf Stream, a significant factor in the rise of the Vikings. Sweden has severe winters but a warm, dry climate in the summer. In Norway the coastal areas, though wet, can be quite mild. Denmark, though the smallest country, has the highest proportion of good agricultural land. In Viking times, Denmark contained the highest population and was the most politically advanced. The sea was an important factor in everyday life and the scarcity of land made fishing essential to survival. Boatbuilding and seamanship were necessary skills.

Norwegian Vikings sailed mostly to the west, to the British Isles, Iceland, and Greenland. The Danes headed largely for England, France, and the Baltic Coast, while the Swedes headed east along the great river systems of Russia.

VIKING HEARTLAND

■ Denmark (or under Danish control)
■ Sweden
■ Norway
∿ Defensive wall
— Trade route

Borg
LAPPS
Arctic Circle
Gulf of Bothnia
NORWAY
Trondhiem
Trondhiem
FINNS
Gulf of Finland
Hortha-Land
Svear
SWEDEN
Aland
Uppsala
Sigtuna
Borre
Oslo
Birka
Gulf of Riga
Götar
Gotland
Vastergarna
Skagerrak
Kopingsvirk
Oland
Baltic Sea
BALTIC
Kattegat
Viborg
DENMARK
Jelling
Roskilde
Lund
Ribe
Odense
Bornholm
Hedeby
Rügen
ABODRITES
KINGDOM OF GERMANY
POLAND

0 — 100 km
0 — 100 miles

972 – 1095   KIEVAN RUSSIA

KIEVAN RUSSIA

Kievan Russia was the creation of a warrior merchant class, the Varangians, or Varyagi, a Slav term to describe the Norse Viking. They exploited the great river systems of European Russia, establishing a trading capital at Novgorod. They later moved their capital to the city of Kiev, which provided a more strategic location on the great River Dnieper.

By 1030 Kievan Russia had expanded to include most of the eastern Slav and some non-Slav tribes, forming the largest federation in Europe. This creation could not, however, hold on to its vast territories, and the lands fell under the control of various nomadic groups.

KIEVAN RUSSIA

- Russ, 972
- Russ, 1054
- → Vladimir's invasion of the Crimea 990
- Main trade route

EUROPE 1095

EUROPE 1095

Feudalism developed in medieval Europe as a result of the social conditions that had existed for hundreds of years. Settled states were continually under threat by hostile Norse invaders from the north, Muslims from the south or Magyars from the east. The obvious way to structure this largely rural society was to establish a two-way contract where the Lord protected the people and in return the people provided services, especially military service. The Lord in turn would hold his land from a great and noble family, who held their patrimony from the King. Each person in this chain will have made an oath that his tenure of the land was conditional on the service that he rendered to his overlord. At the top of the chain were the Holy Roman Emperor and the Pope. They were responsible to God.

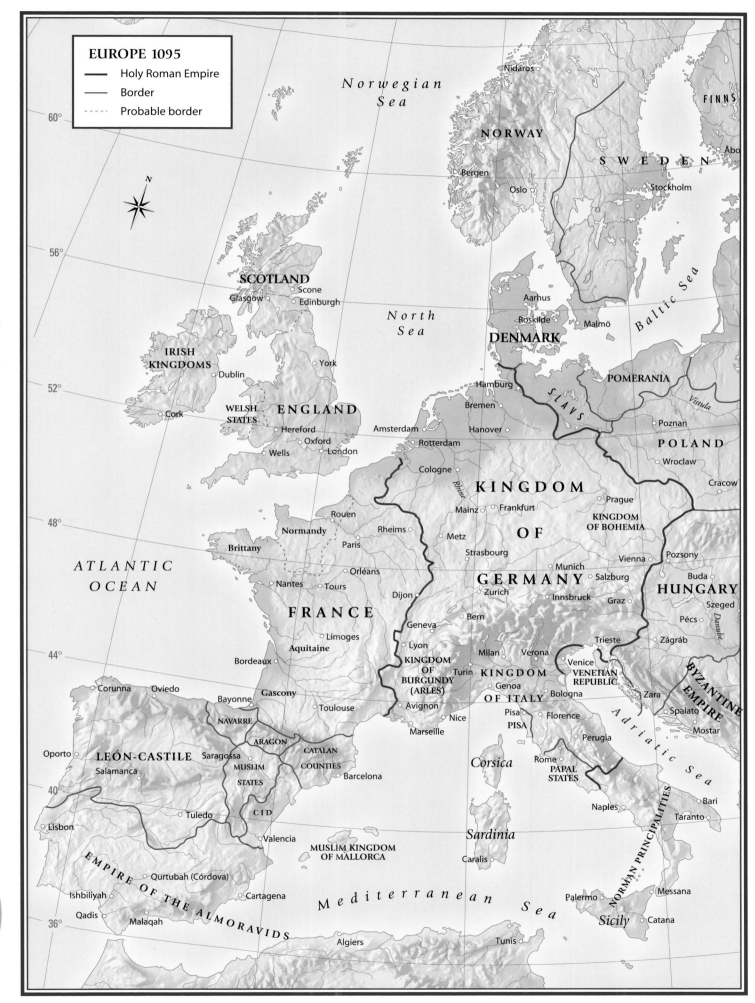

EUROPE 1095
— Holy Roman Empire
— Border
--- Probable border

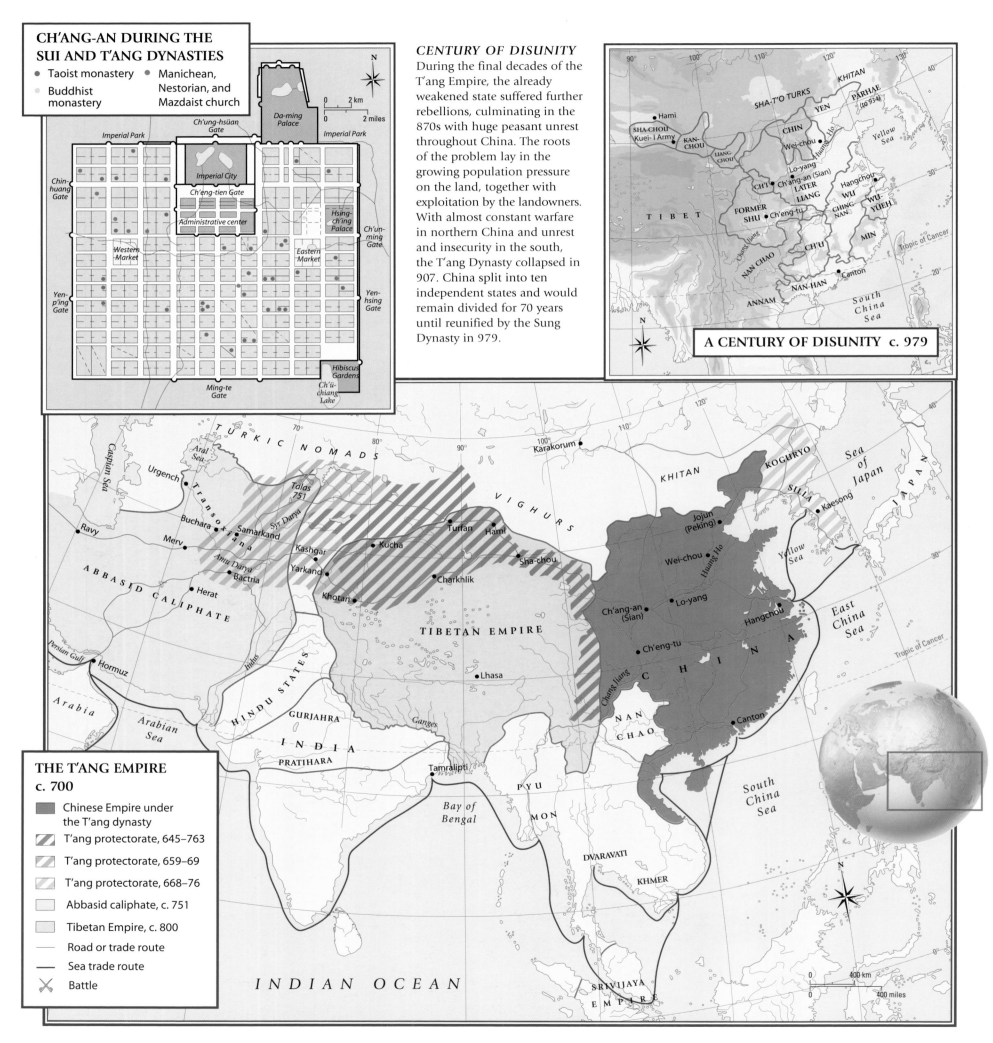

CH'ANG-AN DURING THE SUI AND T'ANG DYNASTIES

- ● Taoist monastery
- ● Buddhist monastery
- ● Manichean, Nestorian, and Mazdaist church

Da-ming Palace
Ch'ung-hsüan Gate
Imperial Park
Imperial Park
Chin-huang Gate
Imperial City
Ch'eng-tien Gate
Administrative center
Western Market
Eastern Market
Hsing-ch'ing Palace
Ch'un-ming Gate
Yen-p'ing Gate
Yen-hsing Gate
Hibiscus Gardens
Ming-te Gate
Ch'ü-chiang Lake

0   2 km
0   2 miles

N

CENTURY OF DISUNITY

During the final decades of the T'ang Empire, the already weakened state suffered further rebellions, culminating in the 870s with huge peasant unrest throughout China. The roots of the problem lay in the growing population pressure on the land, together with exploitation by the landowners. With almost constant warfare in northern China and unrest and insecurity in the south, the T'ang Dynasty collapsed in 907. China split into ten independent states and would remain divided for 70 years until reunified by the Sung Dynasty in 979.

A CENTURY OF DISUNITY c. 979

KHITAN
SHA-T'O TURKS
YEN
PARHAE (to 934)
Hami
SHA-CHOU Kuei- I Army
KAN-CHOU
LIANG-CHOU
CHIN
Wei-chou
Yellow Sea
Lo-yang
CH'I
Ch'ang-an (Sian)
LATER LIANG
Hangchou
WU
CHING-NAN
WU-YÜEH
TIBET
FORMER SHU
Ch'eng-tu
NAN CHAO
CH'U
MIN
NAN-HAN
Canton
ANNAM
South China Sea
Tropic of Cancer

N

THE T'ANG EMPIRE c. 700

- Chinese Empire under the T'ang dynasty
- T'ang protectorate, 645–763
- T'ang protectorate, 659–69
- T'ang protectorate, 668–76
- Abbasid caliphate, c. 751
- Tibetan Empire, c. 800
- — Road or trade route
- — Sea trade route
- ✕ Battle

TURKIC NOMADS
Aral Sea
Caspian Sea
Urgench
Talas 751
Transoxiana
Syr Darya
Buchara
Samarkand
Ravy
Merv
Amu Darya
Kashgar
Yarkand
Bactria
ABBASID CALIPHATE
Herat
Kucha
Turfan
Hami
VIGHURS
Sha-chou
Charkhlik
Khotan
TIBETAN EMPIRE
Karakorum
KHITAN
KOGURYO
Sea of Japan
SILLA
Kaesong
JAPAN
Jojun (Peking)
Wei-chou
Huang Ho
Yellow Sea
Ch'ang-an (Sian)
Lo-yang
Hangchou
East China Sea
Ch'eng-tu
CHINA
Tropic of Cancer
Persian Gulf
Hormuz
HINDU STATES
Indus
Lhasa
Chung Jiang
Canton
Arabia
Arabian Sea
GURJAHRA
Ganges
NAN CHAO
PRATIHARA
INDIA
Tamralipti
South China Sea
Bay of Bengal
PYU
MON
DVARAVATI
KHMER
INDIAN OCEAN
SRIVIJAYA EMPIRE

SUNG CHINA; SOUTHERN CHUN AND CH'IN EMPIRE

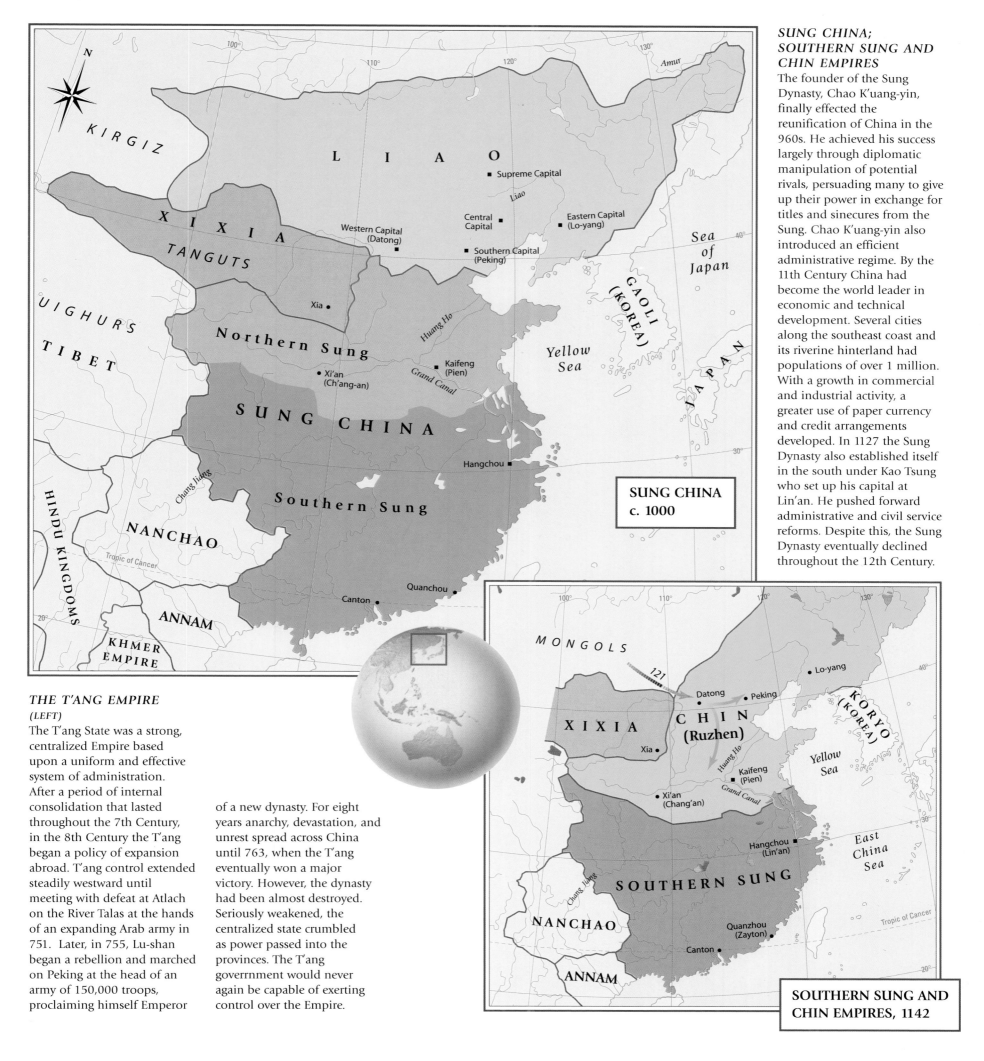

SUNG CHINA c. 1000

SOUTHERN SUNG AND CHIN EMPIRES, 1142

SUNG CHINA; SOUTHERN SUNG AND CHIN EMPIRES

The founder of the Sung Dynasty, Chao K'uang-yin, finally effected the reunification of China in the 960s. He achieved his success largely through diplomatic manipulation of potential rivals, persuading many to give up their power in exchange for titles and sinecures from the Sung. Chao K'uang-yin also introduced an efficient administrative regime. By the 11th Century China had become the world leader in economic and technical development. Several cities along the southeast coast and its riverine hinterland had populations of over 1 million. With a growth in commercial and industrial activity, a greater use of paper currency and credit arrangements developed. In 1127 the Sung Dynasty also established itself in the south under Kao Tsung who set up his capital at Lin'an. He pushed forward administrative and civil service reforms. Despite this, the Sung Dynasty eventually declined throughout the 12th Century.

THE T'ANG EMPIRE
(LEFT)

The T'ang State was a strong, centralized Empire based upon a uniform and effective system of administration. After a period of internal consolidation that lasted throughout the 7th Century, in the 8th Century the T'ang began a policy of expansion abroad. T'ang control extended steadily westward until meeting with defeat at Atlach on the River Talas at the hands of an expanding Arab army in 751. Later, in 755, Lu-shan began a rebellion and marched on Peking at the head of an army of 150,000 troops, proclaiming himself Emperor of a new dynasty. For eight years anarchy, devastation, and unrest spread across China until 763, when the T'ang eventually won a major victory. However, the dynasty had been almost destroyed. Seriously weakened, the centralized state crumbled as power passed into the provinces. The T'ang government would never again be capable of exerting control over the Empire.

646 – 1485 MUSLIM INDIA

MUSLIM INDIA

The Arabs first invaded India in the 8th Century, bringing with them their Muslim faith. The first significant invasion came under the command of Sultan Mahmud of Ghazni, who raided India over 20 times between 1000 and 1027, annexing the Punjab. The Ghaznivids, his descendants, were ousted by Muhammed of Ghur, who in turn launched a series of campaigns which culminated in the creation of an Empire that stretched across northern India to the Ganges Delta.

On his death his viceroy, a Turkistan slave, Qutb-ud-Din Aybak, based in Delhi, proclaimed himself Sultan of Delhi. The Delhi Sultanate was consolidated under the rule of Ala-ud-din, who introduced taxation based on acreage and used the revenue to finance his army, which now numbered almost 500,000 men, large enough to defeat two Mongol invasions of 1304 and 1306.

This army was also large enough to extort tribute and recognition of his imperial status from Hindu rulers across India. Ala-ud-din married the daughter of a prominent Hindu family in an attempt to establish Hindu participation in the rule of India. From the 1330s to the 1390s, the Sultanate increasingly fell into disorder with numerous Hindu rebellions against Muslim rule.

In 1398, Tamerlane (sometimes known as Timur), invaded the Delhi Sultanate on the pretext that it was too tolerant of Hinduism. After a four-month campaign, he annexed the Punjab, leaving a much reduced Delhi Sultanate as one of several northern Indian states.

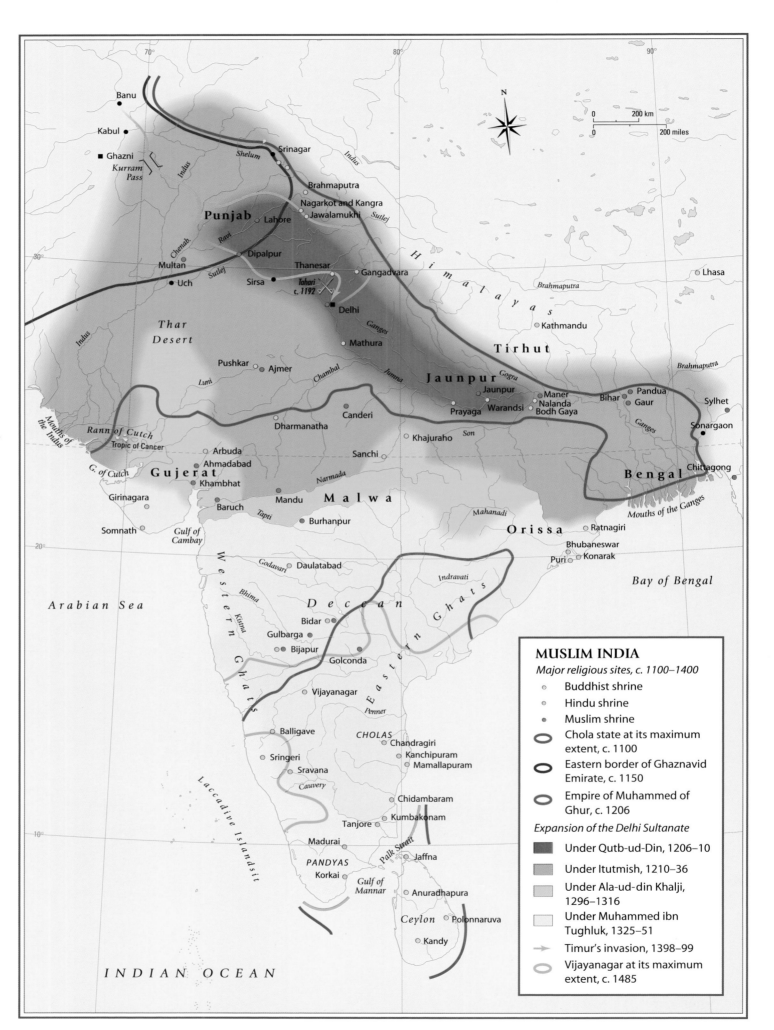

MUSLIM INDIA
Major religious sites, c. 1100–1400
- ● Buddhist shrine
- ● Hindu shrine
- ● Muslim shrine
- ◯ Chola state at its maximum extent, c. 1100
- ◯ Eastern border of Ghaznavid Emirate, c. 1150
- ◯ Empire of Muhammed of Ghur, c. 1206

Expansion of the Delhi Sultanate
- ◼ Under Qutb-ud-Din, 1206–10
- ◼ Under Itutmish, 1210–36
- ◼ Under Ala-ud-din Khalji, 1296–1316
- ◻ Under Muhammed ibn Tughluk, 1325–51
- → Timur's invasion, 1398–99
- ◯ Vijayanagar at its maximum extent, c. 1485

TAIKA REFORMS IN JAPAN; WARRIOR JAPAN

TAIKA JAPAN

The Taika Reforms were edicts aimed at creating the principles of national reorganization. The major point of this new system was the nationalization of land. However, the clan chiefs with their hereditary estates still retained control of their land as a salary for their official position within the state. Later, local and central government was reorganized into a Council of State, with eight ministries each divided into many departments. However, with too many estates enjoying a tax-exempt status, revenue was reduced and the system failed. In 702, in an attempt to suit conditions in Japan, the Fujiwara Clan introduced new civil and penal codes known as the Taika Laws.

WARRIOR JAPAN

In Japan, the years 794 to 1195 are known as the Heian period, the final period of classical Japanese history. During these years the Japanese imperial court reached its zenith of power and achievement, and the period is especially noted for its poetry and literature. The Heian period is also significant for the creation of a uniquely Japanese culture, as Chinese influence declined with the Tang Dynasty. Probably the most important sign of the emergent Japanese culture was the development of the kana, an indigenous writing system. The end of the period was marked by the rise of a number of military clans, and by the end of the 12th century

rivalry between these clans degenerated into outright civil war. Japanese society emerged from this internal strife led by a warrior nobility known as the samurai, which operated under the political control of a shogun, or supreme general of the samurai.

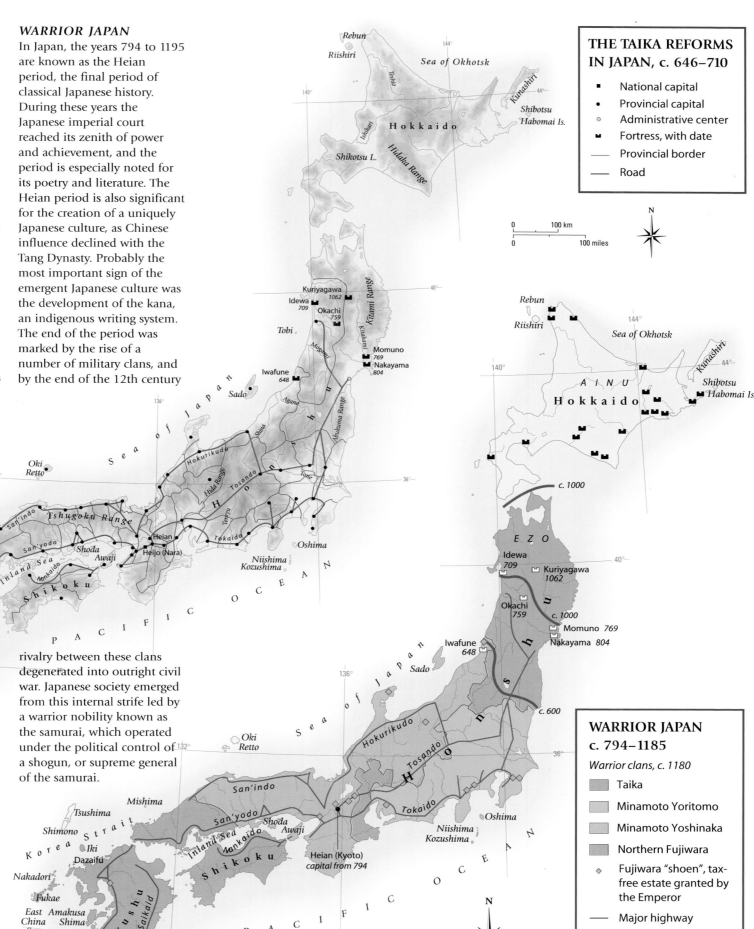

THE TAIKA REFORMS IN JAPAN, c. 646–710

- National capital
- Provincial capital
- Administrative center
- Fortress, with date
- Provincial border
- Road

WARRIOR JAPAN c. 794–1185

Warrior clans, c. 1180
- Taika
- Minamoto Yoritomo
- Minamoto Yoshinaka
- Northern Fujiwara
- Fujiwara "shoen", tax-free estate granted by the Emperor
- Major highway
- Northern frontier, with date
- Fortress, with date
- Ainu hillfort

THE WORLD AD 1000

THE WORLD AD 1000

By the turn of the first millennium many major states across the world had disintegrated. In Europe the Frankish Empire, established by Charlemagne, had been divided into three parts after his death. Henry I, the Saxon successor, eventually came to dominate the German states and conquered most of Italy. His son, Otto I, defeated the nomadic Magyars, becoming the first Holy Roman Emperor in 962. The Byzantine Empire, centered on Constantinople, still maintained its independence, though it was embroiled in a long series of wars, particularly in the Balkans. In Eastern Europe, the Kievan Rus had evolved into the largest state in Europe.

In Asia, the mighty T'ang Empire had finally collapsed, which led to a century of disunity until the 960s, when the rise of the Song partly reunified China.

In the Americas, the Toltecs dominated Central America and had expanded their domains by military conquest, controlling trade routes that reached as far south as modern Columbia and as far north as the emerging Anasazi, Mogollon, and Hohokam cultures of the North American southwest.

In North Africa, the Fatamid rulers made Cairo their capital and declared their lands independent of rule from Baghdad. In West Africa the thriving economy of Ghana was based on the export of gold across the Sahara to the Arabic States along the Mediterranean coast.

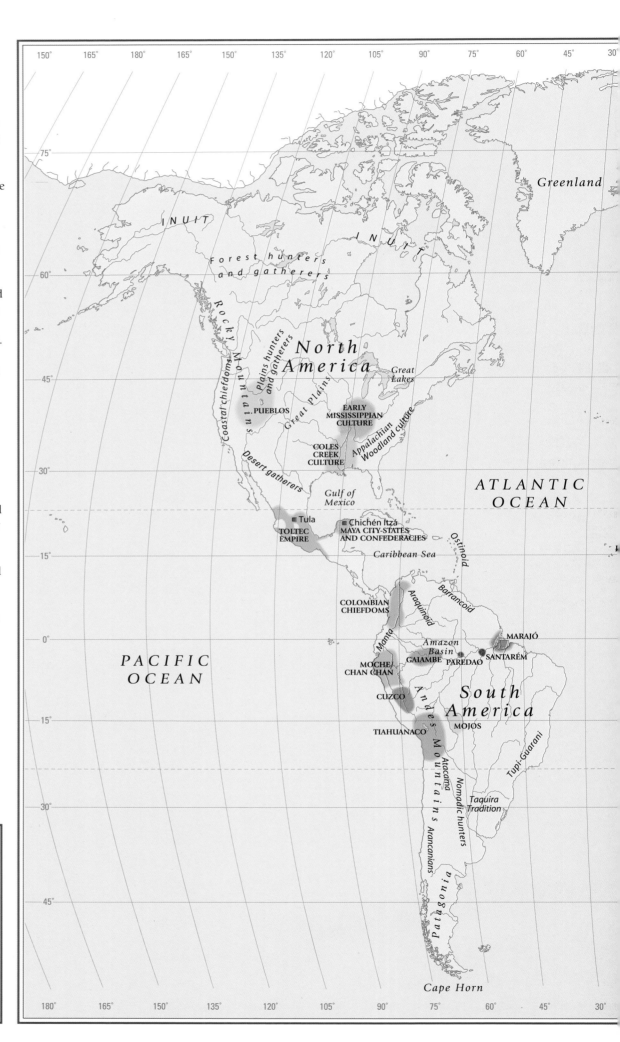

THE WORLD AD 1000

- ■   Major city
- ----   Extent of Abbasid Caliphate under Harun al-Rashid, 786
- ----   Tibet c. 800
- ----   Empire of the Franks under Charlemagne, 814
- ——   Holy Roman Empire

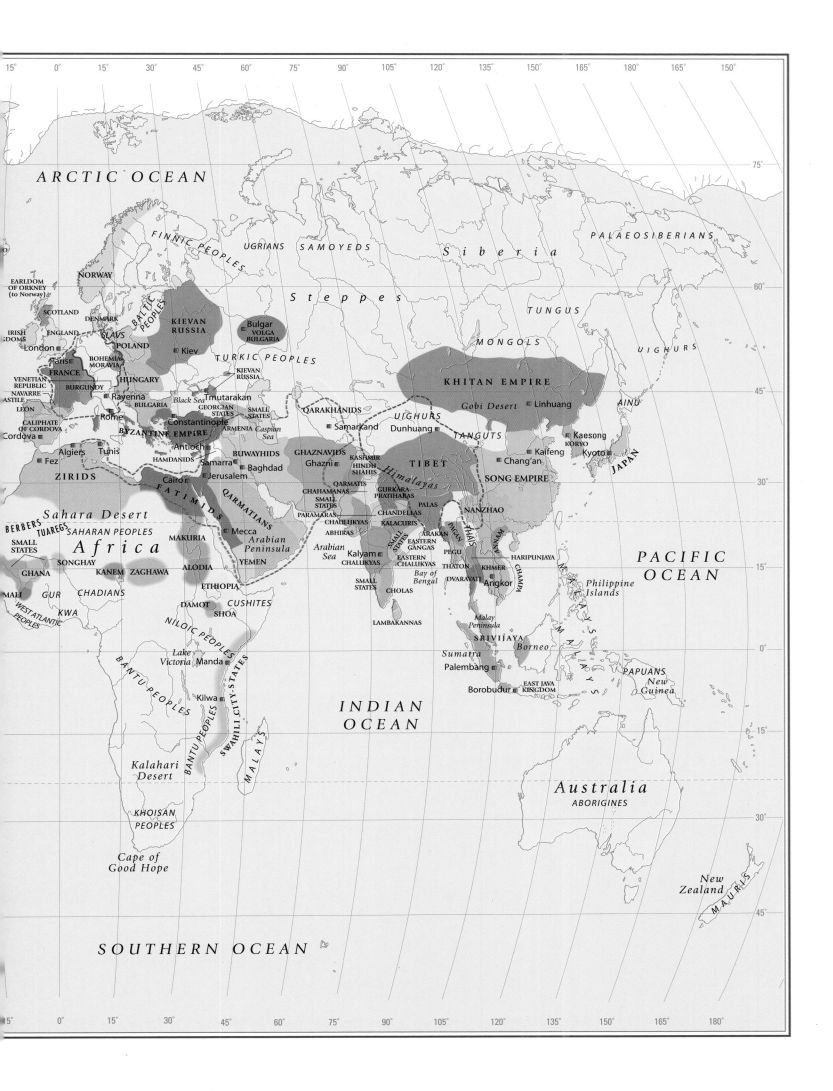

ARCTIC OCEAN

FINNIC PEOPLES

UGRIANS   SAMOYEDS

Siberia

PALAEOSIBERIANS

EARLDOM
OF ORKNEY
(to Norway)

NORWAY

Steppes

TUNGUS

SCOTLAND

DENMARK

BALTIC
PEOPLES

KIEVAN
RUSSIA

Bulgar
VOLGA
BULGARIA

MONGOLS

UIGHURS

IRISH
KINGDOMS

ENGLAND

SLAVS

POLAND

Kiev

TURKIC PEOPLES

KHITAN EMPIRE

AINU

London

Paris

FRANCE

BOHEMIA
MORAVIA

KIEVAN
RUSSIA

Gobi Desert   Linhuang

VENETIAN
REPUBLIC

HUNGARY

NAVARRE

BURGUNDY

Ravenna

BULGARIA

Black Sea

Tmutarakan

GEORGIAN
STATES

QARAKHANIDS

Samarkand

UIGHURS

Dunhuang

Kaesong
KORYO

ASTILE

LEON

Rome

BYZANTINE EMPIRE

Constantinople

ARMENIA

SMALL
STATES

Caspian
Sea

TANGUTS

Kaifeng

Kyoto

CALIPHATE
OF CORDOVA

Antioch

GHAZNAVIDS

KASHMIR

TIBET

Chang'an

JAPAN

Cordova

Algiers   Tunis

HAMDANIDS

BUWAYHIDS

Ghazni

HINDU
SHAHIS

Himalayas

SONG EMPIRE

Fez

Samarra

Baghdad

QARMATIS

GURJARA-
PRATIHARAS

ZIRIDS

Cairo

Jerusalem

FATIMIDS

QARMATIANS

CHAHAMANAS

CHANDELLAS

PARAMARAS

SMALL
STATES

CHAULUKYAS

NANZHAO

BERBERS

TUAREGS

Sahara Desert

SAHARAN PEOPLES

Mecca

Arabian
Peninsula

Arabian
Sea

ABHIRAS

KALACURIS

CHALUKYAS

ARAKAN

PALAS

EASTERN
GANGAS

PAGAN

PACIFIC
OCEAN

SMALL
STATES

Africa

MAKURIA

Kalyam

EASTERN
CHALUKYAS

SMALL
STATES

PEGU

THAIS

ANNAM

HARIPUNJAYA

SONGHAY

ALODIA

YEMEN

THATON

DVARAVATI

KHMER

CHAMPA

GHANA

KANEM   ZAGHAWA

ETHIOPIA

Bay of
Bengal

CHOLAS

Angkor

MALI

GUR

CHADIANS

DAMOT   SHOA

CUSHITES

SMALL
STATES

LAMBAKANNAS

WEST ATLANTIC
PEOPLES

KWA

NILOIC PEOPLES

Malay
Peninsula

SRIVIJAYA

Borneo

Sumatra

INDIAN
OCEAN

Philippine
Islands

PAPUANS
New
Guinea

Lake
Victoria   Manda

BANTU PEOPLES

Palembang

Borobudur

EAST JAVA
KINGDOM

MALAYS

Kilwa

SWAHILI CITY-STATES

Australia
ABORIGINES

Kalahari
Desert

BANTU PEOPLES

MALAYS

KHOISAN
PEOPLES

Cape of
Good Hope

New
Zealand

MAORIS

SOUTHERN OCEAN

NATIVE AMERICAN SOUTHWEST CULTURE; THE MOUNDBUILDERS

NATIVE AMERICAN SOUTHWEST CULTURE
Lacking consistent rainfall, the people in the arid southwest developed new ways to irrigate their crops. The process of solving this problem gave rise to several distinct cultures.

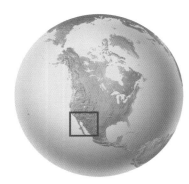

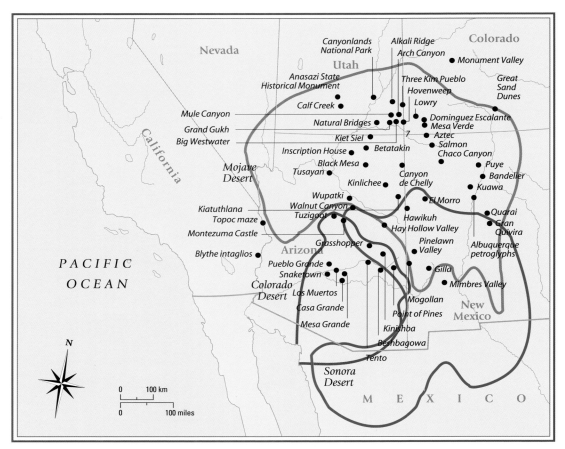

NATIVE AMERICAN SOUTHWEST CULTURE

- ⬭ Anasazi
- ⬭ Hohokam
- ⬭ Mogollon

THE MOUNDBUILDERS
Around AD 700, farming people settled along the Mississippi Valley and began using agricultural implements, particularly the hoe. This, together with new frost-resistant crops, greatly increased agricultural productivity, which freed up a proportion of the population to develop and construct earthen structures. The precise use of these is not known but they could have been used for military or religious purposes.

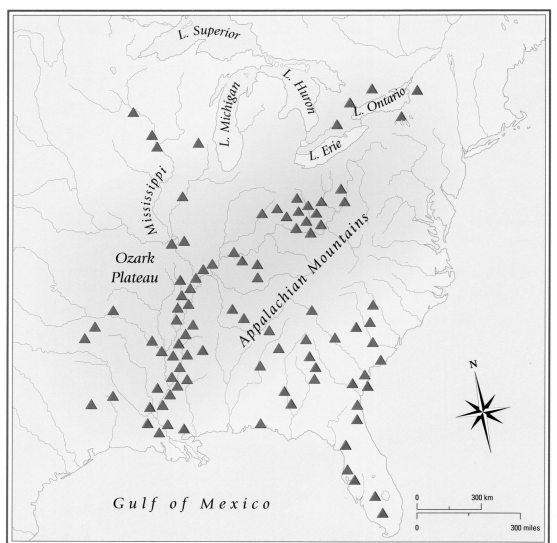

ADENA, HOPEWELL, AND MISSISSIPPIAN MOUNDS

- ▲ Major Adena or Hopewell mounds, 1000 BC–AD 1000
- ▲ Major Mississippian mounds, AD 700–1700

EAST COAST ECONOMY; SAPIR'S THESIS: SIX BASIC INDIAN LANGUAGES

EAST COAST ECONOMY

After the great migration from England in the 1640s, the new settlers traded mainly in timber and furs, which were sent to Britain to pay for much needed British-manufactured goods. As the economy developed, salt fish was sold to the West Indies and barrel staves to the Madeira Islands. This system fitted the triangular trade into which came the vital exports of tobacco, rice, indigo, and naval stores. These were used to pay for manufactured goods and, from Spain, fruit and wine.

By 1770, ports along the east coast like Boston, New York, and Charlestown were locked into a mutually profitable economic system.

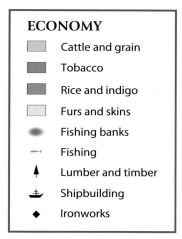

ECONOMY

- Cattle and grain
- Tobacco
- Rice and indigo
- Furs and skins
- Fishing banks
- Fishing
- Lumber and timber
- Shipbuilding
- Ironworks

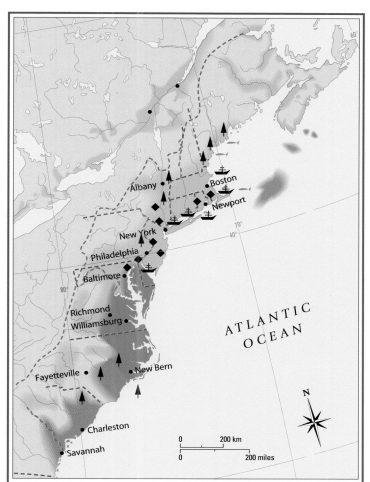

SAPIR'S THESIS: SIX BASIC INDIAN LANGUAGES

The German-born linguist, Edward Sapir (1884–1939), proposed that the many languages spoken by Native Americans could be classified into six basic divisions such as Eskimo-Aleut, spoken in the extreme north, and Macro Siouam-Hokan, spoken mainly in the south.

SAPIR'S THESIS: SIX BASIC INDIAN LANGUAGES

- Eskimo-Aleut
- Na-dene
- Macro Algonquian
- Macro Siouan-Hokan
- Penutian
- Aztec-Tanoan

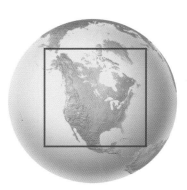

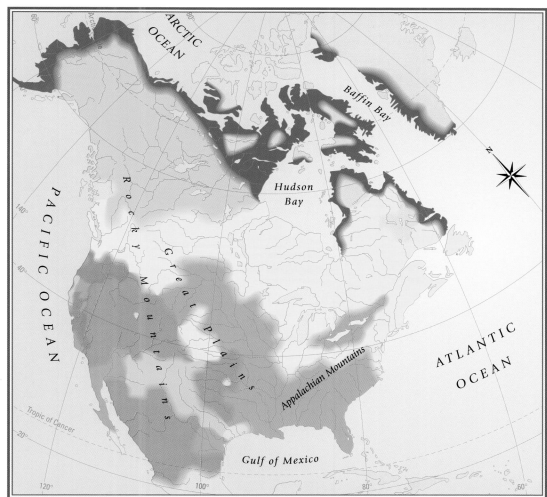

AFRICAN LANGUAGES

AFRICAN LANGUAGES

It is estimated that there are around 1500 languages across Africa, ranging from those spoken by millions of people, like Arabic or Hausa, to those spoken by a few hundred. The map is based on the classifications created by J.H. Greenberg whose work identified four main language families: khoisan, the languages which include the click sound of the San in the south; niger-kordofanian, originally spoken west of Lake Chad but now spoken over large areas of central and southeast Africa; nilo-Saharan; and afro-asiatic, spoken in the north and northeast.

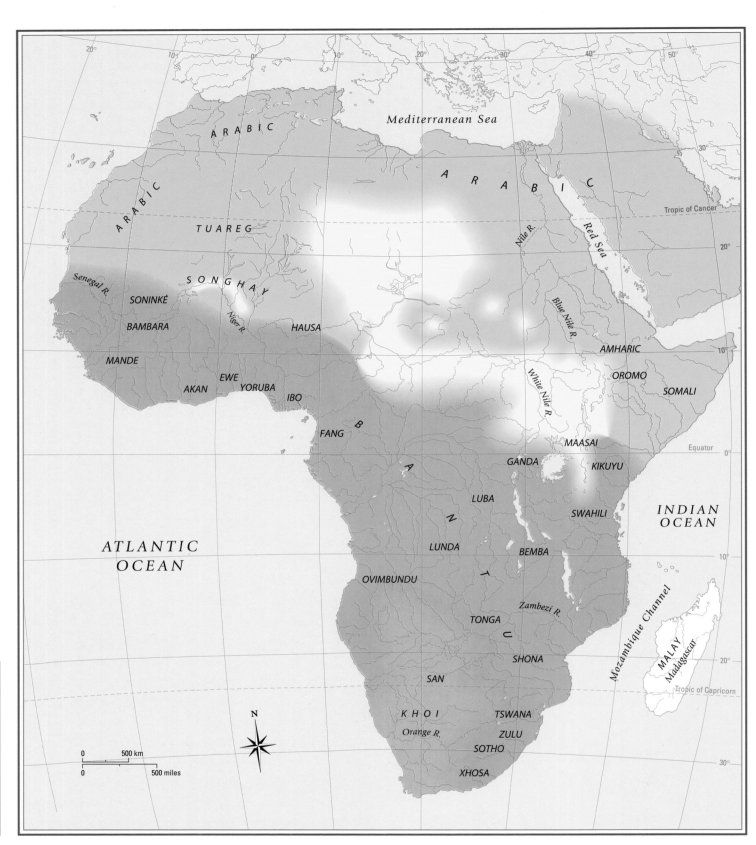

AFRICAN LANGUAGES AD 1000

- ▦ Niger-Kordofanian (inc. Bantu)
- ☐ Nilo-Saharan
- ▧ Afro-Asiatic
- ▨ Khoisan
- ☐ Not known

GHANA AND MALI EMPIRES (RIGHT)

The Empire of Ghana originated as a coalition of agricultural and iron-working communities that coalesced to form the original Kingdom. Ghana's position astride the Saharan trade routes provided horses, and these, combined with locally made iron weapons, gave the new state a decisive military advantage over its neighbors. Having control of the thriving trade and income from the Banbuk and Wangara goldfields, the Ghanian capital at Kumbi-Saleh prospered. The Empire reached its height at around 1050 when it occupied Awdaghust, a Berber trading stronghold to the north. In 1055, the Berbers retook Awdaghust as the first step in conquering and occupying the Ghanaian Empire. By the 12th Century, the much reduced Ghanaian Empire was in decline.

GHANA AND MALI EMPIRES; ALMORAVID EMPIRE

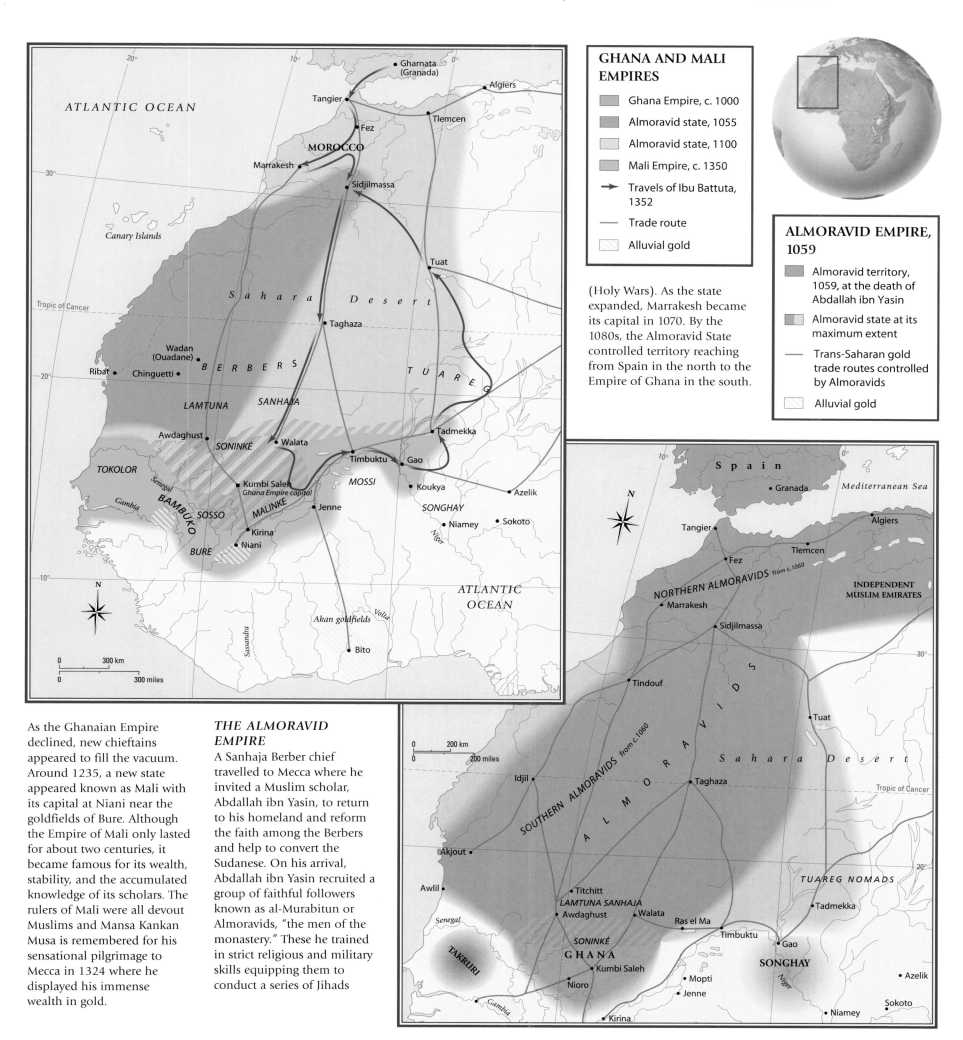

GHANA AND MALI EMPIRES

- Ghana Empire, c. 1000
- Almoravid state, 1055
- Almoravid state, 1100
- Mali Empire, c. 1350
- → Travels of Ibn Battuta, 1352
- — Trade route
- Alluvial gold

ALMORAVID EMPIRE, 1059

- Almoravid territory, 1059, at the death of Abdallah ibn Yasin
- Almoravid state at its maximum extent
- — Trans-Saharan gold trade routes controlled by Almoravids
- Alluvial gold

(Holy Wars). As the state expanded, Marrakesh became its capital in 1070. By the 1080s, the Almoravid State controlled territory reaching from Spain in the north to the Empire of Ghana in the south.

As the Ghanaian Empire declined, new chieftains appeared to fill the vacuum. Around 1235, a new state appeared known as Mali with its capital at Niani near the goldfields of Bure. Although the Empire of Mali only lasted for about two centuries, it became famous for its wealth, stability, and the accumulated knowledge of its scholars. The rulers of Mali were all devout Muslims and Mansa Kankan Musa is remembered for his sensational pilgrimage to Mecca in 1324 where he displayed his immense wealth in gold.

THE ALMORAVID EMPIRE

A Sanhaja Berber chief travelled to Mecca where he invited a Muslim scholar, Abdallah ibn Yasin, to return to his homeland and reform the faith among the Berbers and help to convert the Sudanese. On his arrival, Abdallah ibn Yasin recruited a group of faithful followers known as al-Murabitun or Almoravids, "the men of the monastery." These he trained in strict religious and military skills equipping them to conduct a series of Jihads

FATIMID NORTH AFRICA; MAMELUKE SULTANATE

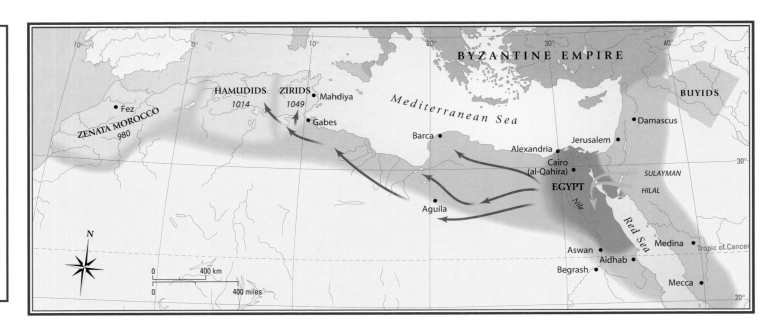

FATIMID NORTH AFRICA TO c. 1000

- Fatimid caliphate at its maximum extent, c. 1000
- Breakaway principalities, with date
- Movement of Arab peoples (Banu Hilal and Banu Sulayman), c. 1000
- Fatimid caliphate, c. 1055
- Sulayman and Hilal attacks, encouraged by the Fatimids

MAMELUKE SULTANATE

The Mameluke Sultanate, founded by the legendary Salah al-Din (Saladin) in 1171, presided over a period of increased prosperity based on agricultural production and trade between the cities of the Red Sea and the eastern Mediterranean. Eventually, due to the combined effects of the Black Death and the fact that the Mamelukes had abandoned the military nature of their regime, the Ottoman Turks were allowed to conquer Egypt in 1517.

MAMELUKE SULTANATE 1171–1517

- Mameluke territory, c. 1400
- Territory recaptured by the Mameluke from European crusaders by 1291
- Trade route

SPREAD OF ISLAM

FATAMID NORTH AFRICA (left)

The Fatamids, (descendants of Fatima, prophet Muhammad's daughter), occupied and ruled Egypt from 969. The Fatamids initially gained control of the north African coast as far west as Morocco. In 973 the Fatamid Caliph, Al-Mu'izz, moved the capital from the Maghrib to Cairo, and in doing so he lost control of the western part of his state. The Fatamid Caliphate, now based in Egypt, went on to build up a large trading empire. Its currency, the Fatamid dinar minted in gold, was imported across the Sahara from the states of Western Africa. The Fatamid State depended on a largely Berber army but this also included large numbers of Mamluk (Turkish slave horsemen). On the death of the last Fatamid Caliph in 1171, Salah al-Din, known to the West as Saladin, a Mameluke General, took power, founding the Ayyubid dynasty.

SPREAD OF ISLAM (below)

The Islamization of Africa first began in the north in the 7th Century. Prior to its arrival most of the population of the Mediterranean coast of Africa were Christian. Further south, across the Sahara, people held their own traditions and beliefs usually focused on nature and the land. After Islam became established in Egypt, and over the next three centuries, Christianity was almost completely obliterated. Islam continued to spread across the trans-Saharan trade routes establishing itself in western and central Sudan. Meanwhile, Arab traders, sailing along the east coast of Africa, established their religion as far south as Sofala in southern Africa and the northern parts of Madagascar.

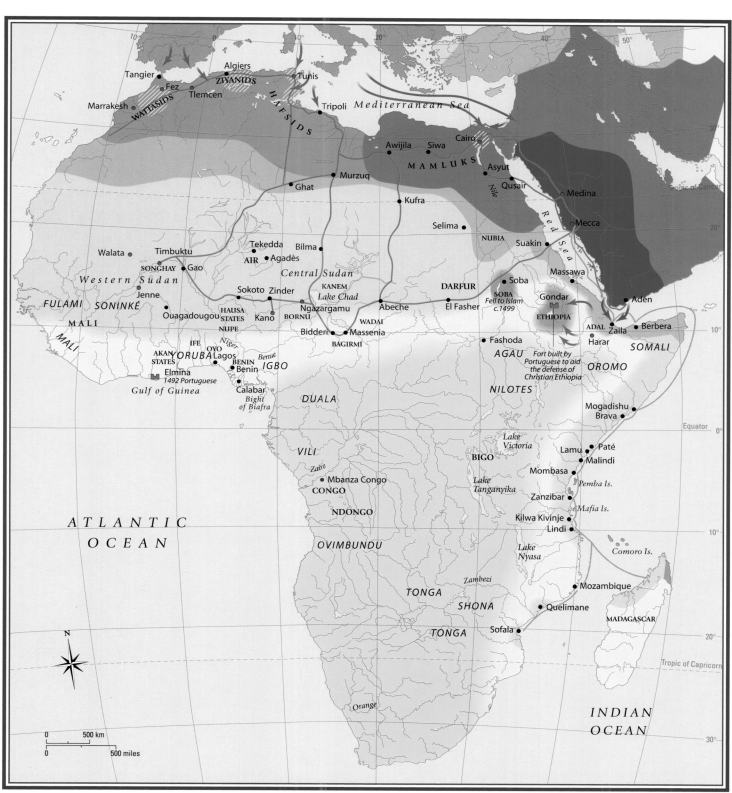

SPREAD OF ISLAM TO c. 1500

- Extent of Islam at the death of Muhammad, 632
- Extent of Islam at the death of Uthman, 650
- Extent of Islam at the end of the Umayyad dynasty, 750
- Extent of Islam, 1250
- Extent of Islam, 1500
- Christian state, 1500
- Animist religions, 1500
- Areas of Africa's Jewish settlers, 1492–96
- Christian crusades, 1096–1570s
- Centers of Islamic learning
- Pilgrimage route developing, 15–16th C.
- Jihad (Holy War) of Ahmad Gran, 1531–43
- Ottoman aid to Jihad
- DARFUR States, c. 1500
- OROMO Major tribe
- Trans-Sahara trade routes

THE CRUSADES

THE CRUSADES

The Crusades were a series of military expeditions launched from Christian Europe from 1095 to 1270. Pope Urban called on the Christian states of central and western Europe to march to the Christians in the east, and this was also to serve as a pilgrimage to Jerusalem. This would be the First Crusade and its aim was to liberate the Holy Land from the Muslim Seljuk Turks. After many trials and tribulations the city of Jerusalem was recaptured among scenes of great brutality in 1099.

"In all the streets and squares of the city, mounds of heads, hands and feet were to be seen. People were walking quite openly over dead men and horses".
Raymond of Aguilers, *eyewitness of the capture of Jerusalem.*

Crusading carried on to the east until the 1270s. There were others to the Baltic and against internal enemies and heretics like the Cathars of southern France.

The Crusading impulse continued in some form until the 16th Century with attempts to hold back the expanding Ottoman Empire.

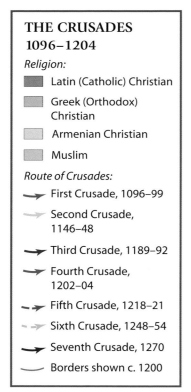

THE CRUSADES
1096–1204

Religion:

- ■ Latin (Catholic) Christian
- ■ Greek (Orthodox) Christian
- ■ Armenian Christian
- ■ Muslim

Route of Crusades:

- ➤ First Crusade, 1096–99
- ➤ Second Crusade, 1146–48
- ➤ Third Crusade, 1189–92
- ➤ Fourth Crusade, 1202–04
- ➤ Fifth Crusade, 1218–21
- ➤ Sixth Crusade, 1248–54
- ➤ Seventh Crusade, 1270
- — Borders shown c. 1200

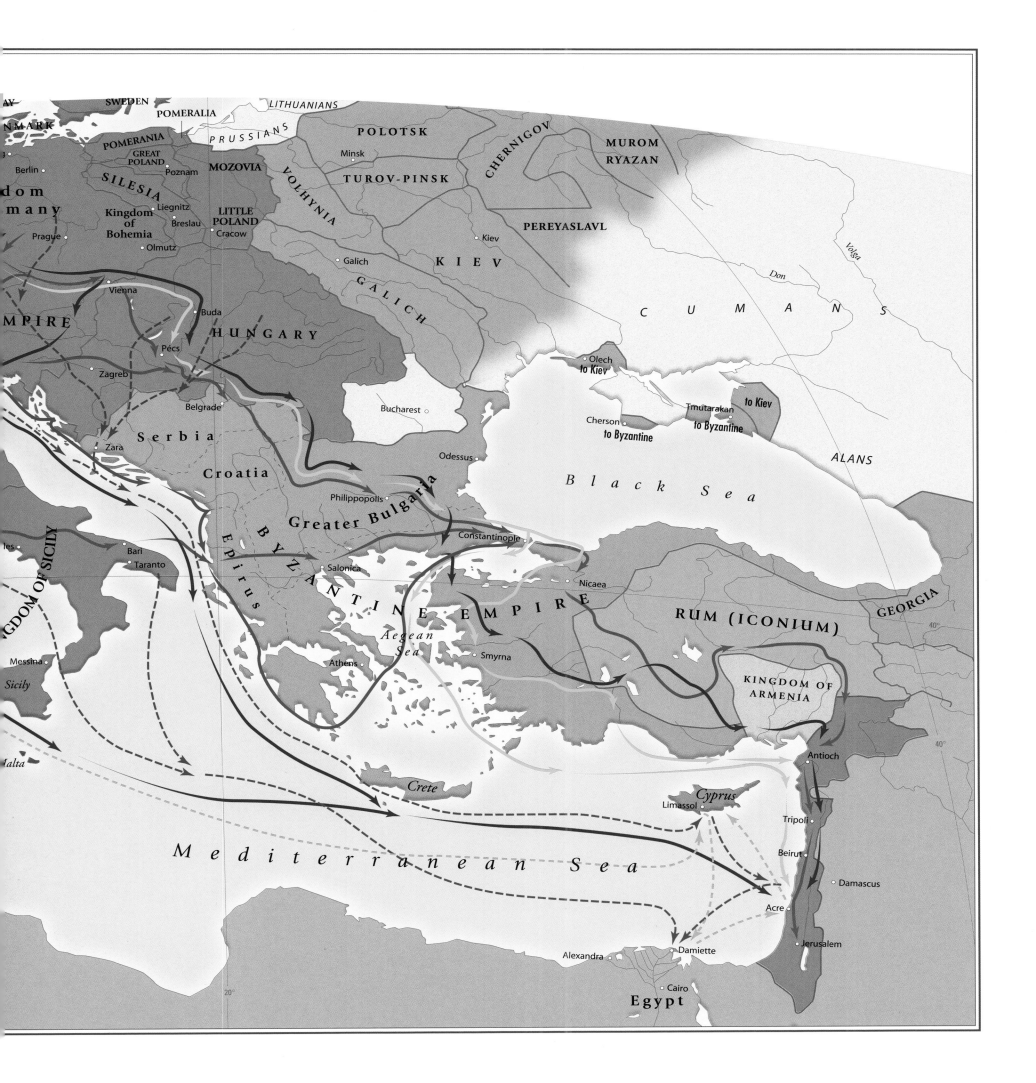

MUSLIM SPAIN; THE CHRISTIAN RECONQUEST

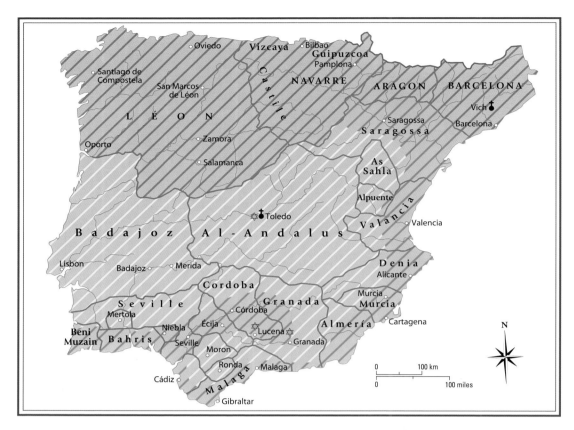

MUSLIM SPAIN

In 711 Tariq ibn Ziyad crossed from north Africa into Spain where he defeated the Visigothic King Roderick. Arab forces launched a campaign of conquest that, by 732, included almost all of modern Spain and Portugal. Islamic dynasties ruled large areas of Spain until 1492 when the last Islamic state fell to the reconquest.

THE CHRISTIAN RECONQUEST

The high tide of Muslim conquest was in 718. However, in the north small areas held out. It was this small territory in which a nucleus of resistance formed. Their first real victory was at Caradonga in 722. Various Christian Kingdoms expanded and united and, with Papal approval and with the help of Christian military orders, mounted a series of Crusades. The Muslims were slowly driven further south until the United Kingdoms of Castile and Aragon finally crushed the Muslim state of Grenada, ending a unique Islamic European culture that had developed over 700 years.

MUSLIM SPAIN
c. 1030

- Christian states
- Caliphate of Cordoba to 1031
- Murcia Islamic (or Party) kingdoms after 1031
- ✝ Archidiocese
- ✡ Important Jewish community

Population
- Christian
- Mostly Berber and converts
- Mostly Arabic

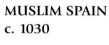

THE CHRISTIAN RECONQUEST

Date of reconquest
- 1080
- 1130
- 1210
- 1250
- 1275
- Muslim domination
- ✝ Archidiocese

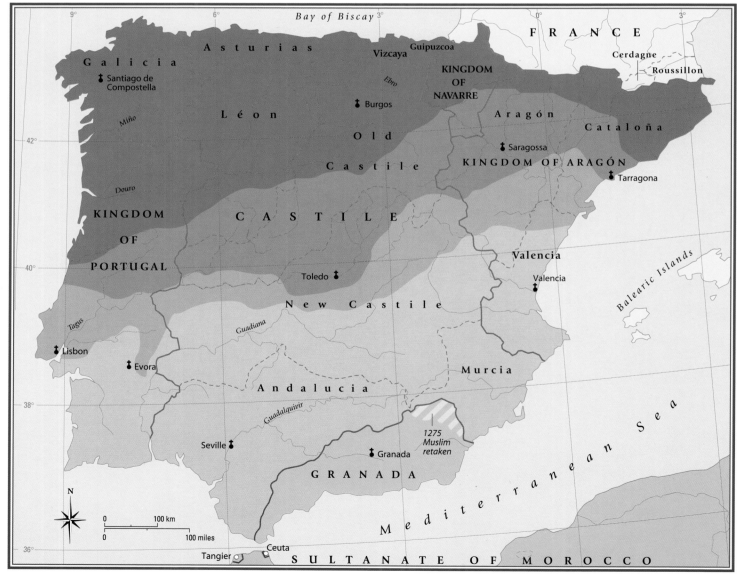

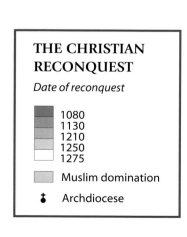

EMPIRE AND THE PAPACY; THE VATICAN CITY

EMPIRE & PAPACY

Henry II conquered Italy in 962, his conquests including the Patrimony of St. Peter and Rome. In Rome, Henry was crowned by Pope John XII, becoming Emperor of a state that was both holy and Roman, combining the ideals of Christianity with the perceived glories of ancient Rome.

In 1059, after a period of imperial consolidation, a rift arose between the Emperor and the Pope as to who was the ultimate God-given authority over western Christendom. This became known as the "Investiture Controversy."

THE EMPIRE AND THE PAPACY

— Empire border, 1152

Kingdom of Germany

Kingdom of Italy

Kingdom of Burgundy

Kingdom of Bohemia

Imperial land in Italy

Hohenstaufen demesne land

Welf demesne land

Ecclesiastical land

• Archdiocese

○ Diocese

■ Lombard League town, 1167

1. St. Peter's Basilica
2. Bernini's Bronze Doors
3. Bernini's Colonnade
4. St. Peter's Square (Piazza San Pietro)
5. Tower of Nicholas V
6. Apostolic Palace
7. Courtyard of San Damaso
8. Courtyard of the Marshal
9. Courtyard of the Parrot
10. Borgia Courtyard
11. Courtyard of the Sentinel
12. Sistine Chapel
13. Borgia Tower
14. Borgia Apartment Collection of Modern Religious Art Raphael Stanze (2nd floor)
15. St. Anne Gate
16. Church of St. Anne of the Palafrenieri
17. Vatican Printing Press
18. Vatican Post Office
19. Tapestry Workshop
20. Church of San Pellegrino
21. Offices of L'Osservatore Romano
22. Lapidary Gallery
23. Courtyard of the Belvedere
24. Vatican Library Sacred Museum Gallery of Maps (2nd floor)
25. Vatican Library
26. Courtyard of the Library
27. Tower of the Winds
28. Braccio Nuovo (New Arm)
29. Chiaramonto Museum
30. Courtyard of the Pine
31. Belvedere Niche
32. Vatican Library Profane Museum Gallery of the Tapastries Gallery of the Candelabra (2nd floor)
33. Gregorian Egyptian Museum Gregorian Etruscan Museum (2nd floor)
34. Pio-Clementine Museum
35. Octagonal Courtyard
36. Belvedere of Innocent VIII
37. Stairs of Bramante

THE VATICAN CITY

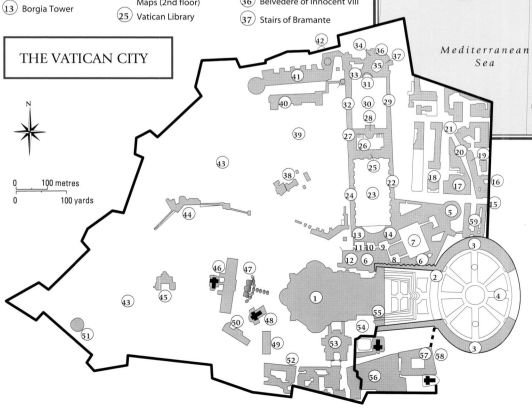

38. Casina of Pius IV
39. Historical Museum (Underground)
40. Pinacoteca (Picture Gallery)
41. Gregorian Profane Museum Pio-Christian Museum Pontifical Missionary-Ethnology Museum
42. Entrance to the Vatican Museums
43. Vatican Gardens
44. Vatican Radio Station
45. Pontifical Ethiopian Museum
46. Palace of the Governorate of Vatican City
47. Floral arrangement in honor of the reigning Pontiff (displaying the Papal Coat of Arms)
48. Church of St. Stephen of the Abyssinians
49. Palace of the Tribunal
50. Mosaic Workshop
51. Tower of St. John
52. Palace of St. Charles
53. Sacristy and Treasury of St. Peter's
54. Piazza of the Protomartyrs
55. Arch of the Bells
56. Audience Hall (Aula)
57. Palace of the Congregation for the Doctrine of the Faith (Holy Office)
58. Holy Office Square
59. Church of San Martino degli Svizzeri (Church of the Swiss Guard)

950 – C.1600 SONGHAY EMPIRE

SONGHAY EMPIRE
A pre-colonial African state centered in eastern Mali, the Songhay Empire was from the early 15th to the late 16th century one of the largest African empires ever seen. Following a civil war fought over succession to the Empire, the Moroccans invaded. During the same period in Morocco itself, the Moorish ruler Abu Abdallah Mohammed II Saadi enlisted the help of his Christian allies in Portugal to overthrow the Islamic Abd Al-Malik, who had deposed him as king. The conflict came to a head on August 4, 1578 at Alcazarquivir, in which the combined troops of the Moors and the Portuguese were utterly routed.

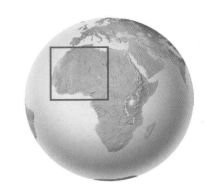

SONGHAY EMPIRE
c. 1540

- Songhay Empire, c. 1520
- Tributary kingdom of Songhay Empire
- Spanish territory
- Portuguese enclave
- Portuguese trading post
- Trade route
- --- Conjectural trade route
- → Commodity flow

Resources
- Alluvial gold
- Tin mining
- Kola nut
- Salt
- Gum
- Copper

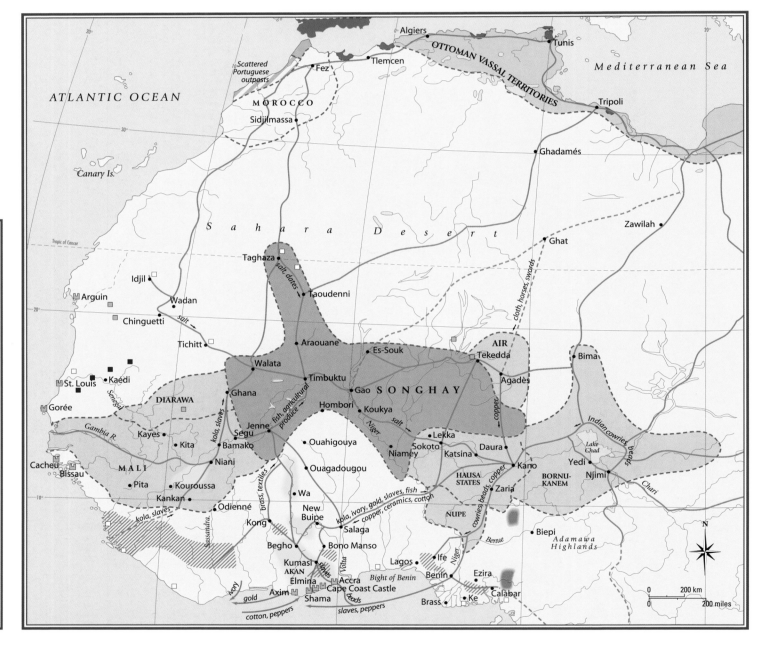

DESERT STATES; THE HORN OF AFRICA

***DESERT STATES AND
THE HORN OF AFRICA***
By the late 16th century the
Spaniards had lost almost all
their African possessions. The
Barbary states, the coastal
regions of Morocco, Algeria,
Tunisia, and Libya, primarily
from the example of the
Moors who had been expelled
from Spain, degenerated into
mere communities of pirates,
and under Turkish influence
civilization and commerce
declined. To the south,
conflicts raged between
Christian and Islamic forces,

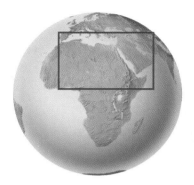

motivated by a combination of
religious and economic factors.

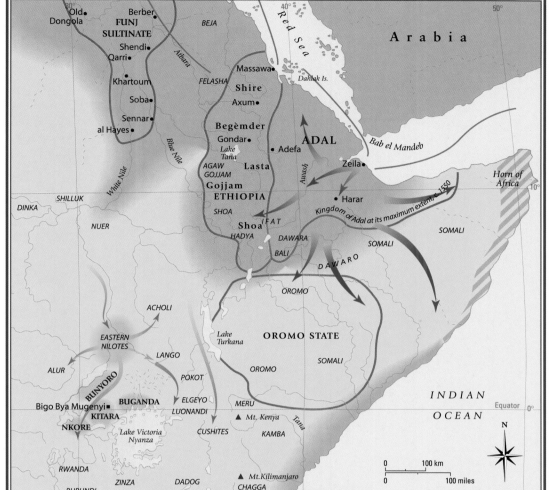

DESERT STATES
c. 1600

→ Migration of Bedouin,
   950–1350

▨ Songhay Empire, c. 1500

▨ Bornu-Kanem, c. 1590

▨ Ottoman Empire by
   c. 1600

• Spanish possessions,
   c. 1540

➤ Slave route

— Trade route

THE HORN OF
AFRICA TO 1500

Religions

▨ Islam, c. 1500

➤ Islam expansion

▨ Christian (Coptic),
   c. 1500

▨ Animist, c. 1500

Tribal movements

➤ Western Nilotes

➤ Southern Nilotes

— Trade route

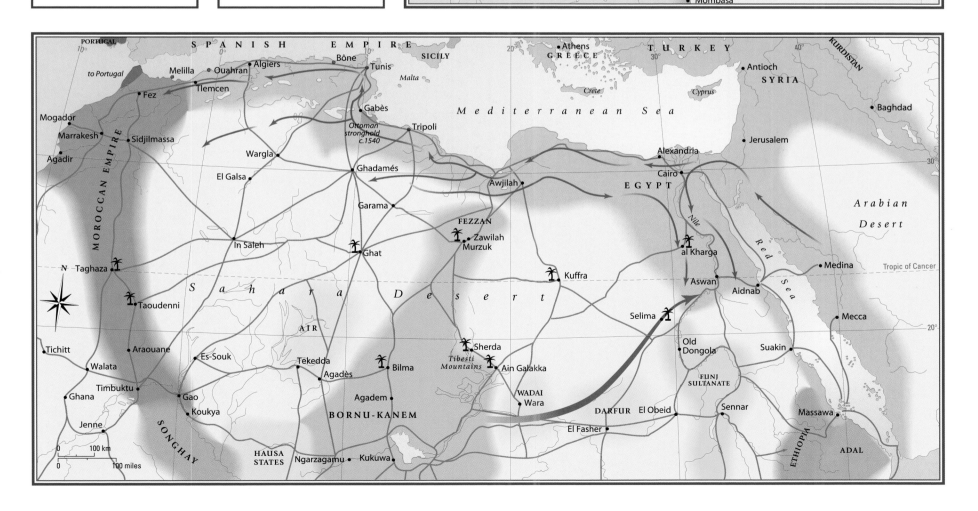

1328 – 1672   EUROPE 1500

EUROPE 1500

⎯ The Holy Roman Empire

EXPANSION OF THE OTTOMAN EMPIRE

EUROPE 1500 (LEFT)
By the Middle Ages the political map of Europe was beginning to take shape, but Central Europe was still made up of a number of small states. For hundreds of years these small feuding states were constantly fighting each other in order to increase their landholdings and wealth. In an attempt to restore some form of order, in the tenth century the Holy Roman Empire was created. Although the Pope crowned each emperor, his authority was not always widely recognized. In spite of this the Empire continued until 1806 when Francis II abdicated during the Napoleonic Wars.

EXPANSION OF THE OTTOMAN EMPIRE
At the beginning of the 13th century what became the Ottoman Empire was a small Turkish State, but it grew to become the center of interactions between Eastern and Western worlds for six centuries. Following the Muslim conquest of Constantinople in 1453 there was a long period of conquest and expansion. The Empire prospered under the rule of a series of committed and effective sultans. At the height of its power during the reign of Suleiman the Magnificent in the 16th century it spanned three continents, controlling much of south-eastern Europe, the Middle East, and North Africa.

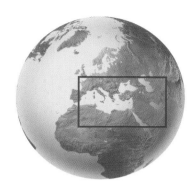

EXPANSION OF THE OTTOMAN EMPIRE 1328–1566

- Ottoman territory, 1328
- Ottoman territory, 1355
- Ottoman vassal from 1394
- Ottoman territory, 1402 (prior to Mongol attack)
- Ottoman territory, 1451
- Ottoman territory, 1481 (Mohammed II)
- Ottoman vassal from 1475
- Ottoman territory, 1520 (Selim I)
- Ottoman vassal from 1541
- Ottoman territory, 1566 (Suleiman I)

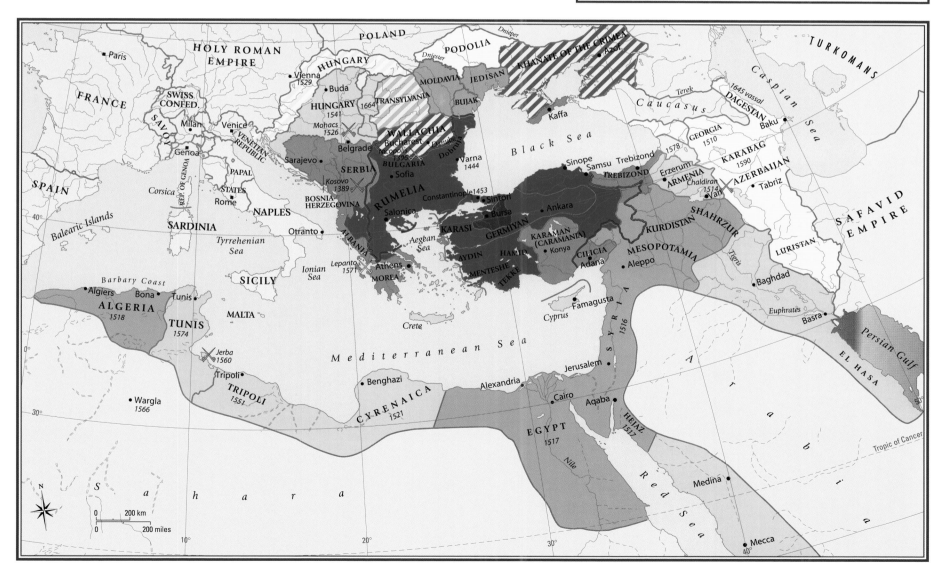

MONGOL CONQUESTS

MONGOL CONQUESTS
The Mongol Empire was the
largest land empire in history.
At its peak it covered around
21 million square miles and
had a population of over 100
million people. It was founded
by Genghis Khan in 1206 and
started out as a Mongol Nation
of unified Central Asian
confederations such as
Mongols, Naimans, Uighurs,
and Merkits, but gradually
expanded outward after
numerous conquests against
Chinese, Middle Eastern, and
European regions. As a result
of Mongolian conquest
commercial and political
connections were established
between Eastern and Western
areas of the world that exist to
this day.

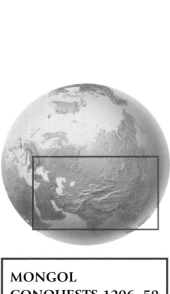

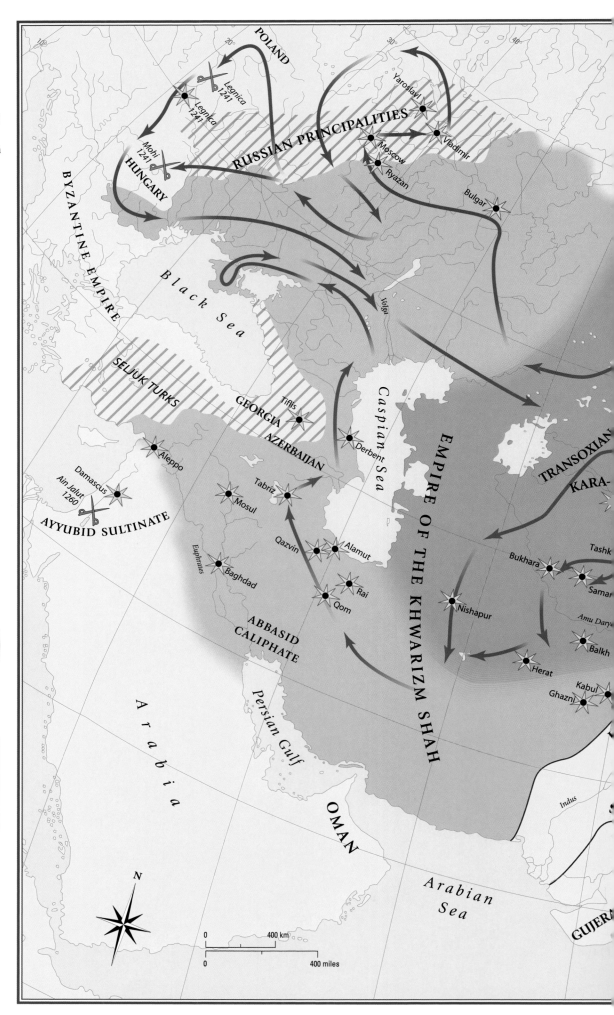

**MONGOL
CONQUESTS 1206–59**

OIROTS Original tribe

▮ Homeland of the
Mongol tribes

▮ Mongol Empire, 1206

▮ Mongol Empire, 1236

▮ Mongol Empire, 1259

▨ Area paying tribute or
under loose Mongol
control

→ Mongol campaign

✳ City sacked by Mongols

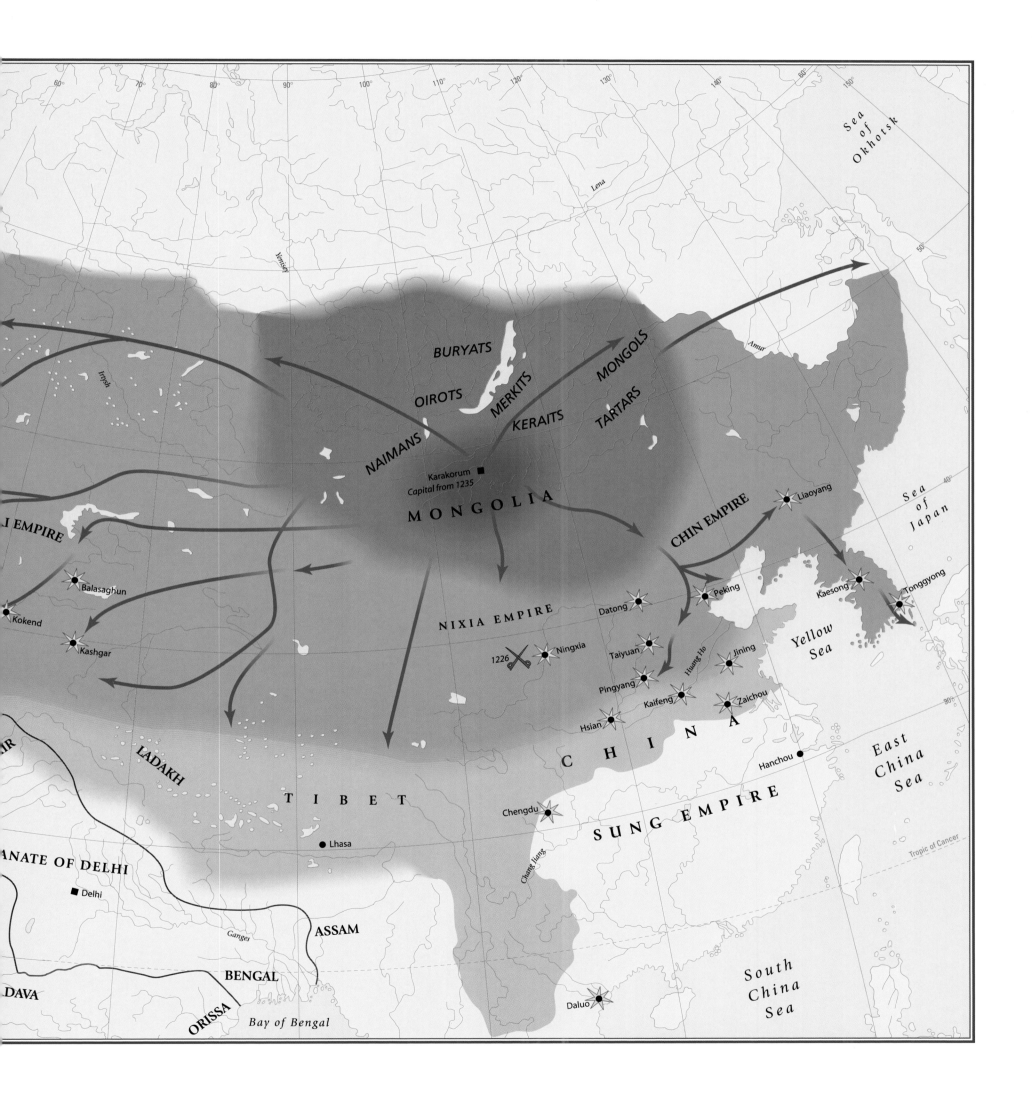

THE EMPIRE OF THE GREAT KHAN

THE EMPIRE OF THE GREAT KHAN

Kublai Khan is remembered as the last Great Khan. He was the grandson of Genghis Khan and was the fifth Khagan of the Mongol Empire and the founder and first Emperor of the Chinese Yuan Dynasty. He was a powerful warrior; his conquest of China is estimated as having killed 18 million people. It was at this time that the Mongol Empire reached its greatest extent. However, he was accused of being too Chinese and he even moved his headquarters to Beijing. His later attempted invasions of Japan and Vietnam were not successful. After his death the Empire broke up.

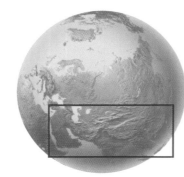

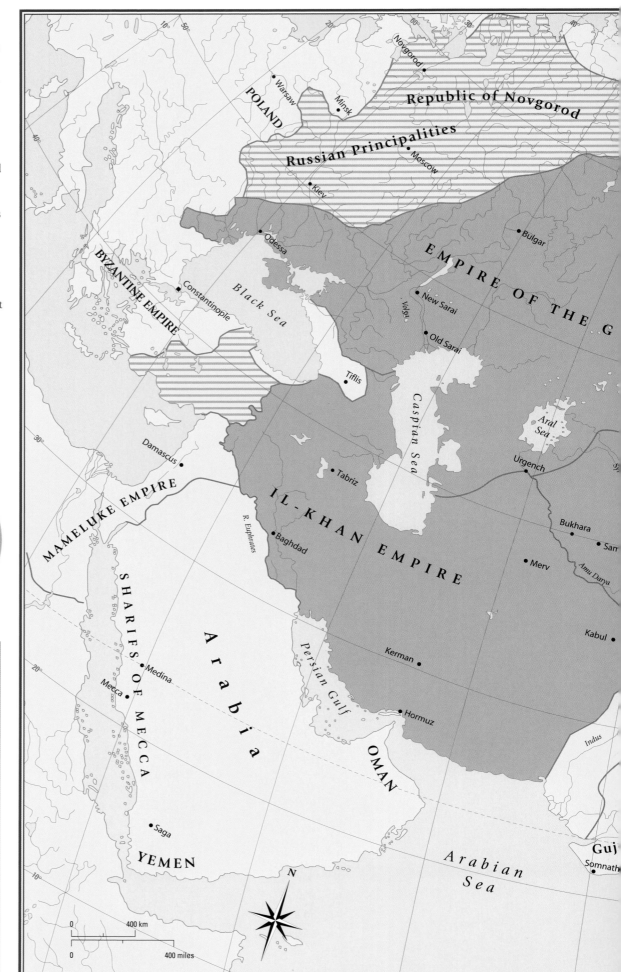

THE EMPIRE OF THE GREAT KHAN, 1260–c. 1300

- The Great Khanate, 1268
- Conquered by the Great Khan (Kublai Khan), 1268–79
- Western khanates owing nominal allegiance to the Great Khan
- Tributary to Mongol state
- → Kublai Khan's campaigns, 1268–79
- → Kublai Khan's campaigns, 1274–92
- → Other Mongol campaign

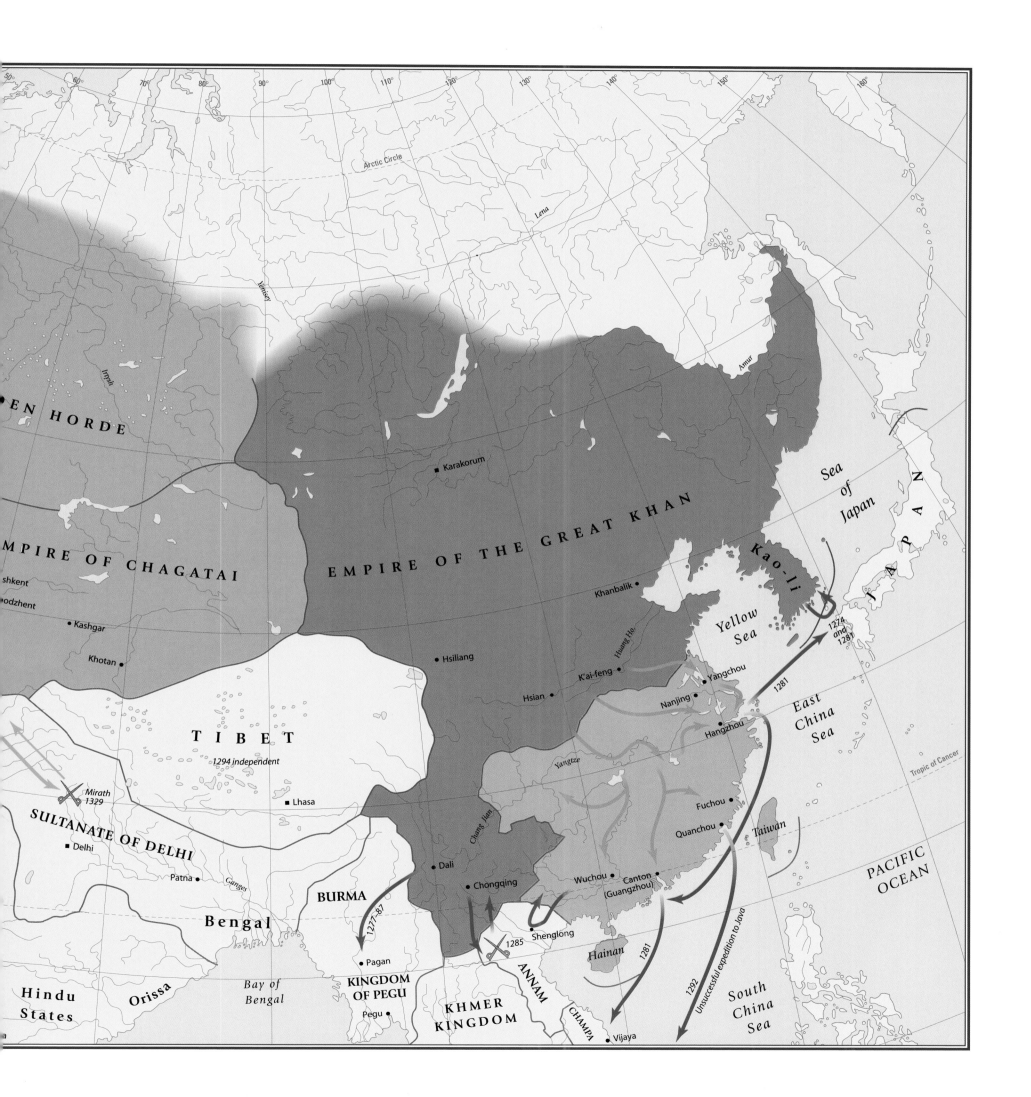

1241

THE BATTLE OF MOHI

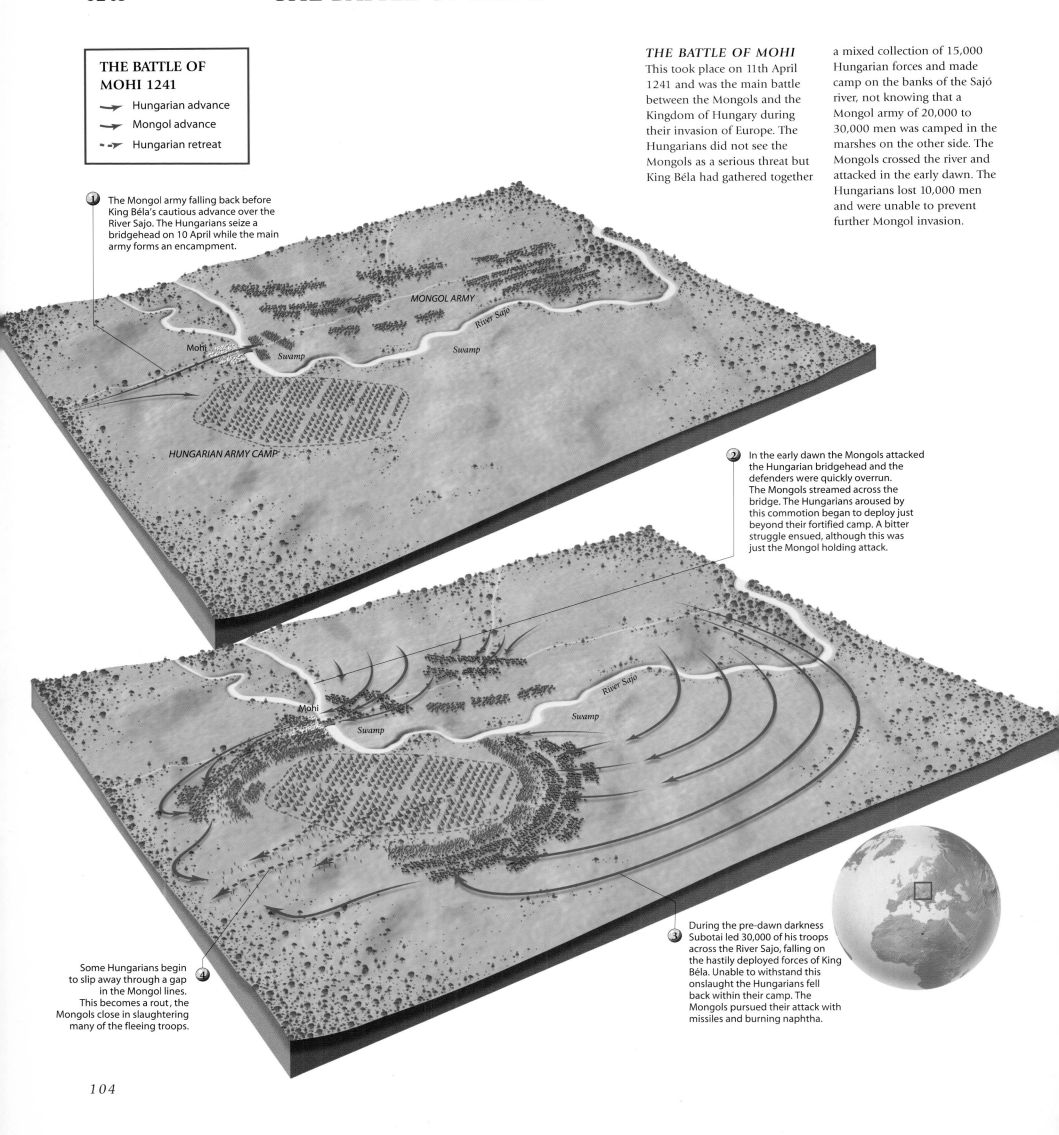

**THE BATTLE OF
MOHI 1241**

→ Hungarian advance

→ Mongol advance

--→ Hungarian retreat

THE BATTLE OF MOHI
This took place on 11th April 1241 and was the main battle between the Mongols and the Kingdom of Hungary during their invasion of Europe. The Hungarians did not see the Mongols as a serious threat but King Béla had gathered together a mixed collection of 15,000 Hungarian forces and made camp on the banks of the Sajó river, not knowing that a Mongol army of 20,000 to 30,000 men was camped in the marshes on the other side. The Mongols crossed the river and attacked in the early dawn. The Hungarians lost 10,000 men and were unable to prevent further Mongol invasion.

① The Mongol army falling back before King Béla's cautious advance over the River Sajo. The Hungarians seize a bridgehead on 10 April while the main army forms an encampment.

MONGOL ARMY

River Sajo

Mohi

Swamp

Swamp

HUNGARIAN ARMY CAMP

② In the early dawn the Mongols attacked the Hungarian bridgehead and the defenders were quickly overrun. The Mongols streamed across the bridge. The Hungarians aroused by this commotion began to deploy just beyond their fortified camp. A bitter struggle ensued, although this was just the Mongol holding attack.

Mohi

River Sajo

Swamp

Swamp

③ During the pre-dawn darkness Subotai led 30,000 of his troops across the River Sajo, falling on the hastily deployed forces of King Béla. Unable to withstand this onslaught the Hungarians fell back within their camp. The Mongols pursued their attack with missiles and burning naphtha.

④ Some Hungarians begin to slip away through a gap in the Mongol lines. This becomes a rout, the Mongols close in slaughtering many of the fleeing troops.

PART 4

EXPLORATION AND FIRST CONTACT

THE WORLD OF EXPLORATION often depended on a combination of naval skill and ship design, coupled with a desire to acquire knowledge and find new products to trade. Following the travels of Marco Polo through the vast Empire of Kublai Khan and Ibn Batuta's journeys through the Muslim world and the Russian steppes to China, Europeans began to look toward the East. Meanwhile, the Chinese Empire's explorations brought them as far west as Mozambique and possibly as far as the Atlantic in ships that dwarfed Christopher Columbus's Santa Maria. Columbus reached the Caribbean in 1492 and established a Spanish presence that rapidly spread into Mexico and the Andes. The Native American population was decimated, unable to defend themselves against the brutality of the new settlers or the new diseases they brought with them. Elsewhere, the French, through the efforts of explorer Samuel de Champlain, successfully established a colony at Quebec. There was also a sprinkling of French settlers along the St Lawrence, and they had established trading forts on the Mississippi and at New Orleans by 1718. The English, thanks to the voyages of Sir Walter Raleigh, established colonies at Roanoke and Jamestown. Jamestown became an important springboard for later ventures in Massachusetts and other New England regions.

1271 – 1776 ROUTE OF MARCO POLO; VOYAGES OF COLUMBUS

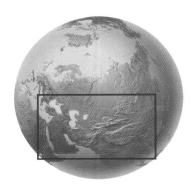

ROUTE OF MARCO POLO 1271

- - -► Route taken by Marco Polo

▨ Over 6000 feet

░ Over 3000 feet

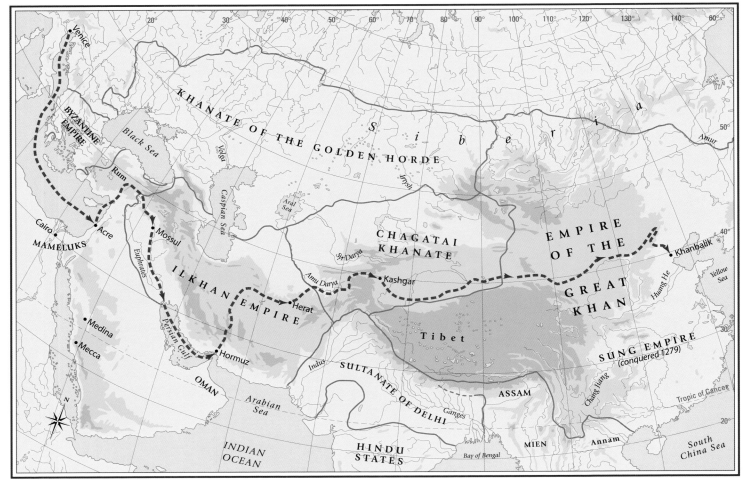

THE ROUTE OF MARCO POLO

Marco Polo came from a family of Venetian merchants and with his father and uncle he traveled to China in 1271.

At that time the Emperor of China was Kublai Khan, the last Great Khan of the Mongol Empire. Marco Polo entered Kublai Khan's diplomatic service and stayed in China for the next 17 years. He journeyed to Yunnan, Burma, Tibet, and along the Yangzi, Yellow, and Mekong river systems.

He was amazed by what he saw on his travels and was particularly impressed by paper money, coal, the postal system, and the size of the Chinese ships, recording his observations in Il Milione.

THE VOYAGES OF COLUMBUS

Christopher Columbus was an Italian navigator who was anxious to explore westward routes across the ocean in the hope of reaching India and China.

When he wanted to finance an expedition he initially approached the Portuguese king, but the Portuguese were mainly interested in developing their route to the East by going around Africa, so turned him down. He was eventually financed by the Spanish, which

meant that Spain basked in the glory of his discoveries. His first expedition was in 1492, but he did not actually set foot on American soil until his third expedition in 1498.

ENGLISH AND FRENCH EXPLORATION

The main thrust of early exploration in the Americas by both the English and the French took place in the two hundred years between 1500 and 1700, although the English carried on for another 80 years.

The French tended to stick to the area around the St Lawrence River and the Great Lakes, while the English went further south and tended to keep to the area between the coast and the Ohio River.

There was some overlap, which obviously led to conflict between the two national groups. There were also a number of encounters with Native Indian groups, many of whom were hostile.

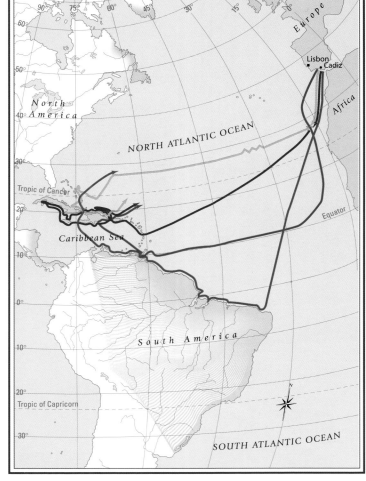

ROUTES OF COLUMBUS 1492–1504

▨ Explored land

☐ Unknown land

→ Columbus, 1492–1493

→ Columbus, 1493–1496

→ Columbus, 1498–1500

→ Columbus, 1502–1504

ENGLISH EXPLORATION; FRENCH EXPLORATION

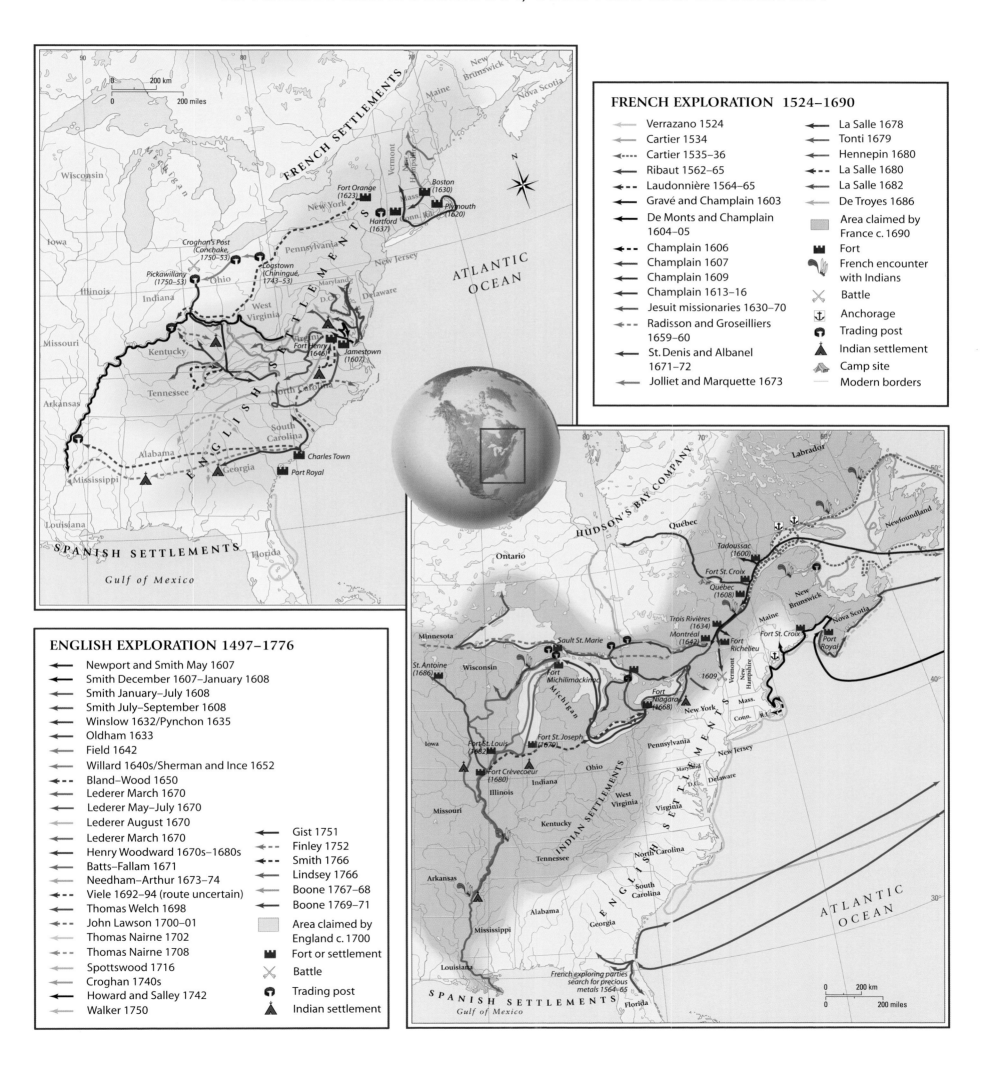

FRENCH EXPLORATION 1524–1690

← Verrazano 1524	← La Salle 1678
← Cartier 1534	← Tonti 1679
◄···· Cartier 1535–36	← Hennepin 1680
← Ribaut 1562–65	◄-·-· La Salle 1680
◄-·-· Laudonnière 1564–65	← La Salle 1682
← Gravé and Champlain 1603	← De Troyes 1686
← De Monts and Champlain 1604–05	▨ Area claimed by France c. 1690
◄-·-· Champlain 1606	🏰 Fort
← Champlain 1607	🖐 French encounter with Indians
← Champlain 1609	✕ Battle
← Champlain 1613–16	⚓ Anchorage
← Jesuit missionaries 1630–70	⚓ Trading post
◄-·-· Radisson and Groseilliers 1659–60	▲ Indian settlement
← St. Denis and Albanel 1671–72	⛺ Camp site
← Jolliet and Marquette 1673	— Modern borders

ENGLISH EXPLORATION 1497–1776

← Newport and Smith May 1607	
← Smith December 1607–January 1608	
← Smith January–July 1608	
← Smith July–September 1608	
← Winslow 1632/Pynchon 1635	
← Oldham 1633	
← Field 1642	
← Willard 1640s/Sherman and Ince 1652	
◄-·-· Bland–Wood 1650	
← Lederer March 1670	
← Lederer May–July 1670	
← Lederer August 1670	
← Lederer March 1670	
← Henry Woodward 1670s–1680s	← Gist 1751
← Batts–Fallam 1671	◄-·-· Finley 1752
← Needham–Arthur 1673–74	← Smith 1766
◄-·-· Viele 1692–94 (route uncertain)	← Lindsey 1766
← Thomas Welch 1698	← Boone 1767–68
◄-·-· John Lawson 1700–01	← Boone 1769–71
← Thomas Nairne 1702	
◄-·-· Thomas Nairne 1708	▨ Area claimed by England c. 1700
← Spottswood 1716	🏰 Fort or settlement
← Croghan 1740s	✕ Battle
← Howard and Salley 1742	⚓ Trading post
← Walker 1750	▲ Indian settlement

1499 – 1800 VOYAGES OF DISCOVERY; WORLD EXPLORATION

VOYAGES OF DISCOVERY 1499–1502

Explored land

Unknown land

→ Vespucci, 1499–1500

→ Cabral, 1500

→ Gaspar Corte-Real, 1500

→ Gaspar Corte-Real, 1501

→ Vespucci, 1501–1502

→ Miguel Corte-Real, 1502

VOYAGES OF DISCOVERY
The first real voyages of exploration began in the 15th Century. Columbus, on behalf of Spain, made several voyages to the Caribbean and Vespucci later followed this up when he sailed along the northeast of South America. A few years after this, in 1519, Magellan set off on an epic voyage around

the world. He sailed around the southern tip of South America, giving his name to the Magellan Straits. After he discovered the Philippines and named them after the King of Spain local islanders killed him. Of the 270 sailors that set out from Spain on this first Round-the-World Voyage, only 18 returned.

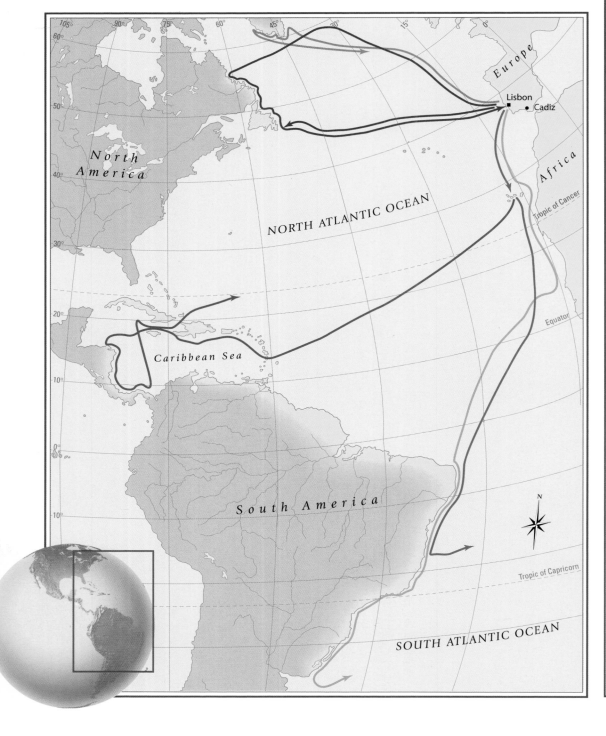

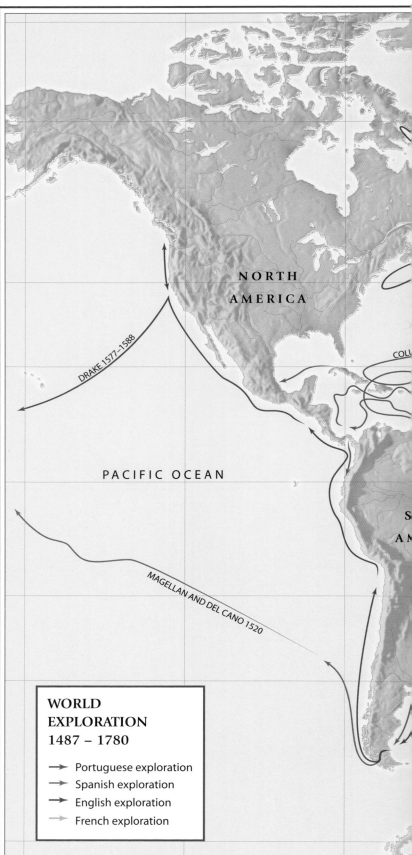

WORLD EXPLORATION 1487 – 1780

→ Portuguese exploration

→ Spanish exploration

→ English exploration

→ French exploration

WORLD EXPLORATION
Captain James Cook (whose voyages can be seen in the inset map below) was another explorer who died at the hands of the people that he had

"discovered." He joined the Royal Navy in 1755 and was a skilled seaman, surveyor, and cartographer. After making the first map of Newfoundland, he embarked on three voyages to

the Pacific Ocean. He was the first European to discover Eastern Australia and made the first circumnavigation of New Zealand. He was also the first European to discover the

Hawaiian Islands. Cook was arguably the last great figure of the 300-hundred year period of global exploration. During this extraordinary time, the great European powers of Britain,

France, Spain and Portugal helped forge the modern world, expanding knowledge and trade, as well as their own empires, laying the foundations for today's global village.

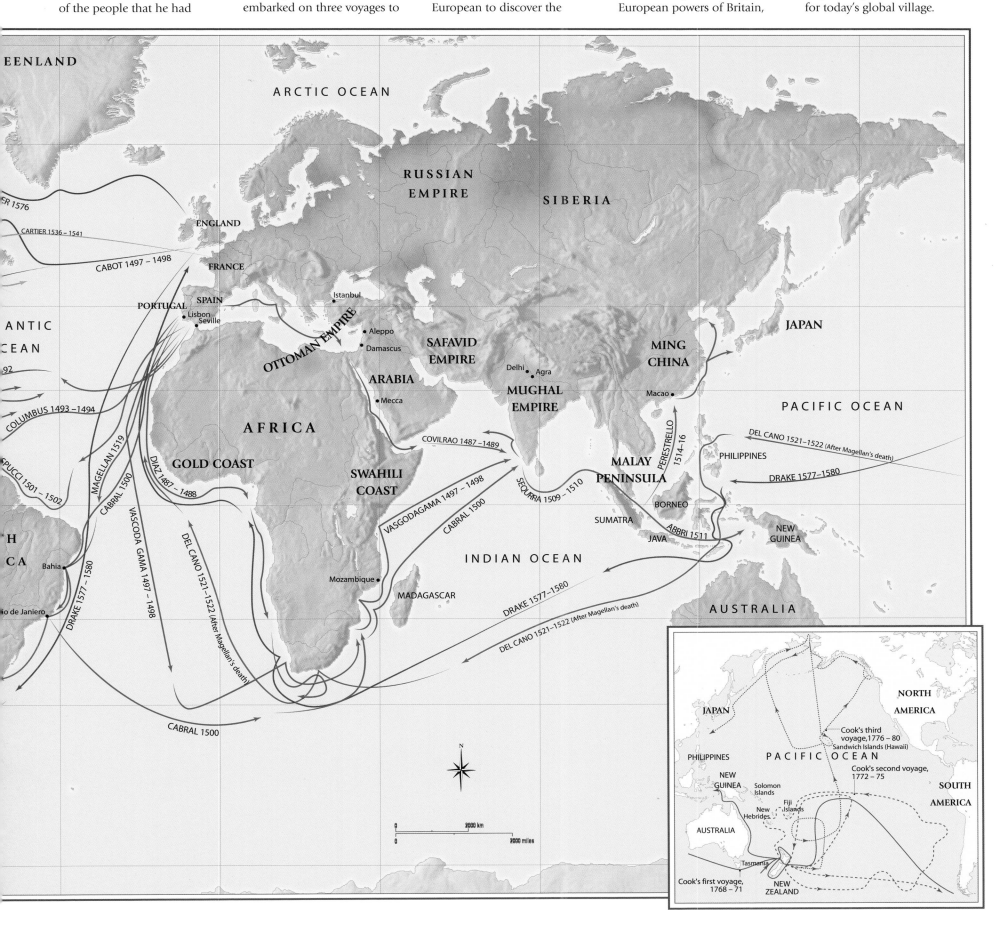

ENGLISH SETTLEMENTS AND COLONIAL GRANTS

ENGLISH SETTLEMENTS AND COLONIAL GRANTS
The early part of the 1600s saw a considerable amount of settlement along the Atlantic seaboard of North America. Many of these settlements were purely commercial ventures financed by a variety of companies. There obviously had to be some structure, so the territory was divided up into zones in an attempt to ensure that companies did not interfere with the commercial interests of each other.

ENGLISH SETTLEMENTS AND COLONIAL GRANTS 1606–35

— London Company 1606

▨ Neutral zone 1606

— Plymouth Company 1606

— Virginia Company of London 1609

— Plymouth Council for New England 1620 (from sea to sea)

- - - Sir William Alexander 1621

- - - John Mason and Sir Fernando Gorges 1622

···· Massachusetts Bay Company 1629

— John Mason 1629

- - - Plymouth Colony 1630

— Lord Baltimore 1632

- - - Lord William Alexander 1635

▨ Main area of English settlement

▨ Other European settlement

THE WORLD 1600

■ Major city or colony

THE WORLD 1600
By the early 17th century there were signs of European colonization, particularly by Spain and Portugal. The Spanish had a major interest in Central America and down the western side of South America. Meanwhile the Portuguese had settled on the Eastern side in what was to become Brazil. The Portuguese had also staked a claim on a number of areas in Africa. Both Spain and Portugal also acquired interests in the Far East. The Ottoman Empire was at its height and it controlled much of the Middle East and the Mediterranean Region.

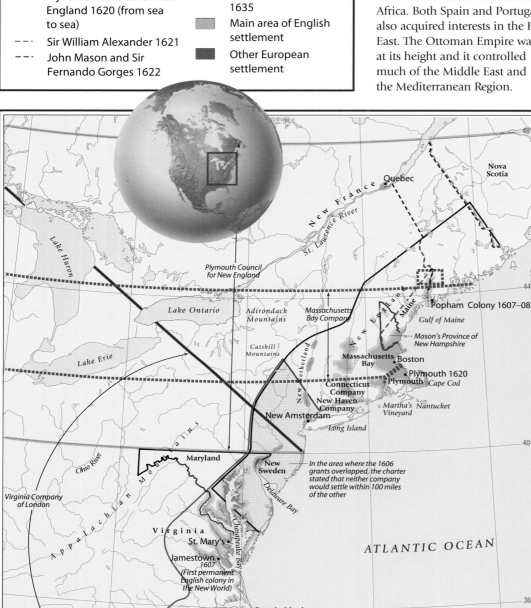

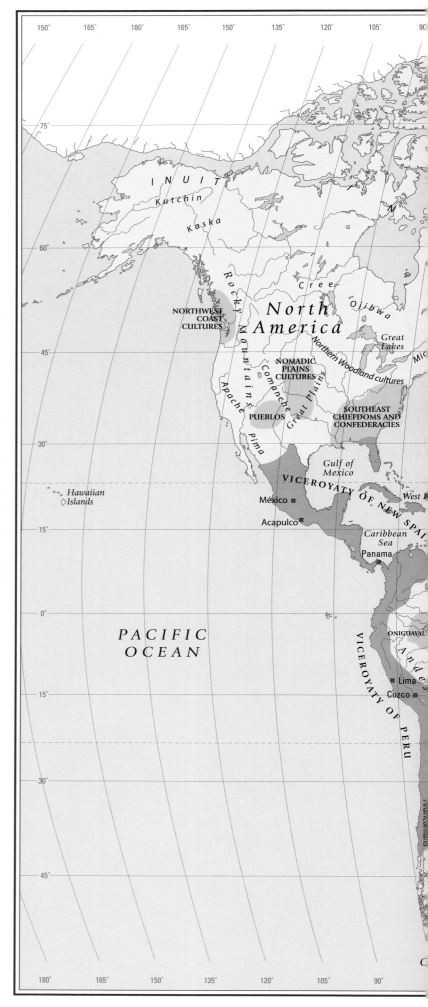

THE WORLD 1600

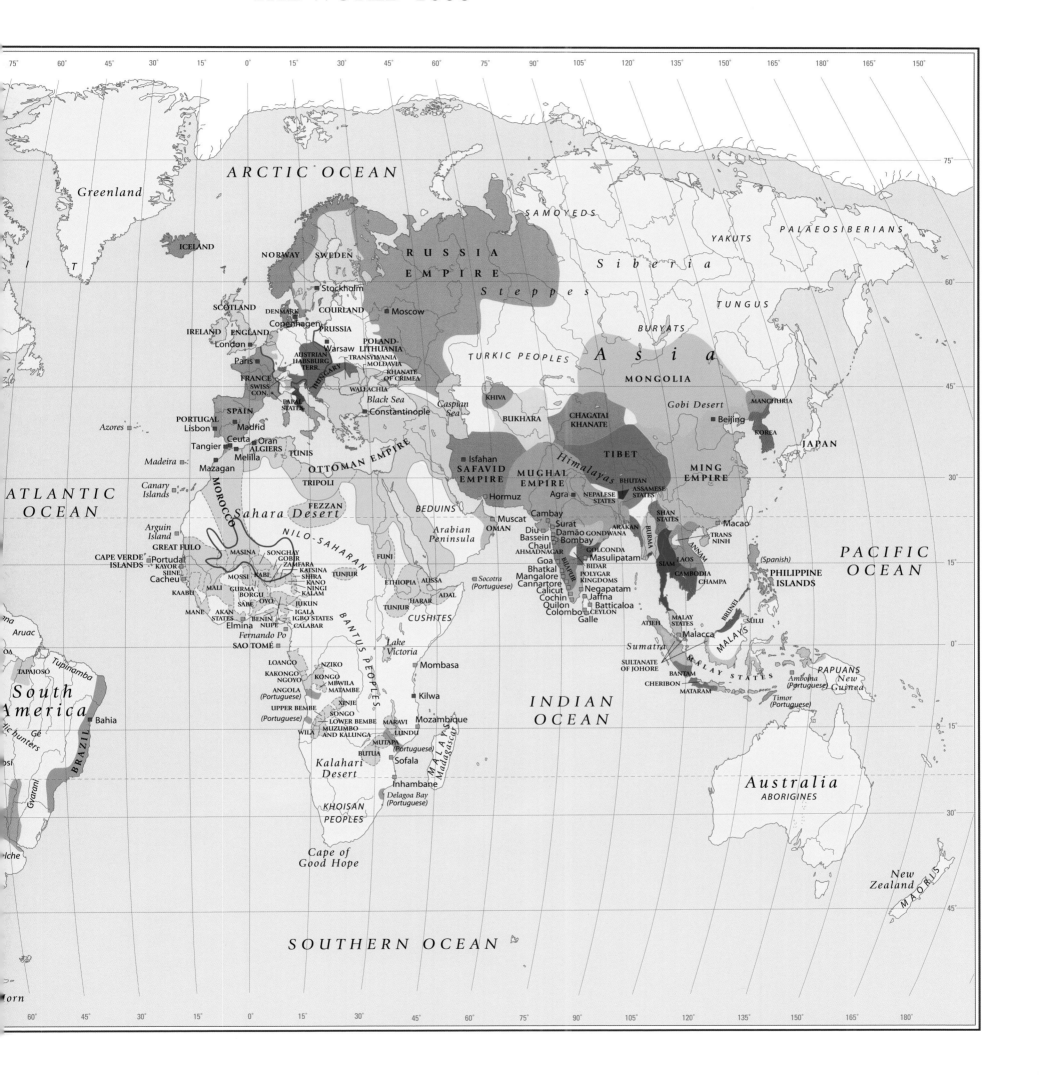

1494 – 1889

EUROPEAN EXPLORERS IN THE CARIBBEAN; TREATY OF TORDESILLAS

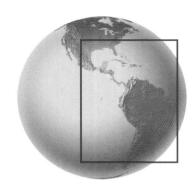

EUROPEAN EXPLORERS IN THE CARIBBEAN

→ Pinzón and Solís, 1508

→ Ojeda (with Cosa), 1509

→ Nicuesa, 1509

→ Balboa, 1513

→ Ponce de León, 1513

→ Córdoba, 1517

→ Grijalva, 1518

→ Cortés, 1518–1521

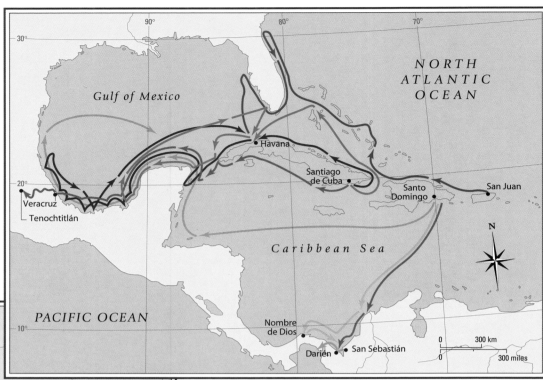

1   Noronha, 1501–02
2   Coelho, 1503
3   Solís, 1515–16
4   Magellan, 1519–21
5   Andagoya, 1522
6   Cortés, 1522
6a   Cortés, 1524–26
6b   Cortés, 1532–35
7   Olid, 1522–24
7a   Olid, 1524
8   Alvarado, 1522–24
8a   Alvarado, 1526
9   Francisco Pizarro, 1524–25
9a   Francisco Pizarro, 1526–28
9b   Francisco Pizarro, 1531–35
10   García, 1524–25
11   Sebastian Cabot, 1526–29
12   Saavedra, 1527
13   Narváez, 1527–28
13a   Narváez and de Vaca, 1528–36
14   Benalcázar, 1533–39
15   Alvarado, 1533–35
16   Almagro, 1535–37
17   Federmann, 1535–39
18   Mendoza, 1535–37
19   Jiménez de Quesada, 1536–37
19a   Jiménez de Quesada, 1569–71
20   Irala, 1537–42
20a   Irala, 1544–56
21   De Soto, 1539–42
21a   De Soto and Moscoso, 1542–43
22   Ulloa, 1539
23   Coronado, 1540–42
23a   Alarcón, 1540–41
23b   Díaz, 1540
23c   Cárdenas, 1540–41
24   Gonzalo Pizarro, 1540–43
25   Valdivia, 1540–47
26   Orellana, 1541–43
27   De Vaca, 1542–44
28   Cabrillo, 1542
29   Villalobos, 1542

EUROPEAN EXPLORERS IN THE CARIBBEAN

The years following the voyages of Christopher Columbus in the 1490s saw a burst of exploratory activity in the Caribbean and the northern coast of Mexico. The Spanish gained a virtual monopoly in the area and the Caribbean became known as the "Spanish Lake." The explorers found rich pickings from the ancient civilizations that they found and conquered, but life was not always easy. Many of the conquistadors never returned to Spain. Some were killed in conflicts with a hostile native population, some were shipwrecked, some fell victim to rivalry and intrigue, while some died from tropical diseases.

THE TREATY OF TORDESILLAS 1494

After Columbus had discovered the New World in 1492 it was clear that conflict would soon arise over land claims by both Spain and Portugal. A treaty was signed in the Spanish town of Tordesillas in 1494 drawing an imaginary line through the mid-Atlantic and South America; Spain could have any unclaimed territory to the west of the line and Portugal could have any territory to the east. In the event Portugal was only given Brazil, but during the next several hundred years Portugal gradually pushed the border of Brazil further westward and the Spanish put up no opposition.

TREATY OF TORDESILLAS 1494

–·–·–   Treaty line

———   Exploration route

EXPLORERS IN AFRICA

EXPLORERS IN AFRICA
Prior to the 1840s Africa was a vast intriguing continent. The coastline had been well charted, but the interior remained largely unknown. There was every good reason for the continent to be known as 'Darkest Africa." There were various reasons that prompted explorers to undertake their journeys. One of the most famous was David Livingstone, who went to Africa as a missionary. His aim was to bring Christianity, commerce, and civilization to Central Africa. Expeditions of this sort were very expensive and sponsors usually needed to be found. One of the chief reasons for financing an expedition was the hope of developing trade.

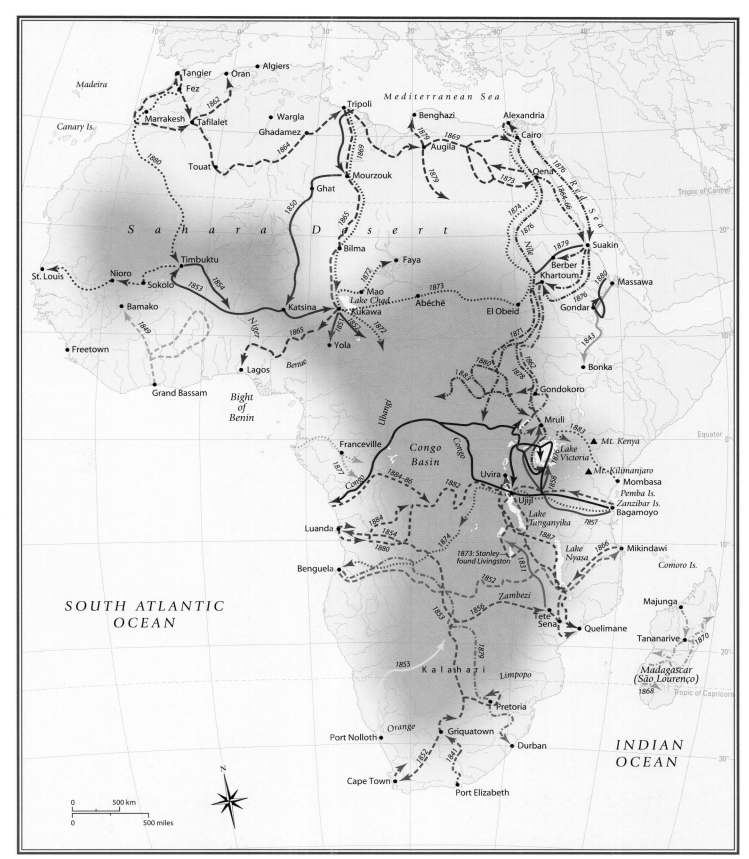

EXPLORERS, 1840–89

Little explored before 19th Century

British explorers
Livingstone, 1840–73

Speke & Burton, 1851–59
Speke & Grant, 1860–63

Baker, 1862–65

Cameron, 1873–75

Thomson, 1883

German explorers
Barth, 1850–55

Rohlfs, 1861–69, 1873–80

Schweinfurth, 1864–74

Nachtigal, 1869–74

Lenz, 1879–80

Junker, 1875–78, 1879–86

Von Wissman, 1880–87

American explorer
Stanley, 1871, 1874–77, 1887–89

French explorers
Brothers d'Abbadie, 1843

Binger, c. 1849

Grandidier, 1868–70

de Brazza, 1876–80

Portuguese explorers
Monteiro, 1831–32

Porto, 1852–53

Serpa-Pinto, 1877–79

Swedish explorer
Anderson, 1851–53

THE STAMP OF SPAIN; AUDIENCIA SYSTEM

**THE STAMP OF SPAIN;
AUDIENCIA SYSTEM**

As the Spanish American
territories grew, it became clear
that there was a need for some
form of government, if only
to control the rivalry between
the various conquistadors.
A series of regional courts
called Audiencias was set
up, following the pattern
established in Spain. The first
permanent Audiencia was in
Santo Domingo in 1526 and
others followed. By the 1550s
the area controlled by Spain
was so extensive that it was
decided to divide it and create
two Viceroyalties; New Spain
to govern the north and Peru
to govern the south. The
Audiencias continued to have
an important role in both
Viceroyalties.

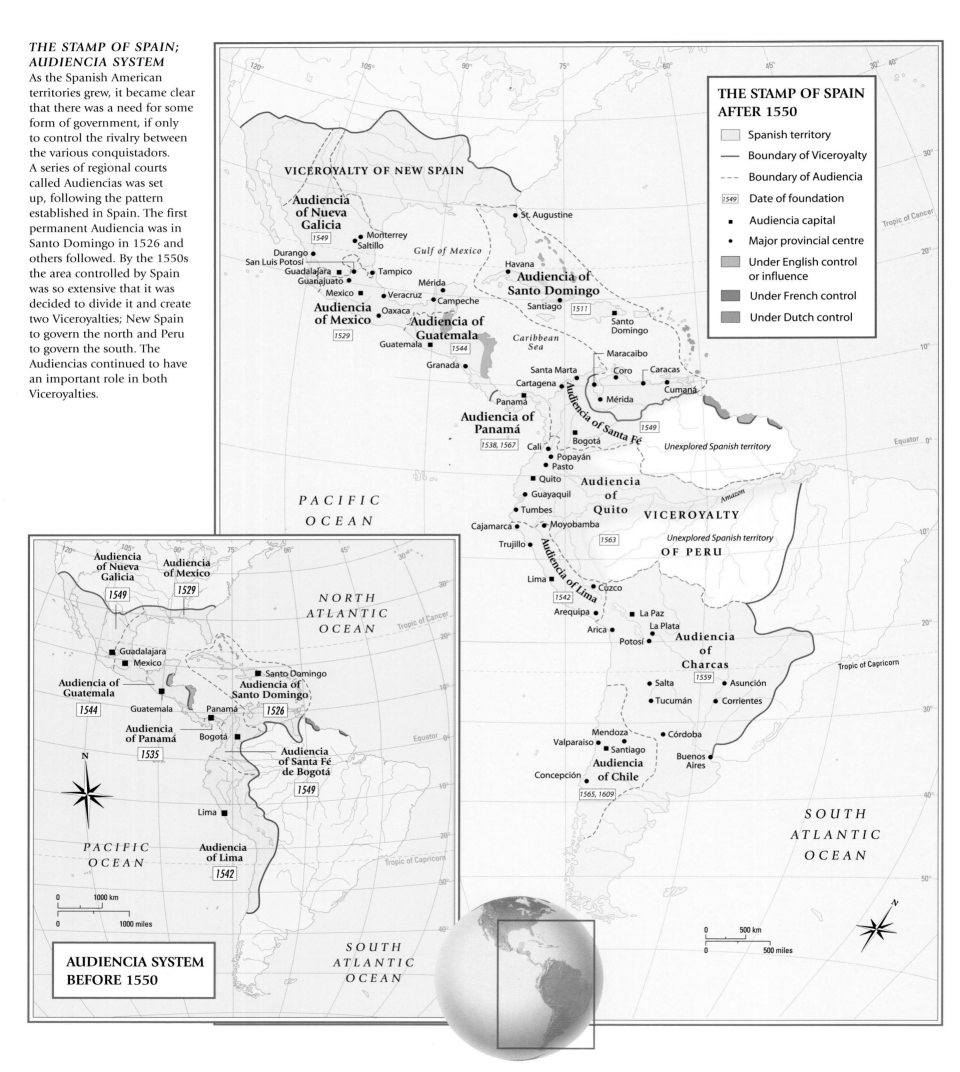

PART 5

THE AGE OF EMPIRE

*I*MPERIALISM HAS BEEN A FORCE in human development from the formation of the first city states, with empires rising and falling ever since. With the acceleration of world exploration in the 15th and 16th centuries, European nations established empires on a global scale. In Central and South America Spanish imperialists ravaged and destroyed native civilization until overthrown by subjects in the early 1800s. Britain settled New England, defeated France and acquired Canada in the process. After the American War of Independence Britain was forced to concentrate on its Caribbean islands and the acquisition of India, Burma, and Malaysia. Britain and France opened up China through the Opium Wars, eventually dividing China into spheres of influence, while France acquired a free hand in Southeast Asia. Africa, too, was partitioned after the Berlin Conference (1885). Originally the source of slaves for the American market, Africa was carved up between Italy, France, Britain, and Germany. Only Liberia and Abyssinia remained independent. Some 80 years after winning its independence, The United States was rent by a civil war, in which the Northern states opposed the Southern states' decision to leave the Union. In the Far East, Japan defeated China (1895) and commenced to build an empire, while a humiliated China overthrew its emperor and established a republic in 1912.

COLONIAL FRONTIERS

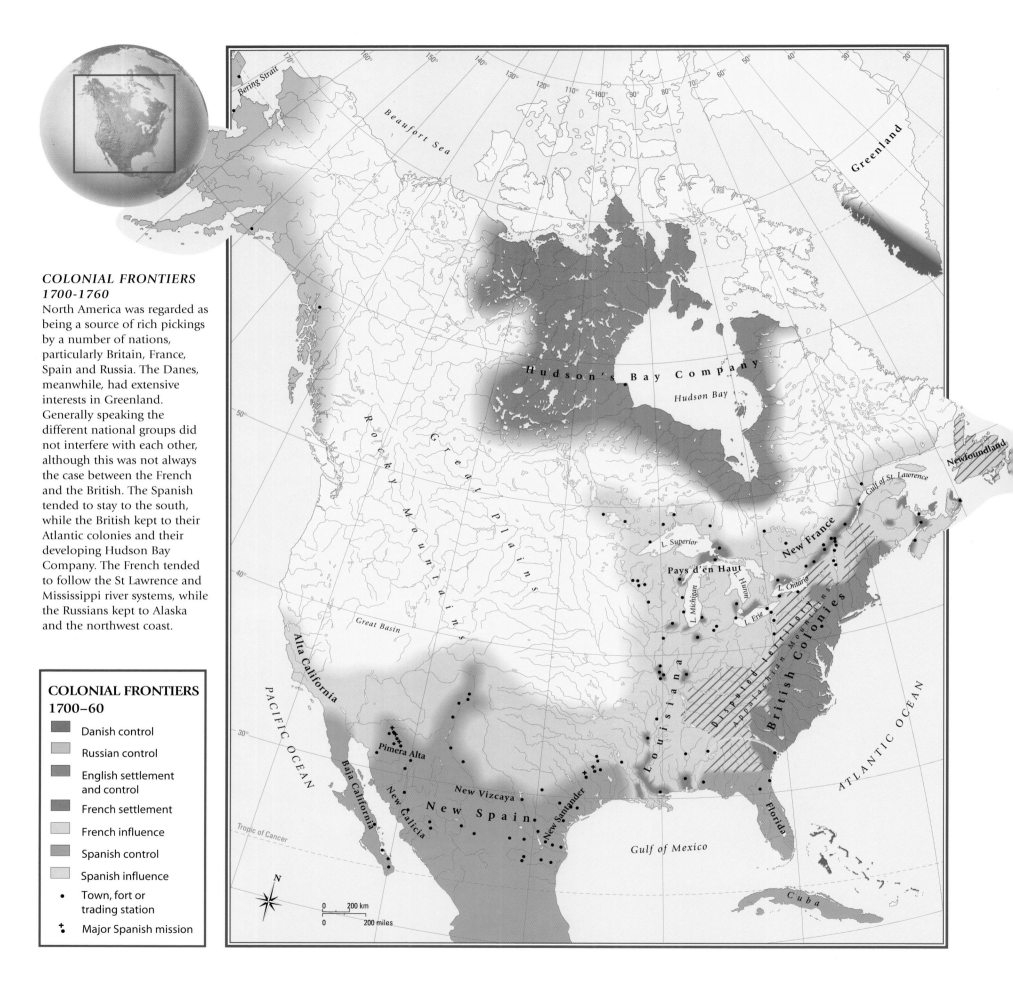

COLONIAL FRONTIERS
1700-1760

North America was regarded as being a source of rich pickings by a number of nations, particularly Britain, France, Spain and Russia. The Danes, meanwhile, had extensive interests in Greenland. Generally speaking the different national groups did not interfere with each other, although this was not always the case between the French and the British. The Spanish tended to stay to the south, while the British kept to their Atlantic colonies and their developing Hudson Bay Company. The French tended to follow the St Lawrence and Mississippi river systems, while the Russians kept to Alaska and the northwest coast.

COLONIAL FRONTIERS
1700–60

- Danish control
- Russian control
- English settlement and control
- French settlement
- French influence
- Spanish control
- Spanish influence
- • Town, fort or trading station
- ⁺ Major Spanish mission

PREDOMINANT IMMIGRATION GROUPS

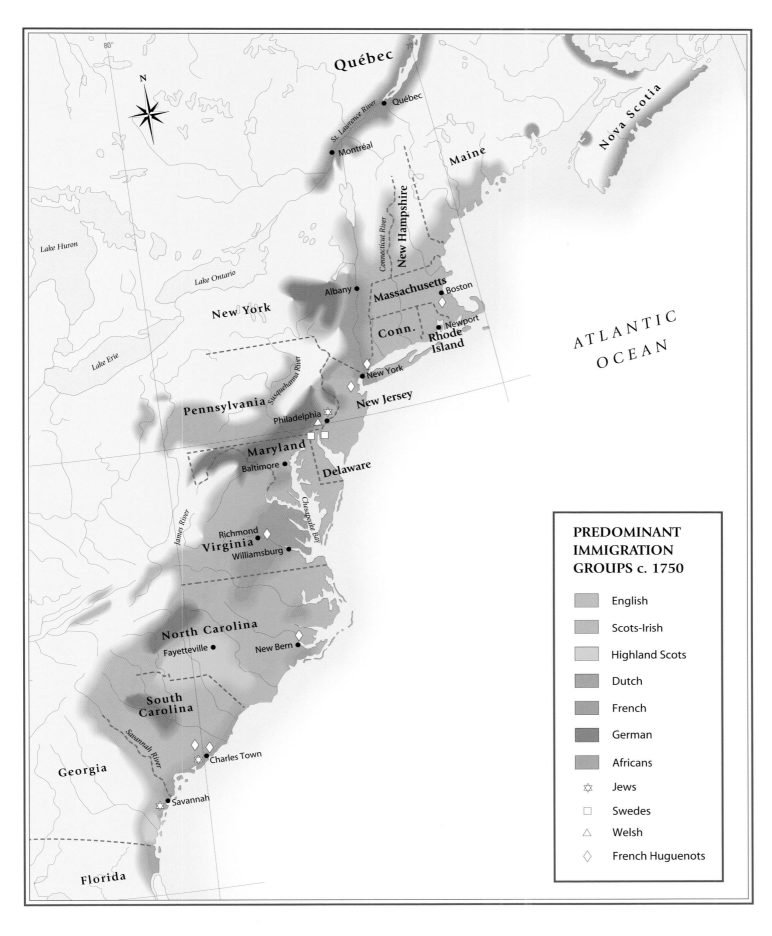

PREDOMINANT IMMIGRATION GROUPS c. 1750

- ▢ English
- ▢ Scots-Irish
- ▢ Highland Scots
- ▢ Dutch
- ▢ French
- ▢ German
- ▢ Africans
- ✡ Jews
- ▢ Swedes
- △ Welsh
- ◇ French Huguenots

PREDOMINANT IMMIGRATION GROUPS

Immigrants went to North America for a variety of reasons. The French were primarily interested in the fur trade and tended to keep to the north. The Dutch went for trade. Many English settlers were seeking religious freedom. These included Roman Catholics, Jews, Quakers, and French Huguenots. Others, such as Highland Scots, had been dispossessed of their homelands. Groups like the Scots-Irish were simply seeking a better life. One group had no choice in the matter—they were the black Africans who were forced to work as slaves in the tobacco plantations of Virginia or the cotton plantations further south.

One of the great centers of immigration into North America was New York. The land on which New York City was built had been inhabited by Europeans since the 1520s, and by 1664 the English had taken the emerging city from Dutch hands. During the next century of British rule New York's importance as a trading port grew enormously. The 19th century saw the city transformed by an increase in immigration, which proved to be the engine of huge economic and cultural development.

1764 – 1780   HISPANIC AMERICA

HISPANIC AMERICA c. 1780

In the 300 years or so since Columbus first landed, Spanish influence had grown to the extent that it controlled vast areas of North and South America. So that this could be governed the Spanish divided the territory into three semi-autonomous Viceroyalties, which were each subdivided into administration areas known as "Intendencies." By 1780 the United States had achieved independence from British rule, but the British continued to control the far north. Portugal had a large part of South America and the northwestern region of North America was jointly claimed by Britain, Spain, and Russia.

HISPANIC AMERICA c. 1780

- ☐ Spanish territory
- ☐ Portuguese territory
- ☐ British territory
- ☐ French territory
- ☐ Dutch territory

Viceroyalty of New Spain
1 Government of New Mexico
2 Intendency of Sonora
3 Intendency of Durango
4 Province of Coahuila
5 Province of Texas
6 Province of Nuevo Santander
7 Province of Nuevo León
8 Intendency of San Luis Potosí
9 Intendency of Zacatecas
10 Intendency of Guadalajara
11 Intendency of Valladolid
12 Intendency of Guanajuato
13 Intendency of Veracruz
14 Intendency of Mexico
15 Intendency of Puebla
16 Government of Tlaxcala
17 Intendency of Oaxaca
18 Intendency of Veracruz
19 Intendency of Chiapas
20 Intendency of Mérida
21 Intendency of Guatemala
22 Intendency of San Salvador
23 Intendency of Comayagua
24 Intendency of León
25 Province of Costa Rica
26 Intendency of Havana
27 Intendency of Puerto Príncipe
28 Intendency of Santiago de Cuba

Viceroyalty of Peru
29 Intendency of Trujillo
30 Intendency of Tarma
31 Intendency of Lima
32 Intendency of Huancavelica
33 Intendency of Huamanga
34 Intendency of Cuzco
35 Intendency of Arequipa
36 Intendency of Potosí
37 Intendency of Santiago
38 Intendency of Concepción

Viceroyalty of Río de la Plata
39 Intendency of La Paz
40 Province of Mojos
41 Intendency of Cochabamba
42 Intendency of Charcas
43 Province of Chiquitos
44 Intendency of Paraguay
45 Province of Misiones
46 Province of Montevideo
47 Intendency of Salta
48 Intendency of Potosí

BRITISH NORTH AMERICA

BRITISH NORTH AMERICA 1764–1776
In the mid-1700s Britain and France were at war, and this spilled over to North America. At its conclusion in 1763, Britain got control of Canada and kept the Thirteen Colonies. The following year the Colonists were angered when Britain introduced new taxes and restrictions. Although some of these were repealed, further taxes and restrictions were progressively added, leading to increased Colonial anger. British troops were mobilized and in 1774 the Colonists formed special groups of militia known as Minute Men. In 1775 George Washington was appointed commander-in-chief of the new army and in 1776 the Colonies declared Independence.

BRITISH NORTH AMERICA 1764–76

- Original Thirteen Colonies
- Other British territories
- Spanish Louisiana, secretly ceded by France in 1763
- Only French possession after Treaty of Paris, 1763
- Fort

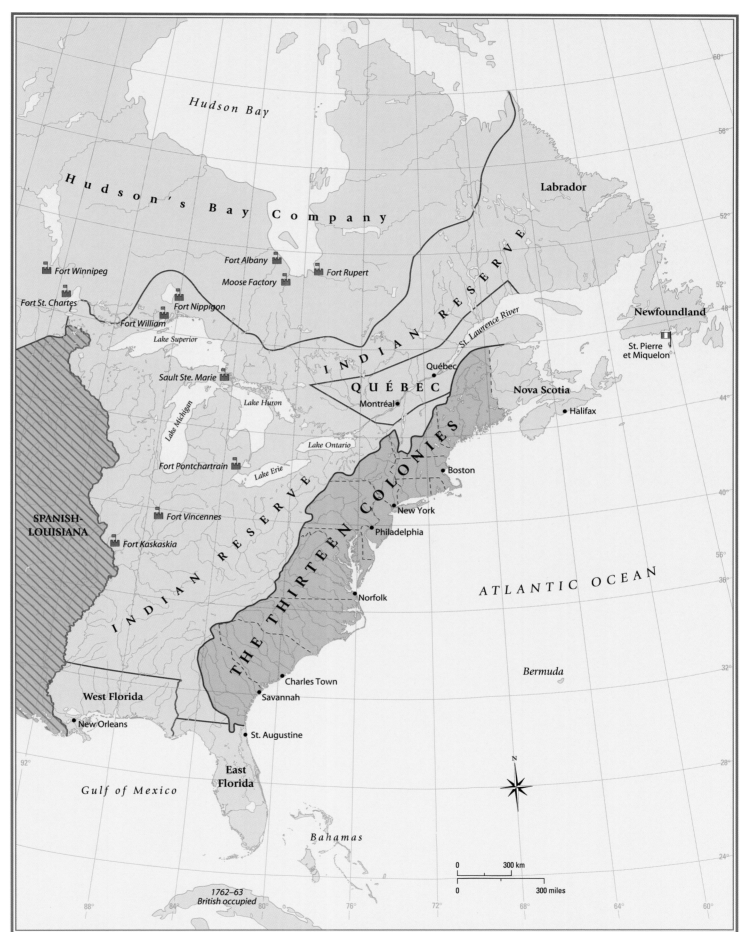

Hudson Bay

Hudson's Bay Company

Labrador

Fort Winnipeg

Fort Albany

Fort Rupert

Moose Factory

Fort St. Charles

Fort Nippigon

Fort William

Newfoundland

INDIAN RESERVE

St. Lawrence River

St. Pierre et Miquelon

Lake Superior

Sault Ste. Marie

QUÉBEC

Québec

Nova Scotia

Montréal

Halifax

Lake Huron

Lake Michigan

Lake Ontario

Fort Pontchartrain

Lake Erie

Boston

SPANISH-LOUISIANA

Fort Vincennes

INDIAN RESERVE

THE THIRTEEN COLONIES

New York

Philadelphia

Fort Kaskaskia

ATLANTIC OCEAN

Norfolk

Bermuda

Charles Town

Savannah

West Florida

New Orleans

St. Augustine

East Florida

Gulf of Mexico

Bahamas

0 300 km
0 300 miles

1762–63 British occupied

THE OTTOMAN THREAT; THE SIEGE OF VIENNA

THE OTTOMAN THREAT 1328–1672

The period up to 1566 was the time of territorial, economic, and cultural growth in the Ottoman Empire. Osman I had extended the frontiers of Ottoman settlement to the edge of the Byzantine Empire and in the century after his death, Ottoman rule began to extend over the Eastern Mediterranean and the Balkans. In 1453 Constantinople was captured by the 21-year-old Mohammed II. He was killed in 1481. Expansion continued under Selim and Suleiman the Magnificent, but Suleiman's death put a stop to this and by the end of the 16th century the period of sweeping conquest was at an end.

THE SIEGE OF VIENNA 1683

The capture of Vienna had long been a strategic target of the Ottoman Empire, and during two months in the late summer

OTTOMAN THREAT 1328–1672

- ■ Ottoman territory, 1328
- ■ Ottoman territory, 1355
- ▨ Ottoman vassal from 1394
- ▢ Ottoman territory, 1402 (prior to Mongol attack)
- ▨ Ottoman territory, 1481 (Mohammed II)
- ▨ Ottoman vassal from 1475
- ▨ Ottoman territory, 1520 (Selim I)
- ▨ Ottoman vassal from 1541
- ▨ Ottoman territory, 1566 (Suleiman I)
- ▢ Ottoman territory, 1660
- ▢ Ottoman territory, 1630–72
- ▢ Ottoman vassal from 1664

of 1683 a large Ottoman army laid siege to the city, cutting off virtually every means of food supply and mining the city walls. The city was only saved after a relief army of some 70,000 men arrived to confront the Ottomans. At the resulting

Battle of Kahlenberg the Ottomans were defeated and Vienna was saved from capture. The Ottomans carried on fighting for another 16 years, but this battle marked the end of Turkish expansion into southeastern Europe.

(1) A 16th-Century brick *enceinte* and a garrison of 10,000 troops protected Vienna, a city of 100,000 people. Georg Rimpler improved the fortifications early in 1683, concentrating on the southern and south-western fronts because the Danube Canal and River Wien refused the north and east. Vienna was successfully defended largely because the 90,000 Turks lacked heavy breaching artillery. As at Candia, the principal threat came from miners.

(2) The Turks attacked the front between the Burg and Löwel bastions. Here, the Burg Ravelin has fallen (2–3 September). On 9 September, Turkish miners demolished the salient and one face of the Löwel Bastion but, three days later, the relieving army under John III Sobieski of Poland and the Duke of Lorraine swept from the Wienerwald and routed the besiegers at the Battle of the Kahlenberg.

THE SIEGE OF VIENNA 1683

Turkish Camp

Turkish Camp

Vienna (1)

(2)

Wien

Danube Canal

River Danube

HOLY ROMAN EMPIRE

Vienna

SWISS CONFED.

SAVOY

Milan

Po

Genoa

Venice

REP. OF GENOA

VENETIAN REPUBLIC

Adriatic Sea

Corsica

Rome

PAPAL STATES

BOS. HER.

SARDINIA

NAPLES

Tyrrhenian Sea

Cetraro

Otrant

Bona

Tunis

SICILY

TUNIS 1574

MALTA

Tripoli

TRIPOLI 1551

Med

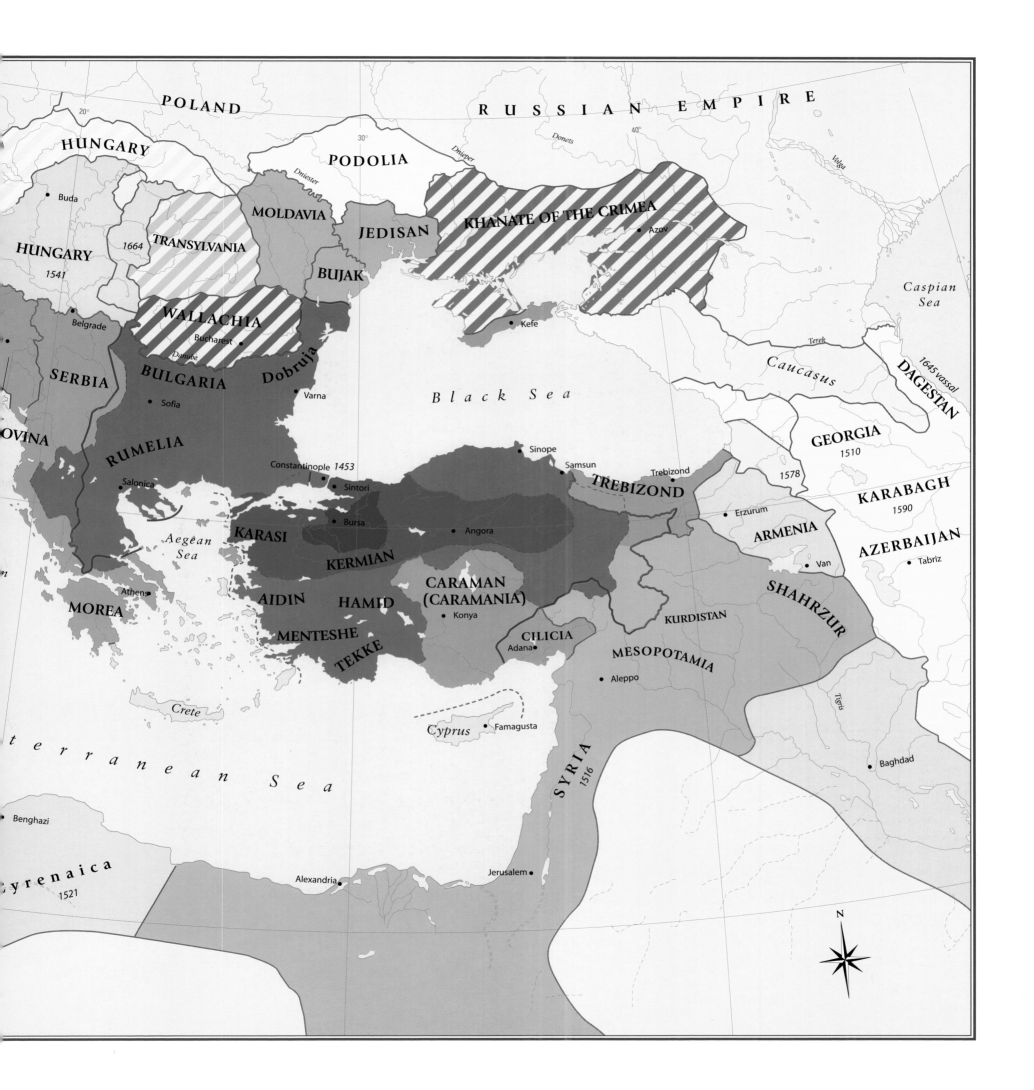

POLAND

RUSSIAN EMPIRE

HUNGARY

PODOLIA

Buda

Dnieper

Donets

40°

20°

30°

Dniester

MOLDAVIA

JEDISAN

HUNGARY
1541

1664

TRANSYLVANIA

KHANATE OF THE CRIMEA

Caspian
Sea

Azov

Belgrade

BUJAK

WALLACHIA

Kefe

1645 vassal

DAGESTAN

SERBIA

Bucharest

BULGARIA

Danube

Dobruja

Caucasus

Terek

·OVINA

Varna

GEORGIA
1510

Sofia

RUMELIA

Black Sea

Sinope

KARABAGH
1590

Salonica

Constantinople 1453

Samsun

Trebizond

TREBIZOND

1578

Sintori

Erzurum

ARMENIA

AZERBAIJAN

KARASI

Bursa

Angora

Aegean
Sea

KERMIAN

Van

Tabriz

MOREA

Athens

AIDIN

HAMID

CARAMAN
(CARAMANIA)

SHAHRZUR

MENTESHE

Konya

KURDISTAN

·n

TEKKE

CILICIA

MESOPOTAMIA

Adana

Crete

Aleppo

Tigris

Cyprus

Famagusta

·terranean Sea

SYRIA
1516

Baghdad

·Benghazi

Alexandria

Jerusalem

·yrenaica
1521

N

121

AFRICA TO c. 1600

AFRICA TO C. 1600
There is a long history of nomadic groups in Africa. The Fulanis of West Africa are the largest nomadic group in the world and the Galla in East Africa are the ancestors of many peoples. Long before European intervention Arab traders had assisted the development of sophisticated African civilizations based on the movement of gold, kola nuts, and slaves in exchange for cloth, utensils, and salt. At its peak in the 15th and 16th centuries, before its defeat by the Moroccans, the Songhay Empire in West Africa was one of the largest African Empires in history. The first Europeans to establish colonies on the continent were the Portuguese.

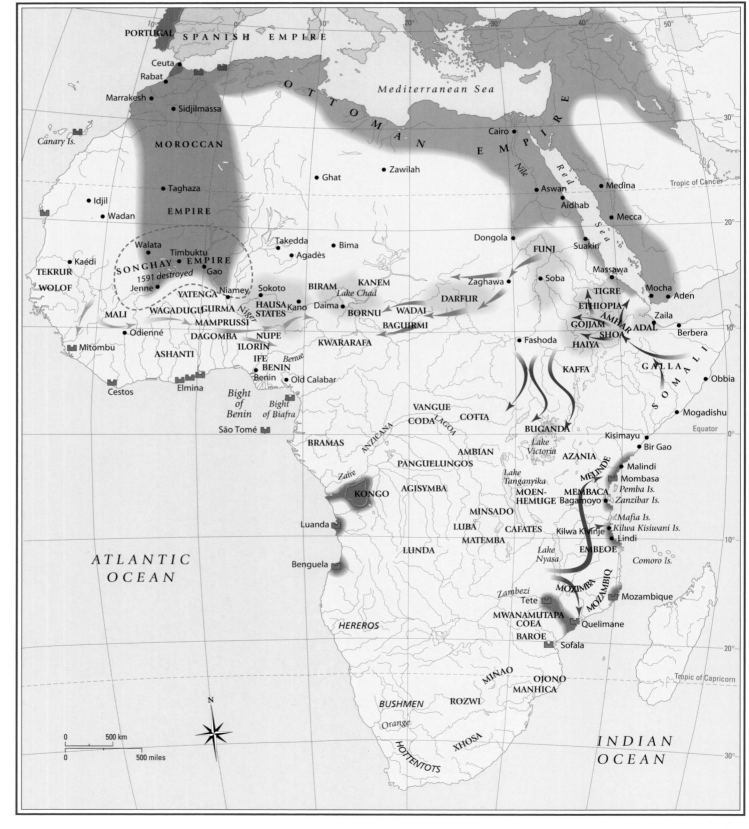

AFRICA TO c. 1600

- ▨ Moroccan Empire, c. 1600
- ▨ Major Kingdoms and Empires
- ⚏ Portuguese/Spanish forts
- ▨ Portuguese territory
- BAROE Other state/kingdom

Movements of peoples

- ➤ Fulani
- ➤ Galla
- ➤ Luo
- ➤ Maravi
- ➤ Shuwa Arabs

AFRICA'S BLACK GOLD

**AFRICA'S BLACK GOLD
1500–1870**
Africa has a long history of
slave trading, but it was the
Atlantic slave trade that made
the greatest impact. This trade
was begun at the end of the
15th century, initially by the
Portuguese and Spanish, and
lasted for about 250 years.
Other countries later joined in.
The Europeans were aware of
the West African practice of
enslaving prisoners and since
they needed a ready source of
labor for their American
plantations, a trade developed
where slaves were exchanged
for guns, rum, and other goods.
The practice was eventually
banned, and the Atlantic trade
was eradicated by the actions
of the British Royal Navy in
the late 19th Century.

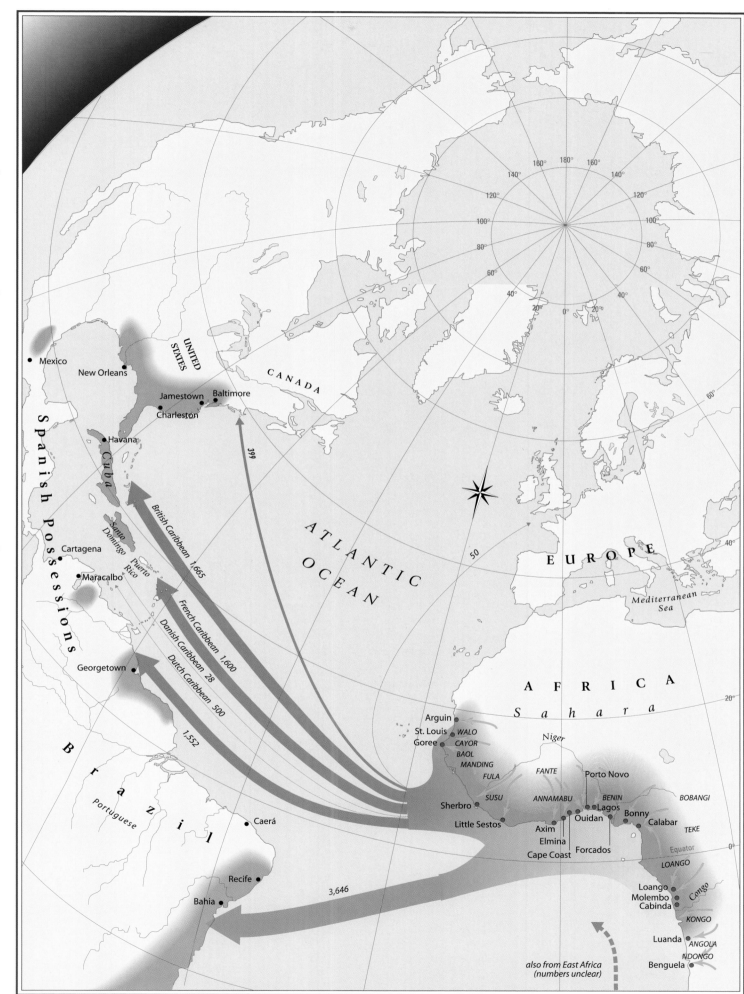

AFRICA'S BLACK GOLD 1500–1870

- Area of origin of slaves
- Area of slave settlement
- → Slave shipping, with numbers in thousands
- *FULA* Supplier tribe
- • Major slave ports
- → Routes for movement of slaves to the coast

INDIAN OCEAN

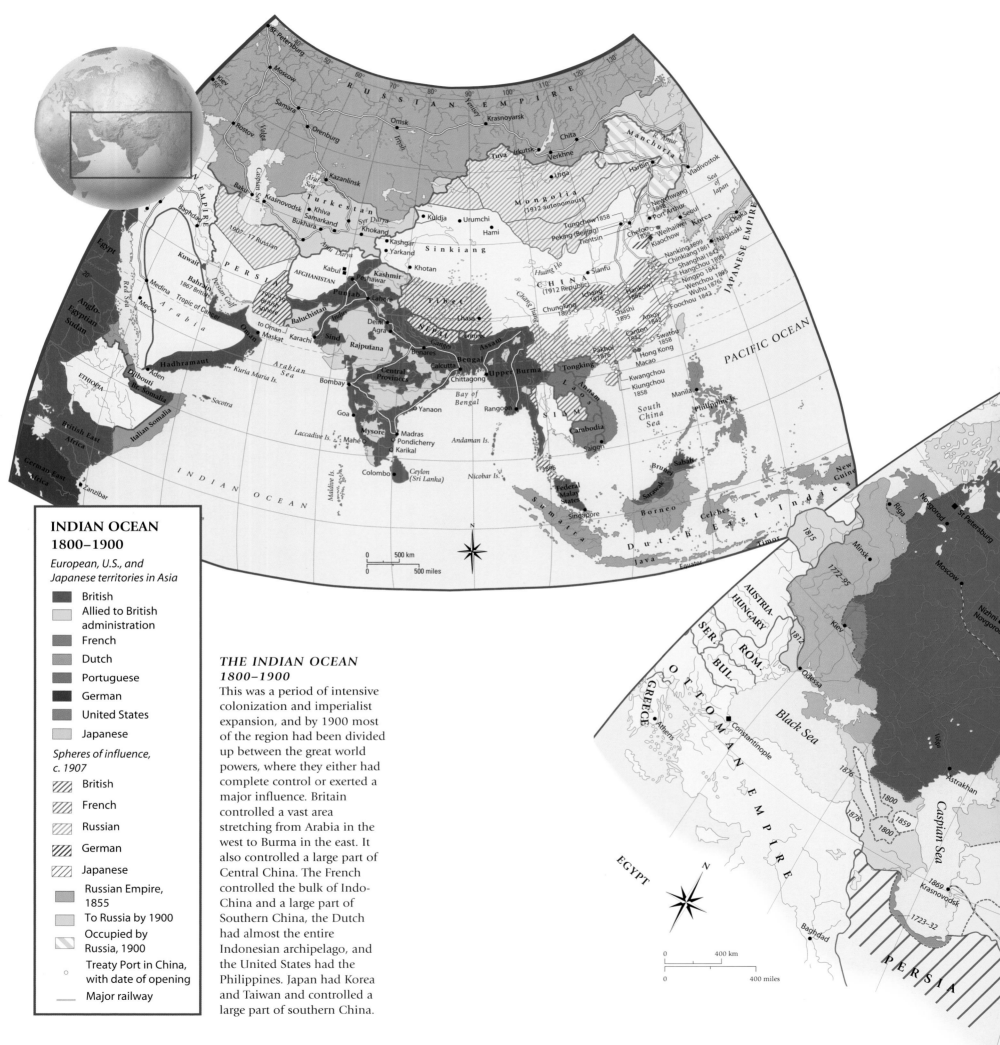

INDIAN OCEAN
1800–1900

European, U.S., and Japanese territories in Asia

- British
- Allied to British administration
- French
- Dutch
- Portuguese
- German
- United States
- Japanese

Spheres of influence, c. 1907

- British
- French
- Russian
- German
- Japanese
- Russian Empire, 1855
- To Russia by 1900
- Occupied by Russia, 1900
- Treaty Port in China, with date of opening
- Major railway

THE INDIAN OCEAN
1800–1900

This was a period of intensive colonization and imperialist expansion, and by 1900 most of the region had been divided up between the great world powers, where they either had complete control or exerted a major influence. Britain controlled a vast area stretching from Arabia in the west to Burma in the east. It also controlled a large part of Central China. The French controlled the bulk of Indo-China and a large part of Southern China, the Dutch had almost the entire Indonesian archipelago, and the United States had the Philippines. Japan had Korea and Taiwan and controlled a large part of southern China.

RUSSIAN EXPANSION INTO ASIA

RUSSIAN EXPANSION INTO ASIA 1581–1900
Unlike the western European countries, Russia's geography prevented it from developing a tradition of maritime exploration. In Russia's case territorial expansion was over land. The conquest of Siberia had been periodically taking place since the 16th century, but apart from looting, exacting tribute, and territorial gain, the only real interests had been to develop the fur trade and to increase commerce with China. By the 19th century Russia was a multilingual and multireligious empire and was continuing to expand at a furious rate. It was only pressure of competitive empire builders such as Great Britain and Japan that eventually limited this expansion.

RUSSIAN EXPANSION INTO ASIA 1581–1900

- Russian Empire, 1598
- Acquisitions, 1598–1689
- Acquisitions, 1689–1725 (Peter "the Great")
- Acquisitions, 1725–1796
- Acquisitions, 1796–1855
- Acquisitions, 1855–1900
- Russian sphere of influence in Mongolia, China (1900–14) and Persia (1907–21)
- Strategic railways into Asia constructed by 1900

1800

THE WORLD

THE WORLD 1800
By 1800 the major maritime powers had firmly established colonies and settlements for trade and development. Spain controlled enormous territories in North and South America, while Portugal had the huge mass of Brazil in South America. Britain had lost much of its American territory following the American War of Independence, but had gained large areas of the embryonic Canada from France. Portugal also had substantial colonies in Africa, and Britain had acquired the Cape Colonies and much of India. New South Wales in Australia had been claimed as a colony by Britain and from January 1788 convicts and settlers began to arrive.

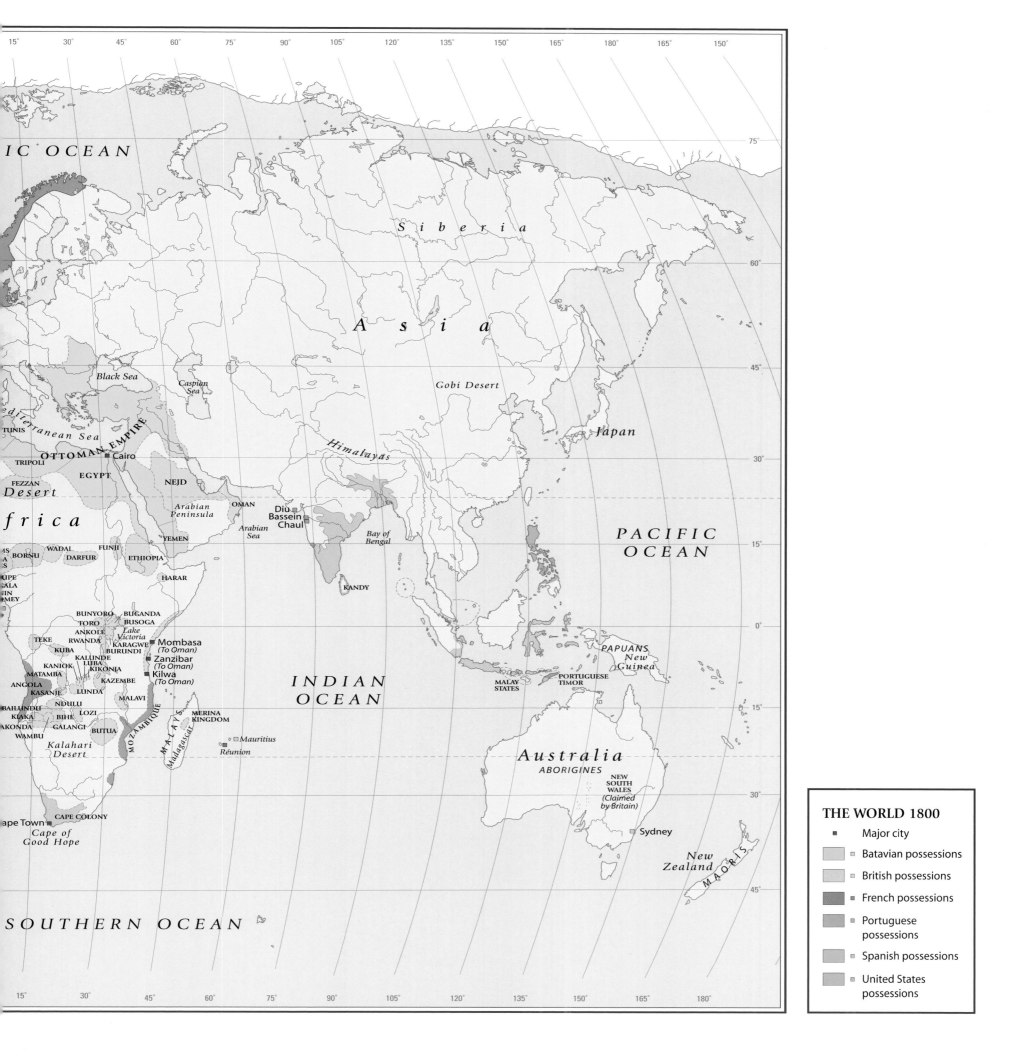

IC OCEAN

Siberia

A s i a

Black Sea

Caspian Sea

Gobi Desert

Japan

Mediterranean Sea
TUNIS
OTTOMAN EMPIRE ■ Cairo
TRIPOLI
Himalayas
FEZZAN
EGYPT
NEJD
Desert
OMAN
Diu
rica
Arabian Peninsula
Bassein
Chaul
Arabian Sea
Bay of Bengal
PACIFIC OCEAN

YEMEN
MS
BORNU
WADAI
FUNJI
AS
DARFUR
ETHIOPIA
PE
SALA
HARAR
KANDY
IN
MEY
15°

BUNYORO BUGANDA
TORO BUSOGA
ANKOLE
Lake Victoria
TEKE RWANDA KARAGWE
KUBA BURUNDI
KALUNDE Mombasa
KANIOK LUBA KIKONJA *(To Oman)*
MATAMBA KAZEMBE Zanzibar
(To Oman)
ANGOLA LUNDA Kilwa
KASANJE *(To Oman)*
BAILUNDU NDULU
KIAKA LOZI MALAVI
AKONDA GALANGI
WAMBU BIHE BUTUA
Kalahari Desert

PAPUANS
New Guinea

MALAY STATES
PORTUGUESE TIMOR

INDIAN OCEAN

M A L A Y S
MOZAMBIQUE
Madagascar
MERINA KINGDOM
□ *Mauritius*
Réunion

Australia
ABORIGINES

NEW SOUTH WALES
(Claimed by Britain)

Cape Town ■ CAPE COLONY
Cape of Good Hope

■ Sydney

New Zealand
MAORIS

SOUTHERN OCEAN

THE WORLD 1800

■ Major city

▫ Batavian possessions

▫ British possessions

■ French possessions

▫ Portuguese possessions

▫ Spanish possessions

▫ United States possessions

1739 – 1890 · INDIA – INVASIONS AND REGIONAL POWERS

INDIA – INVASIONS AND REGIONAL POWERS 1739–1760

In the mid-1700s the Maratha Empire dominated India. It was a Hindu state and at its height it ruled over 600,000 square miles of land, or one third of South Asia. It was strong enough to resist the Mughal invasions from the north and to keep the British at bay. This came to an end after the Afghans defeated the Maratha army in 1761, which started the fragmentation of the empire. Britain already controlled Bengal, the area around Madras, and the Northern Circars and was just waiting for an opportunity to annex more territory.

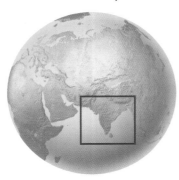

INDIA, INVASIONS AND REGIONAL POWERS 1739–60

- English base, 1700
- Portuguese base, 1700
- French base, 1700
- Dutch base, 1700
- British territory c. 1785
- Maratha territory, c. 1785
- Mysore territory, c. 1785
- Center of Gurkha power, c. 1785

Campaigns

- Nadir Shah of Persia
- Ahmed Khan Abdali of Afghanistan
- Haidar Ali of Mysore
- Gurkhas
- Chinese
- Marathas
- Battle sites

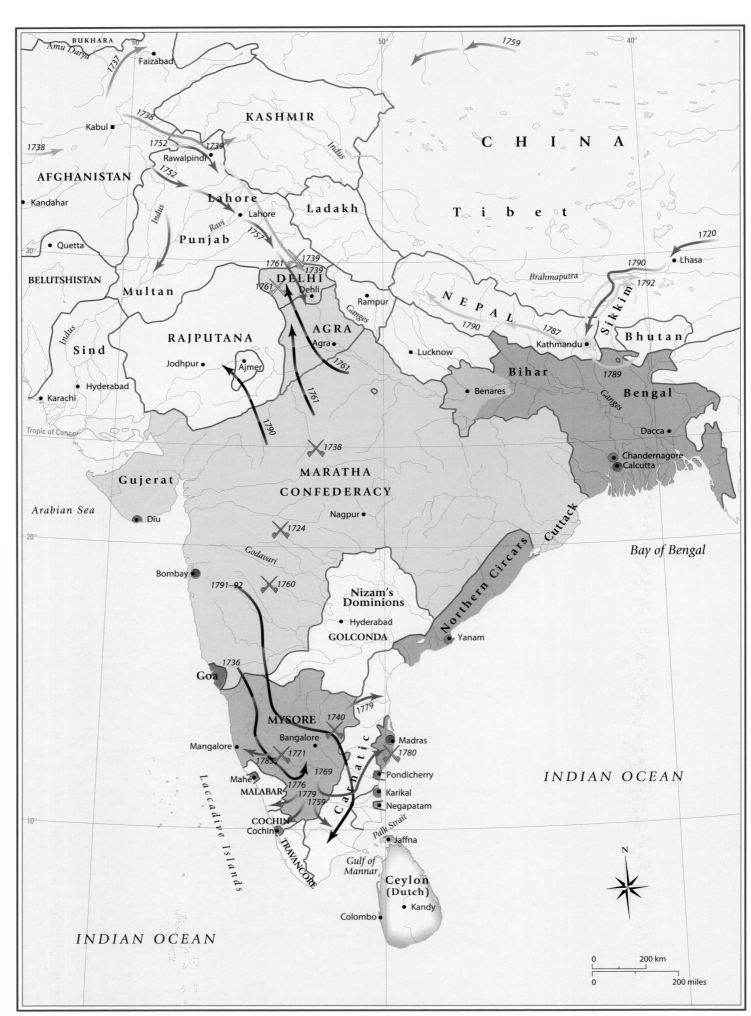

BUKHARA
Amu Darya
1737
Faizabad
1759
KASHMIR
CHINA
1738
Kabul
Tibet
1752
Rawalpindi
1739
AFGHANISTAN
1752
Ladakh
Kandahar
Lahore
Lahore
1757
Indus
Ravi
Punjab
1720
Quetta
Lhasa
1790
Brahmaputra
1792
Multan
1761 *1739*
BELUTSHISTAN
1739
DELHI
1761
Dehli
NEPAL
Bhutan
Sind
Indus
RAJPUTANA
AGRA
Rampur
Kathmandu
Sikkim
Agra
1790
1787
1789
Jodhpur
1761
Lucknow
Bihar
Ajmer
Bengal
Karachi
Hyderabad
1761
Ganges
Benares
Tropic of Cancer
Dacca
1790
Gujerat
1738
Chandernagore
Calcutta
MARATHA CONFEDERACY
Arabian Sea
Nagpur
Diu
Godavari
1724
Bay of Bengal
Bombay
1791–92
1760
Northern Circars
Cuttack
Nizam's Dominions
Hyderabad
GOLCONDA
Yanam
1736
Goa
MYSORE
1740
1779
Bangalore
Madras
Mangalore
1771
1780
Carnatic
1785
1769
Pondicherry
Mahé
1776
Karikal
MALABAR
1779
Negapatam
1759
COCHIN
Cochin
Palk Strait
Jaffna
TRAVANCORE
Gulf of Mannar
INDIAN OCEAN
Ceylon (Dutch)
Colombo
Kandy
Laccadive Islands
INDIAN OCEAN
N

0 200 km
0 200 miles

BRITISH CONQUEST IN INDIA

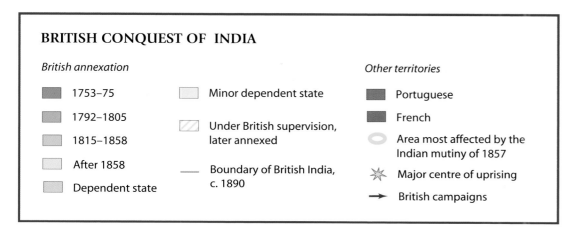

BRITISH CONQUEST OF INDIA

British annexation

- 1753–75
- 1792–1805
- 1815–1858
- After 1858
- Dependent state

- Minor dependent state
- Under British supervision, later annexed
- Boundary of British India, c. 1890

Other territories

- Portuguese
- French
- Area most affected by the Indian mutiny of 1857
- Major centre of uprising
- British campaigns

BRITISH CONQUEST OF INDIA

The British East India Company had a monopoly of all trade with the East Indies. It gradually grew from being a trading company to the virtual ruler of India. It acquired governmental and military functions and had a very large private army. The decline of the Mughal Empire allowed the Company to expand its territories. It fought many wars during this conquest, but by the 1850s it ruled over most of the Indian subcontinent. In 1857 the Company was blamed for the disastrous mutiny and the British government took over control of India, which it retained until independence was granted in 1948.

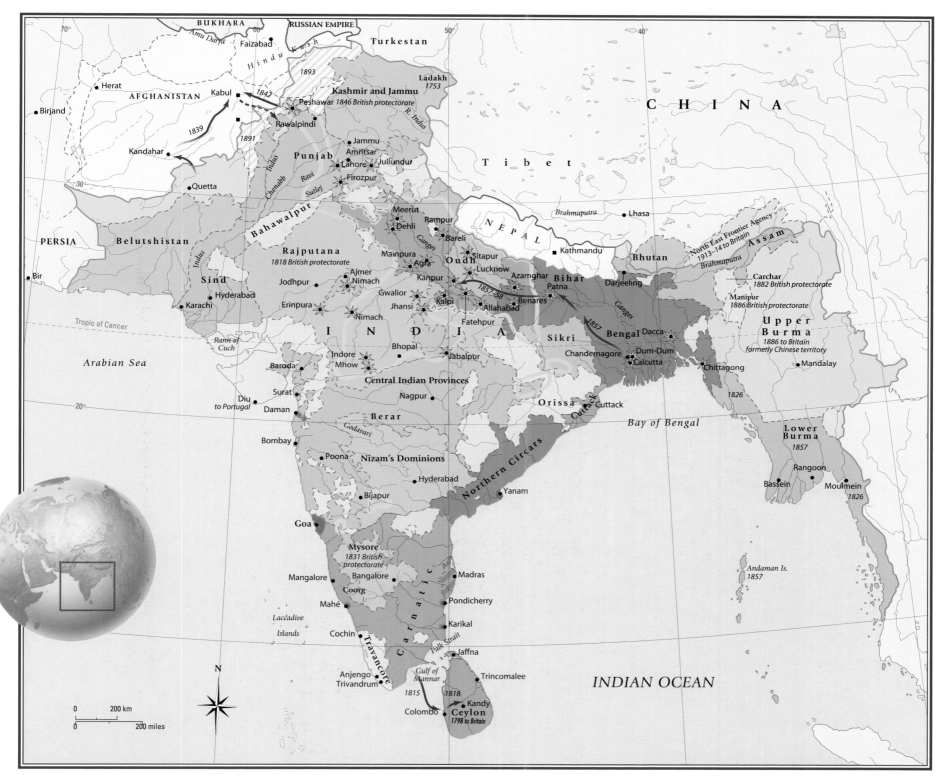

THE AMERICAN CIVIL WAR CAMPAIGNS OF 1863

THE AMERICAN CIVIL WAR CAMPAIGNS 1863
The early years of the war saw many victories for the southern Confederate forces, with General Robert E. Lee running an effective military campaign and seeing off a succession of Union generals. Significant Confederate victories during 1862 included Second Bull Run, part of the Northern Virginia Campaign, and the Battle of Fredericksburg on December 13, 1862, when over 12,000 Union soldiers were killed or wounded during repeated futile frontal assaults against Marye's Heights. Confederate momentum carried over into 1863 when, outnumbered by more than two to one, Robert E. Lee's forces won the Battle of Chancellorsville in May 1863. However, defeat two months later at Gettysburg, in July 1863, stemmed Confederate progress and reversed Union fortunes. The Battle of Gettysburg is considered to be the turning point of the American Civil War.

THE CAMPAIGNS OF 1863

→ Union offensive

→ Confederate offensive

--▶ Confederate retreat

✕ Union victory

✕ Confederate victory

⛵ Union blockade

▢ Union state

▢ Slave state staying loyal to the Union

▢ Confederate state

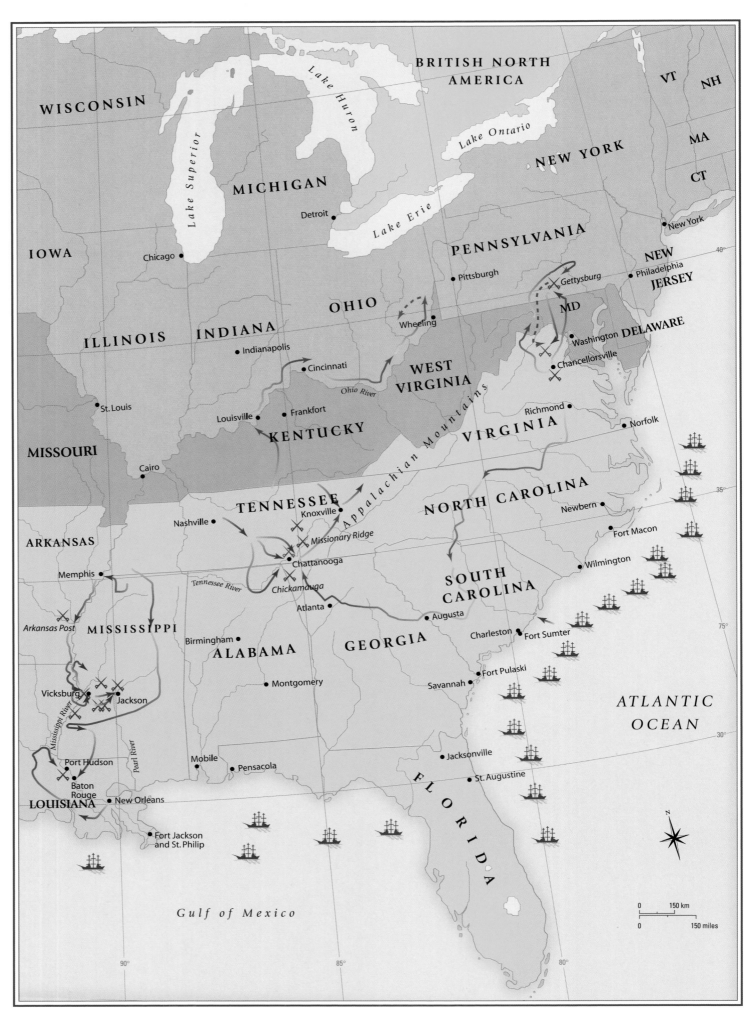

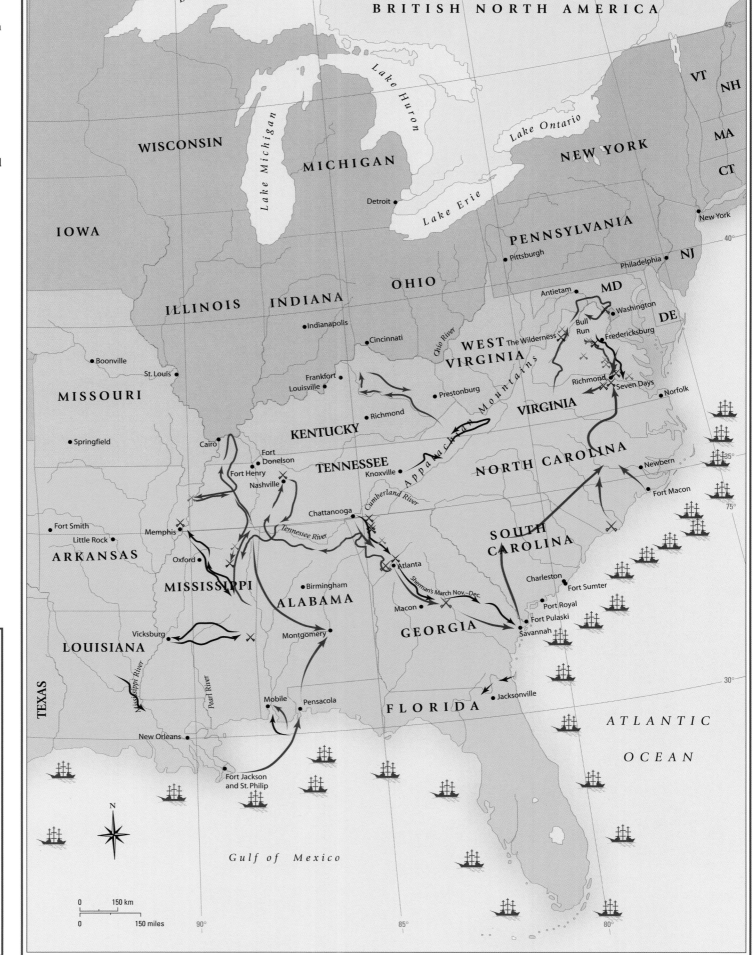

THE AMERICAN CIVIL WAR CAMPAIGNS 1864–1865

At the beginning of 1864 Union President Lincoln made Ulysses S. Grant commander of all Union armies and gave William T. Sherman command of most of the Western armies. Grant, Sherman, and Lincoln understood the concept of total war and believed that utter defeat of Confederate forces and their economic base was the only way to achieve victory. Grant devised a coordinated strategy that resulted in a number of battles, with enormous casualties on both sides. Huge areas of the South were laid to waste as the Confederates were gradually overrun. The final ceasefire was signed at Fort Towson on 23rd June, 1865.

THE CAMPAIGNS OF 1864–1865

Union blockade
Union state
Slave state staying loyal to the Union
Confederate state

CAMPAIGNS 1864
Union offensive
Confederate offensive
Union victory
Confederate victory

CAMPAIGNS 1865
Union offensive
Union victory

THE SINO–JAPANESE WAR

THE SINO-JAPANESE WAR 1894–95

Railroad concessions

— Russian

— British

— German

— French

— Japanese

— Under Chinese control

Spheres of influence

▨ Russian

▨ British

▨ German

▨ French

▨ Japanese

▨ Occupied or ceded to Japan, 1895

▨ Occupied by Russia, 1900

□ Leased territory

○ Treaty port

● British

● French

○ Japanese

● German

○ Portuguese

● U.S.

● Chinese control

***THE SINO-JAPANESE
WAR 1894–1895***

This war was fought between
the Chinese Qing Dynasty and
the Japanese Empire over the
control of Korea. The Korean
Government had asked for
Chinese help to suppress a
rebellion. The Japanese also
sent a force. The situation
rapidly escalated and the
Japanese entered Seoul and
seized the Korean Emperor.
This led to a formal declaration
of war. The war came to
symbolize the degeneration
and enfeeblement of the
Chinese against the successful
modernization of Japan. The
principle results were a shift
in regional dominance in
Asia from China to Japan and
a fatal blow to the Qing
Dynasty and the Chinese
classical tradition.

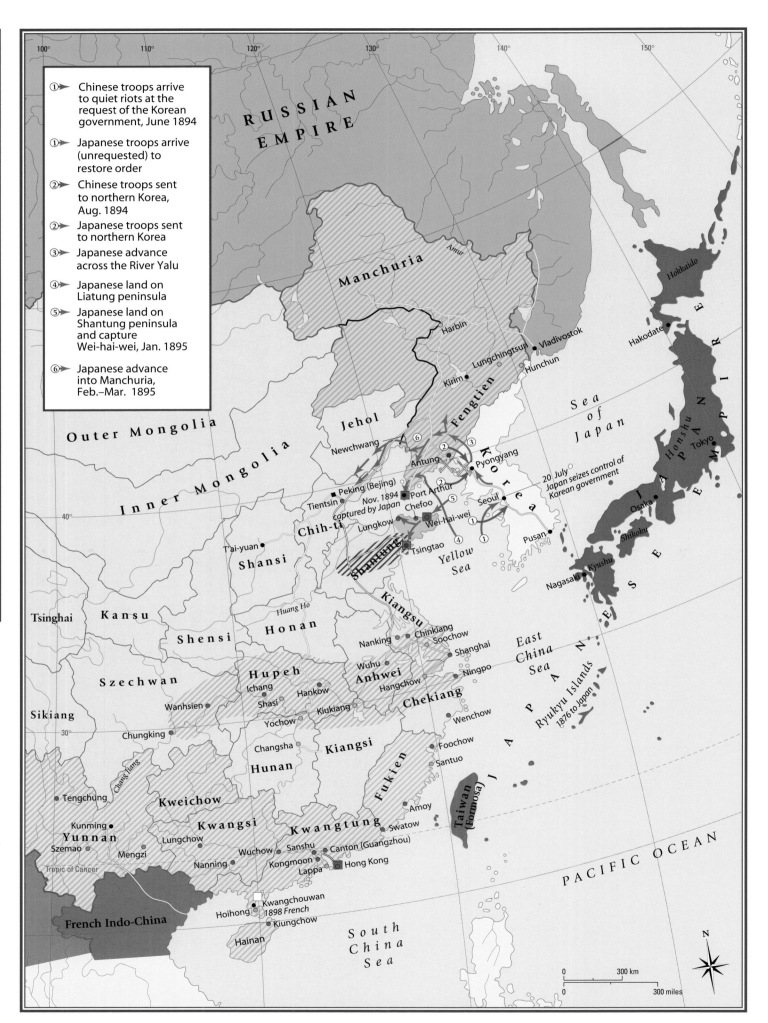

① Chinese troops arrive to quiet riots at the request of the Korean government, June 1894

① Japanese troops arrive (unrequested) to restore order

② Chinese troops sent to northern Korea, Aug. 1894

② Japanese troops sent to northern Korea

③ Japanese advance across the River Yalu

④ Japanese land on Liatung peninsula

⑤ Japanese land on Shantung peninsula and capture Wei-hai-wei, Jan. 1895

⑥ Japanese advance into Manchuria, Feb.–Mar. 1895

PART 6

GLOBALIZATION

*T*HE NINETEENTH TO TWENTY-FIRST centuries witnessed conflict on a scale not previously seen, with nations fighting wars over territory and ideology. While the two world wars overshadow this period of history, nations also became increasingly reliant on one another, with economic interdependence growing. The 19th Century saw the unification of Italy and Germany, with the latter assuming much responsibility for the alliance systems that led to World War I. In Russian, war damage and a failed government engendered the Bolshevik Revolution, leading ultimately to Stalinist excesses. After World War I Europe was redesigned by the Versailles Treaty which destroyed old empires while building new, fragile states.

In the 1920s and 1930s fascist Italy had ambitions for a new Roman Empire in Africa, while Germany under the Nazi regime sought to reverse Versailles and build a Germanic empire in Europe. In China, Japan's quest for expansion led to the acquisition of Manchuria, which sparked a conflict that became part of World War II. The defeat of Nazi Germany and her allies in 1945 ushered in a Cold War between the dominant superpowers of the USA and USSR. The collapse of the Soviet Union in the 1990s has led to a period marked by far less certainty than the previous half century. It has been dominated by conflicts in the Middle East and an increased terrorist threat in much of the West.

MANHATTAN 1880-1884

MANHATTAN 1880–1884

200 years earlier Manhattan had been little more than a trading post protected by a defensive wall that followed present-day Wall Street. With the increase in immigration in the 19th century, the city rapidly grew and the population exploded beyond all predictions. The distinctive gridiron pattern of streets was established in the early 19th century and by 1820 Broadway had become a commercial thoroughfare. The period between 1880 and 1884 was a time of massive immigration. During these four years some 2 million people arrived. Many were cruelly exploited and most were forced to live in tenements and to find work in one of the many sweatshops that sprang up in the city.

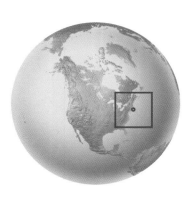

**MANHATTAN
1880–1884**

◻ Tenement area

◼ Entertainment area

THE WORLD 1900

The World of 1900 was dominated by the British Empire, with many areas on the map colored in pink. Canada, Australasia, India, and large areas of Africa, together with many smaller territories, were all British. Alaska now belonged to the United States, while the Russian Empire had continued to grow. France had large African territories and Germany, Italy, Portugal, and Spain were also represented in Colonial Africa. France also had Indochina. Spain had lost its former American colonies, as had Portugal. The declining Ottoman Empire was still hanging on in the Middle East and the Dutch still had its East Indies.

THE WORLD 1900

◼ Major city

◻ British possessions

◼ French possessions

◼ German possessions

◼ Italian possessions

◼ Portuguese possessions

◼ Russian possessions

◻ Spanish possessions

◼ United States possessions

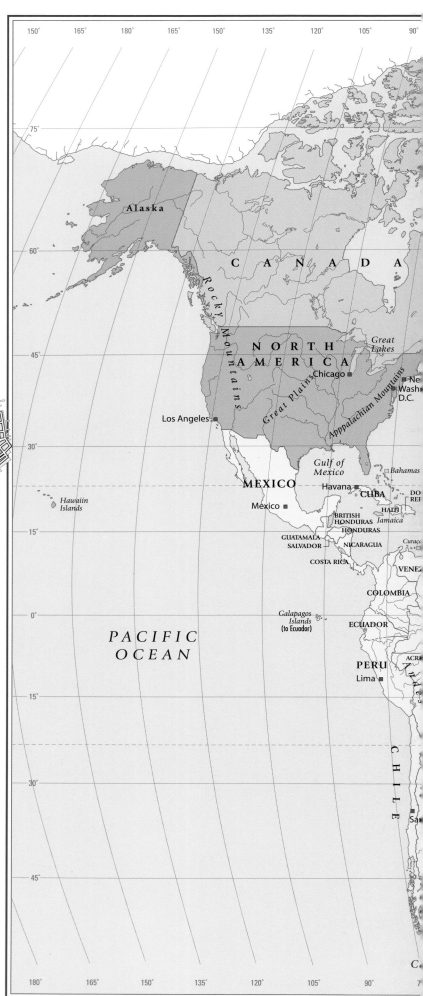

THE WORLD 1900

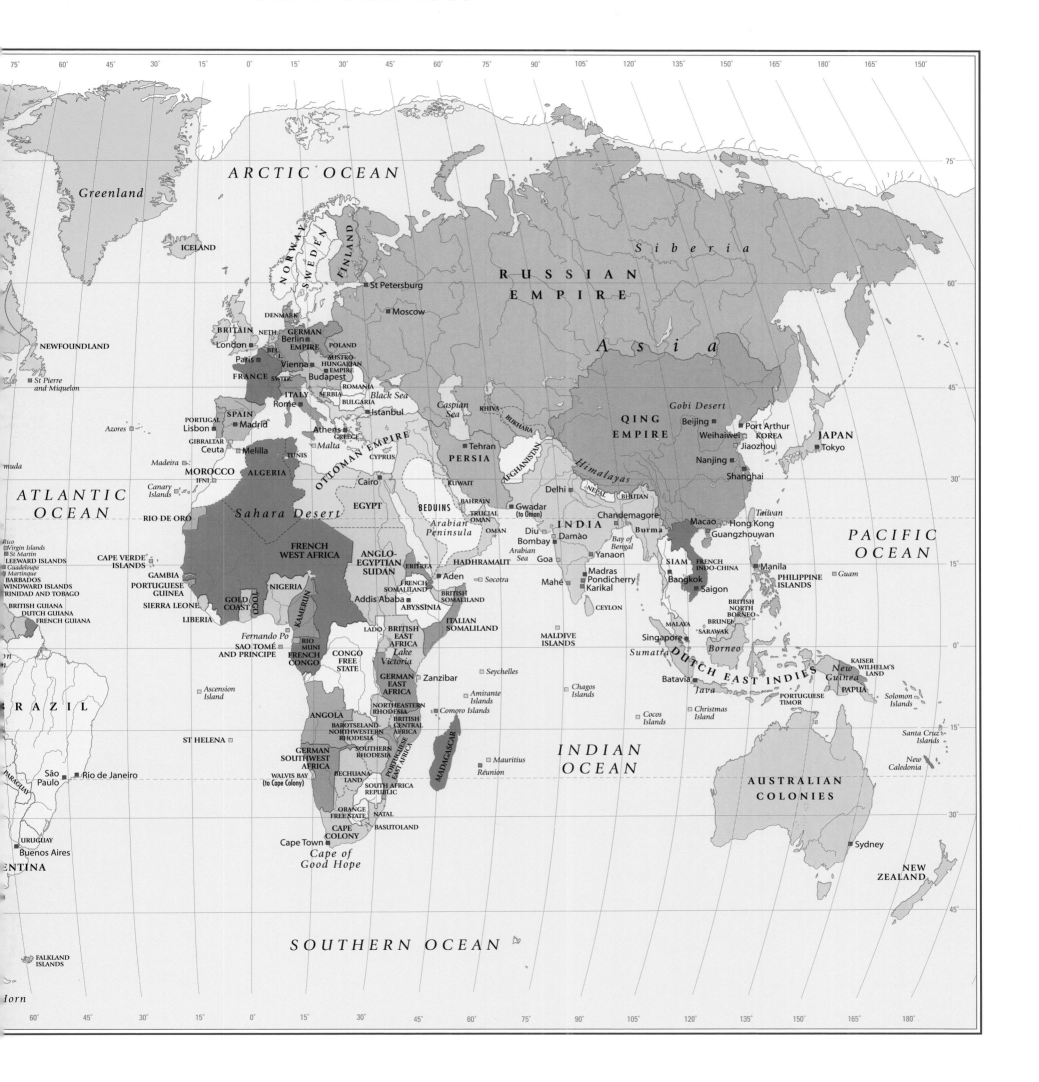

ARCTIC OCEAN

Greenland

ICELAND

NORWAY

SWEDEN

FINLAND

St Petersburg

Moscow

Siberia

RUSSIAN EMPIRE

Asia

DENMARK

BRITAIN
London
NETH.
BEL.
GERMAN EMPIRE
Berlin
POLAND
Paris
FRANCE
SWITZ.
AUSTRO-HUNGARIAN EMPIRE
Vienna
Budapest
ROMANIA
SERBIA
BULGARIA
ITALY
Rome
Black Sea

Gobi Desert

QING EMPIRE
Beijing
Port Arthur
Weihaiwei
KOREA
Jiaozhou
Nanjing
Shanghai

JAPAN
Tokyo

NEWFOUNDLAND

St Pierre and Miquelon

Azores

PORTUGAL
Lisbon
SPAIN
Madrid
Athens
GREECE
Istanbul
Caspian Sea
KHIVA
BUKHARA
PERSIA
Tehran
AFGHANISTAN
Himalayas

Taiwan

PACIFIC OCEAN

Madeira
GIBRALTAR
Ceuta
Melilla
Malta
CYPRUS
TUNIS

ATLANTIC OCEAN

muda

Canary Islands
MOROCCO
IFNI
ALGERIA
OTTOMAN EMPIRE
Cairo
EGYPT
KUWAIT
BEDUINS
BAHRAIN
TRUCIAL OMAN
Gwadar (to Oman)
OMAN
Delhi
NEPAL
BHUTAN
INDIA
Chandemagore
Macao
Hong Kong
Guangzhouwan

RIO DE ORO
Sahara Desert
Arabian Peninsula
Diu
Bombay
Damão
Bay of Bengal
Burma

Rico
Virgin Islands
St Martin
LEEWARD ISLANDS
Guadeloupe
Martinique
WINDWARD ISLANDS
BARBADOS
TRINIDAD AND TOBAGO
BRITISH GUIANA
DUTCH GUIANA
FRENCH GUIANA

CAPE VERDE ISLANDS
GAMBIA
PORTUGUESE GUINEA
SIERRA LEONE
LIBERIA
FRENCH WEST AFRICA
NIGERIA
GOLD COAST
TOGO
KAMERUN
ANGLO-EGYPTIAN SUDAN
ERITREA
FRENCH SOMALILAND
Addis Ababa
ABYSSINIA
Aden
HADHRAMAUT
Socotra
Goa
Yanaon
Arabian Sea
Mahé
Madras
Pondicherry
Karikal
CEYLON
MALDIVE ISLANDS
SIAM
FRENCH INDO-CHINA
Bangkok
Saigon
Manila
PHILIPPINE ISLANDS
Guam
BRITISH NORTH BORNEO
BRUNEI
SARAWAK
MALAYA
Singapore

Fernando Po
SÃO TOMÉ AND PRINCIPE
RIO MUNI
FRENCH CONGO
CONGO FREE STATE
LADO
BRITISH EAST AFRICA
Lake Victoria
GERMAN EAST AFRICA
Zanzibar
Seychelles
Amirante Islands
Chagos Islands
Cocos Islands
Christmas Island

Ascension Island

BRAZIL

Sumatra
DUTCH EAST INDIES
Batavia
Java
Borneo
PORTUGUESE TIMOR
New Guinea
KAISER WILHELM'S LAND
PAPUA
Solomon Islands

NORTHEASTERN RHODESIA
BRITISH CENTRAL AFRICA
BAROTSELAND NORTHWESTERN RHODESIA
SOUTHERN RHODESIA
PORTUGUESE EAST AFRICA
MADAGASCAR
Comoro Islands
Mauritius
Réunion

INDIAN OCEAN

Santa Cruz Islands

ST HELENA

ANGOLA

GERMAN SOUTHWEST AFRICA
WALVIS BAY (to Cape Colony)
BECHUANALAND
SOUTH AFRICA REPUBLIC
ORANGE FREE STATE
NATAL
BASUTOLAND
CAPE COLONY

New Caledonia

AUSTRALIAN COLONIES

Sydney

PARAGUAY
São Paulo
Rio de Janeiro

URUGUAY
Buenos Aires
ENTINA

Cape Town
Cape of Good Hope

NEW ZEALAND

FALKLAND ISLANDS

Iorn

SOUTHERN OCEAN

WORLD WAR I; RUSSIAN REVOLUTION

WORLD WAR I

The trigger for the first truly global conflict in history was the assassination in Sarajevo of the heir to the Austro-Hungarian throne, Archduke Ferdinand. All the countries of Europe at that time were tied into alliances and the assassination set off a chain reaction that effectively divided Europe into two opposing groups; the Allies and the Central Powers, or Axis. Both sides predicted that the war would be swift and over very quickly; in the event, with both sides fairly evenly matched, the result was stalemate. There were a number of set piece battles involving infantry charges, but these were usually disasters, resulting in enormous numbers of casualties.

WORLD WAR I

▨ Central Powers	→ Allied attack, 1915–17
▨ Allied Powers	— Front line, mid-1917
▨ Joining Allied Powers at a later date	→ Central Powers occupation of Russia, Feb.–May 1918 and occupation of Georgia by Ottoman Empire, May 1918
✕ Declaration of war ⚔ Surrender	→ Allied attack, 1918
→ Central Powers attack, 1914	— Front line, Nov. 1918
→ Allied attack, 1914	✳ Naval battle
— Front line, late 1914	
→ Central Powers attack, 1915–17	

THE RUSSIAN REVOLUTION

THE RUSSIAN REVOLUTION

By late 1916, after 14 months of war, Russia had lost nearly 5,000,000 men. There was considerable hardship, and widespread discontent was growing in all areas at the inefficiency and corruption of the Tsarist regime. Tsar Nicholas II was strongly advised to put a constitutional form of government in place, but he ignored this advice. The Russian Revolution of 1917 was a series of political and social upheavals beginning with the overthrow of the Tsar and ultimately leading to the establishment of Soviet power by the Bolshevik party, led by Vladimir Lenin, and the formation of the USSR.

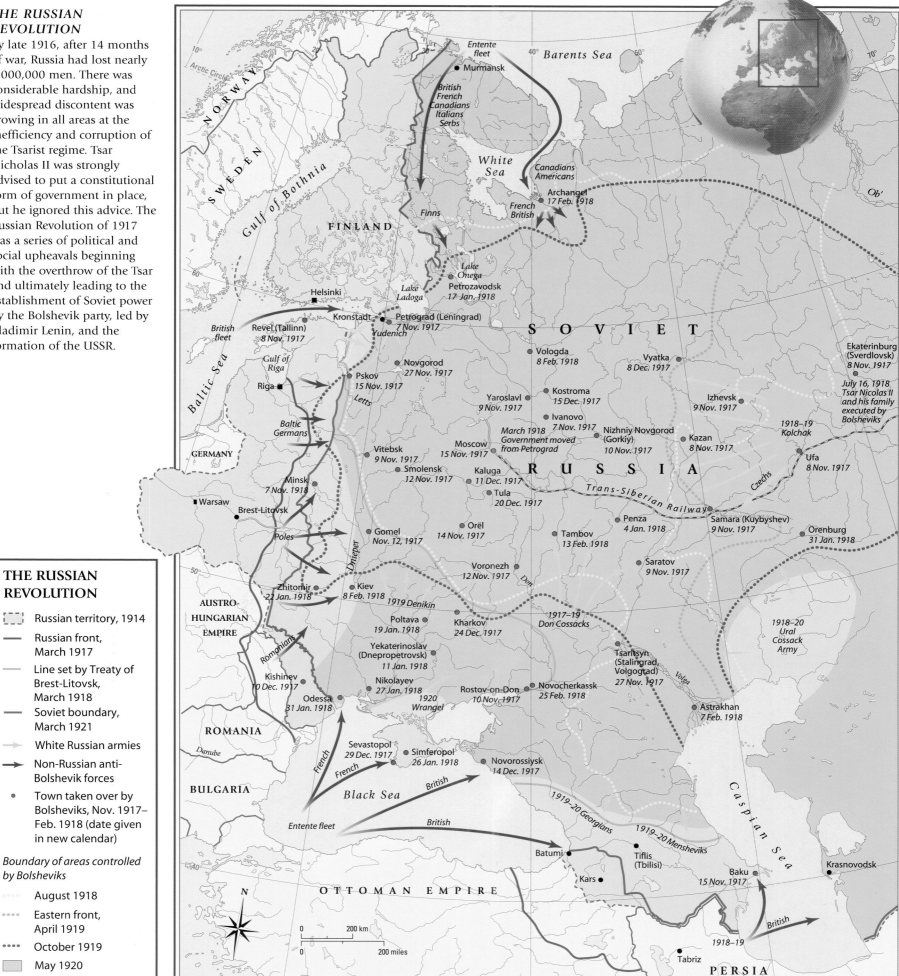

THE RUSSIAN REVOLUTION

- Russian territory, 1914
- Russian front, March 1917
- Line set by Treaty of Brest-Litovsk, March 1918
- Soviet boundary, March 1921
- White Russian armies
- Non-Russian anti-Bolshevik forces
- Town taken over by Bolsheviks, Nov. 1917–Feb. 1918 (date given in new calendar)

Boundary of areas controlled by Bolsheviks

- August 1918
- Eastern front, April 1919
- October 1919
- May 1920

EUROPE 1914/1919

REVOLUTION AND INVASION IN CHINA 1912–1939 (RIGHT)

By the beginning of the 20th century Imperial China was in terminal decline. The Emperor was overthrown and a republic was founded, but a power struggle resulted in many years of conflict during which China was ruled by warlords. Control was finally established in 1927 and a Nationalist government was set up in Nanjing. The following year Beijing was annexed and China once again was unified. Meanwhile the communists under Mao Zedong were uniting the peasants and setting up their own base in the northwest. At the same time Japan had invaded, seizing Manchuria and inner Mongolia, and by 1939 they occupied most of China's east coast.

EUROPE IN 1919

EUROPE IN 1914

EUROPE IN 1914

In 1914 Central Europe was dominated by the vast German and Austro-Hungarian Empires. Germany was a relatively young power, having only been united after a series of wars in 1871. Germany's Chancellor, Bismarck, always maintained that in any dispute among the five Great Powers, Germany must be in a majority of three. When Kaiser Wilhelm II came to power he retired Bismarck and upset the balance of power by refusing to renew Germany's friendship with Russia. Germany soon found itself in a minority of two, with its only ally being the weakest of the Great Powers, Austria-Hungary.

EUROPE IN 1919

World War I was regarded as the "war to end all wars" and at the Peace Congress at Versailles in 1919, a prime aim was to prevent a similar war in the future. With scant concern toward its population, the map of Europe was redrawn. Germany and Russia were both reduced in size, as Poland was restored and the Baltic States and Finland regained independence.

The vast, but crumbling, Austro-Hungarian Empire was broken up to create independent states such as Czechoslovakia, Hungary, and Austria. Yugoslavia also emerged, being a hotchpotch of smaller countries including the previously independent Serbia and Montenegro.

REVOLUTION AND INVASION IN CHINA

REVOLUTION AND INVASION IN CHINA 1912–39

Areas of China under warlord control, 1920s

- Chang Tsao-lin
- Feng Yü-hsiang ⎫ Chihli
- Sun Ch'üan-fang ⎭ faction
- Wu Pei-fu
- Kwangsi clique (group of local warlords)
- T'ang Chi-yao

Kuomintang control

- Under Kuomintang control, 1926
- → Kuomintang (with Communist allies) campaign, 1926–27
- Under Kuomintang control, 1928
- 1937 Date province brought under Kuomintang control or influence

Japanese intervention

- → Japanese troops advance and occupy, 1927–29
- Invaded, 1931
- Invaded, 1933
- Attempt to set up North China state, 1935

Communist activities

- ◯ Communist self-governed area, 1927–35
- → The Long March, 1934–35

1922 – 1936

THE DEPRESSION IN EUROPE; UNEMPLOYMENT AND RELIEF BY STATE

THE DEPRESSION IN EUROPE

The Great Depression began in Europe in 1929, exactly midway between the two catastrophic wars of the first half of the twentieth century. Europe was still struggling to rebuild its economy and few realized at this time the interdependence of world markets. The 1920s had generally been beset by unemployment and galloping inflation, and in Germany this had been extreme. The German government had responded by reducing public expenditure, which simply made matters worse. In Britain there was the General Strike in 1926, which led to fears of a class war. France and Britain both suffered because they were unable to find foreign markets for their manufactured goods.

UNEMPLOYMENT AND RELIEF BY STATE 1934

The Great Depression was the worst economic slump in US history and was to have repercussions throughout the industrialized world. It began in late 1929 and recovery took

about ten years. Many factors contributed to this situation, but the main cause was a combination of unequal distribution of wealth between the working class and the rich or middle class, and extensive and excessive stock market speculation. Factories closed, jobs were lost, and intense hardship forced many families to move and seek a better life elsewhere. At the same time prairie agriculture suffered from the devastating effects caused by intensive agriculture and prolonged drought.

THE DEPRESSION IN EUROPE

Percentage of industrial workers unemployed

- 31.7
- 28
- 23
- 18
- 13
- No data

★ Strike waves

☆ Sit-down strikes

✦ Riot, demonstration or single strike

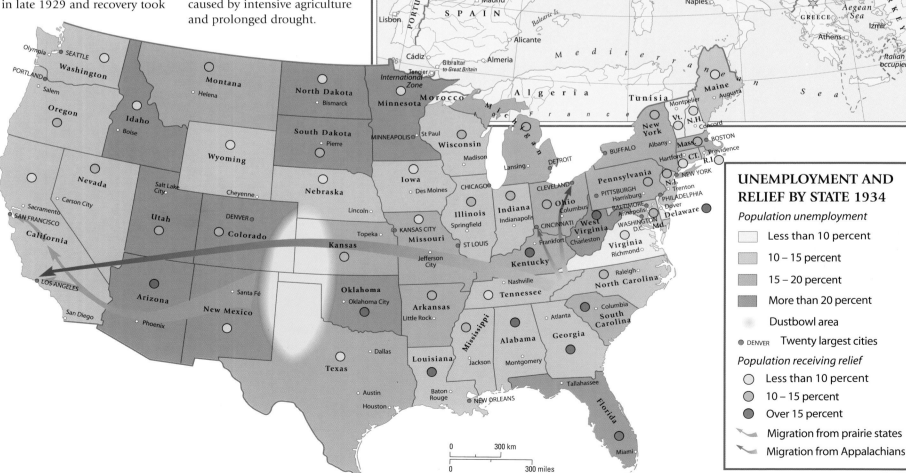

UNEMPLOYMENT AND RELIEF BY STATE 1934

Population unemployment

- Less than 10 percent
- 10 – 15 percent
- 15 – 20 percent
- More than 20 percent
- ✦ Dustbowl area
- ● DENVER Twenty largest cities

Population receiving relief

- ○ Less than 10 percent
- ◐ 10 – 15 percent
- ● Over 15 percent
- Migration from prairie states
- Migration from Appalachians

THE FASCIST STATES

Democratic countries

Repressive or
conservative countries

Fascist countries

Communist
dictatorship

Right-wing activity

THE FASCIST STATES
1922–1936

The growth of Fascism was a
feature of the 1920s and
1930s. The name was
originally coined by Mussolini
of Italy in 1922, and his idea
was that individuals would be
bound together in a strong
state and that their individual
needs would be subordinate to
the needs of the nation.
Fascism sought to forge a type
of national unity, based on
ethnic, cultural, or racial
attributes. This form of
government was adopted by
Germany and Spain, and to a
lesser extent, by a number of
other European countries.
Others, like Britain and
France, continued to follow
democratic principles, while
the Communist USSR,
although far from being
democratic, was bitterly
opposed to Fascism.

1938 – 1945   THE AXIS EXPANSION

THE AXIS EXPANSION 1938–1942

In the late 1930s, Hitler's Third Reich began to expand following his avowed intent to unite all the German-speaking peoples of Europe. Austria and a large part of Czechoslovakia were the first to be absorbed into the Reich and Poland followed. At this point the Allies declared war on Germany in an attempt to put a stop to Hitler's intentions. Germany countered this by continuing to move its borders outward to eventually include France, the Low Countries, Denmark, Norway, Russia, and the Balkans. Some countries remained neutral, while others were Axis satellites.

THE AXIS EXPANSION 1938–42

- ■ Germany, 1939
- → German invasion of Poland, 1938–39
- → Soviet attack on Baltic states and Poland
- ■ Added to the Reich, 1936–40
- ■ Axis satellites, 1939–44
- → Invasion of Denmark and Norway, April 1940
- → Allied landing in Norway and withdrawal
- → Invasion of Netherlands, Belgium and France, 10 May 1940
- → British attack on Libya from Egypt, 1940
- ■ Western states conquered, 1940
- → Invasion of Yugoslavia and Greece, April 1941
- ⇒ Allied landing in Greece, withdrawal to Crete then Egypt, 1941
- → Italian advance, 1941
- ■ Eastern territories and Balkans conquered, 1941
- → German support of Italy, campaigns to Egypt, Feb. 1941– Sept. 1942
- → Invasion of Russia, June 1941
- – → Soviet industrial plants move east, 1941–42
- ■ Conquered, 1942
- ■ Controlled by Vichy, 1942
- ■ Allied controlled, late 1942
- ■ Neutral states

THE AXIS COLLAPSE

THE AXIS COLLAPSE
1942–1945
By 1942 the Allies had begun to fight back. Initially this was in North Africa but gradually the armies moved on to Sicily and up through Italy. The following year the Soviet army began to regain some of the ground that had earlier been lost to the German advance. The South of France was invaded and the Allies began moving up through France, and in 1944 the main Second Front invasion force landed in Normandy. Gradually the Allies moved in from all sides. There were a few German counterattacks and a few pockets of resistance, but the eventual end was inevitable.

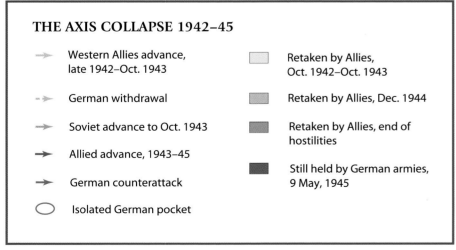

THE AXIS COLLAPSE 1942–45

- → Western Allies advance, late 1942–Oct. 1943
- → German withdrawal
- → Soviet advance to Oct. 1943
- → Allied advance, 1943–45
- → German counterattack
- ◯ Isolated German pocket

- Retaken by Allies, Oct. 1942–Oct. 1943
- Retaken by Allies, Dec. 1944
- Retaken by Allies, end of hostilities
- Still held by German armies, 9 May, 1945

1941 – 1945   WORLD WAR II IN ASIA

**WORLD WAR II IN ASIA
1941–1943**
Japan had invaded Manchuria and China, and in 1940 it signed a Tripartite Pact with Germany and Italy, thus becoming part of the "Axis." The United States imposed sanctions on Japan in the hope that it would withdraw from China and Manchuria. Japan countered by launching a surprise attack on Pearl Harbor. The US promptly declared war on Japan and, due to Japan's pact with Germany, the US also entered the European war. Japan achieved a long series of military successes, but the turning point came at the Battle of Midway in 1942. After heavy losses the Japanese fleet was turned back.

**WORLD WAR II IN ASIA
1943–1945**
In August 1942 the Americans attacked the Solomon Islands and the following February the Japanese were forced to make a costly withdrawal from the island of Guadalcanal. Allied forces were now slowly gaining naval and air superiority in the Pacific and began to move from island to island, conquering them but often sustaining significant casualties. Late in 1944 American forces liberated the Philippines and began massive air attacks on Japan. British forces recaptured Burma. In 1945, in spite of heavy casualties, the Americans captured the strategic islands of Iwo Jima and Okinawa. The war ended after atomic bombs were dropped on two Japanese cities, Hiroshima and Nagasaki, forcing the Japanese to surrender.

WORLD WAR II IN ASIA, 1941–43

- ◼ Japanese, 1933
- ◼ Japanese gain, 1937
- ◻ Japanese perimeter, July 1942
- → Major Japanese attacks, 1941–43
- — Planned Japanese perimeter "co-prosperity sphere"
- ◻ British and Commonwealth territory
- ◻ USSR and area of influence
- → Allied attacks, 1942–43

① 7 December 1941
   Japanese attack Pearl Harbor.

② 8 December 1941
   Japanese land in the Philippines.

③ 8 December 1941
   Japanese land on Malay coast.

④ 27 February 1942
   Battle of Java Sea; Allied fleet destroyed.

⑤ 5–9 May 1942
   Battle of Coral Sea; Japanese fleet repulsed.

⑥ 25 May – 3 June 1942
   Battle of Midway; Japanese invasion force defeated.

⑦ August 1942 – February 1943
   Guadalcanal, U.S. forces drive back Japanese invasion forces.

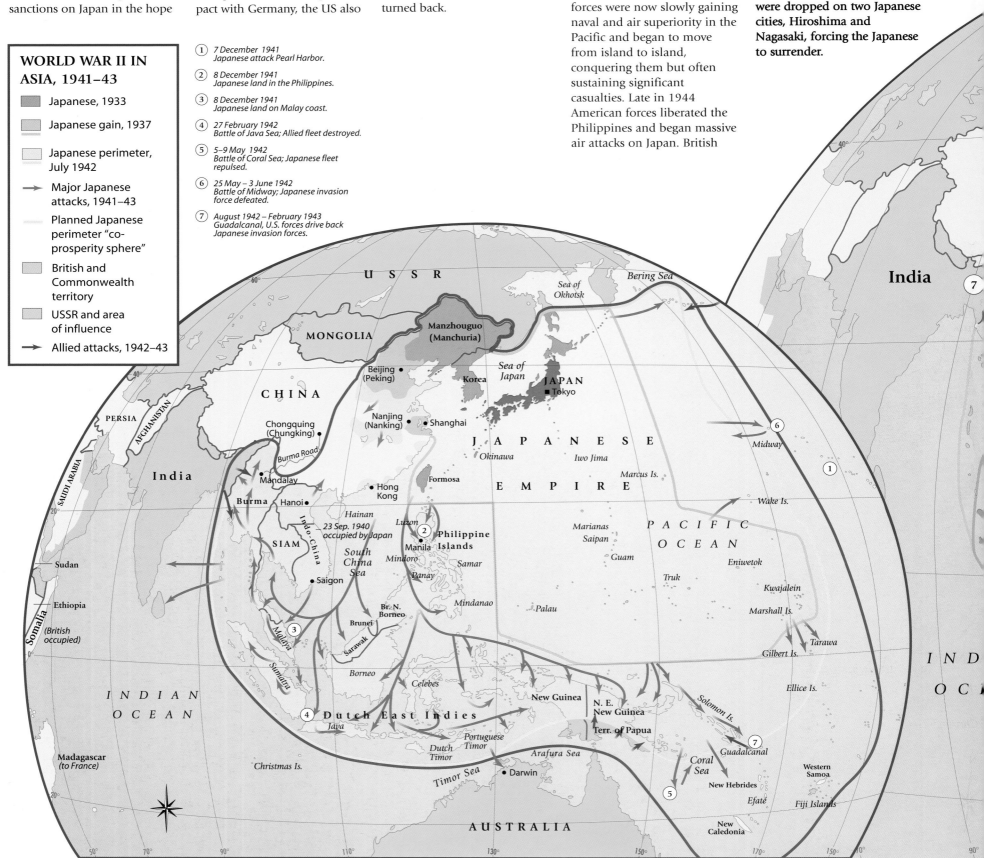

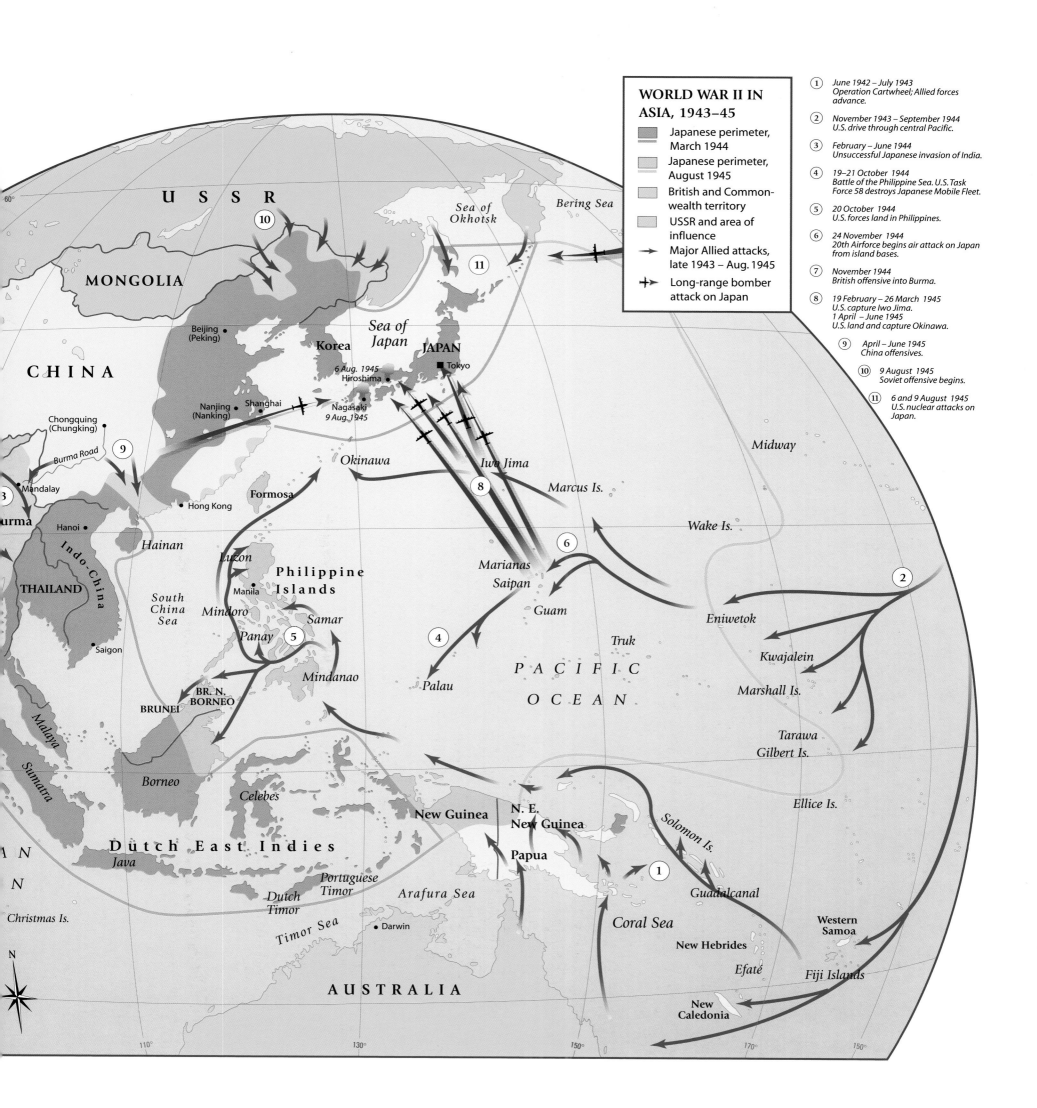

WORLD WAR II IN ASIA, 1943–45

- Japanese perimeter, March 1944
- Japanese perimeter, August 1945
- British and Commonwealth territory
- USSR and area of influence
- → Major Allied attacks, late 1943 – Aug. 1945
- ✈ Long-range bomber attack on Japan

① *June 1942 – July 1943*
Operation Cartwheel; Allied forces advance.

② *November 1943 – September 1944*
U.S. drive through central Pacific.

③ *February – June 1944*
Unsuccessful Japanese invasion of India.

④ *19–21 October 1944*
Battle of the Philippine Sea. U.S. Task Force 58 destroys Japanese Mobile Fleet.

⑤ *20 October 1944*
U.S. forces land in Philippines.

⑥ *24 November 1944*
20th Airforce begins air attack on Japan from island bases.

⑦ *November 1944*
British offensive into Burma.

⑧ *19 February – 26 March 1945*
U.S. capture Iwo Jima.
1 April – June 1945
U.S. land and capture Okinawa.

⑨ *April – June 1945*
China offensives.

⑩ *9 August 1945*
Soviet offensive begins.

⑪ *6 and 9 August 1945*
U.S. nuclear attacks on Japan.

Map labels:

USSR · MONGOLIA · Beijing (Peking) · CHINA · Chongquing (Chungking) · Burma Road · Mandalay · Burma · Hanoi · Indo-China · THAILAND · Hainan · Saigon · Malaya · Sumatra · Java · Dutch East Indies · Borneo · BRUNEI · BR. N. BORNEO · Celebes · Christmas Is. · Dutch Timor · Portuguese Timor · Timor Sea · Darwin · AUSTRALIA · Arafura Sea · Coral Sea

Korea · Sea of Japan · JAPAN · Tokyo · 6 Aug. 1945 Hiroshima · Nanjing (Nanking) · Shanghai · Nagasaki 9 Aug. 1945 · Sea of Okhotsk · Bering Sea · Formosa · Hong Kong · Okinawa · Iwo Jima · Marcus Is. · Luzon · Manila · Philippine Islands · Mindoro · Panay · Samar · South China Sea · Mindanao · Marianas · Saipan · Guam · Palau · Truk · PACIFIC OCEAN · Midway · Wake Is. · Eniwetok · Kwajalein · Marshall Is. · Tarawa Gilbert Is. · Ellice Is.

New Guinea · N. E. New Guinea · Papua · Solomon Is. · Guadalcanal · New Hebrides · Efaté · New Caledonia · Fiji Islands · Western Samoa

N

THE BERLIN AIRLIFT; THE WORLD 1950

THE BERLIN AIRLIFT JUNE 1948 TO MAY 1949
After World War II Germany was partitioned into four zones, the British, American, French, and Russian. The capital, Berlin, was situated in the Russian Zone, and that was also partitioned. In June 1948 the Russians cut off all road and rail links through Soviet-controlled territory. It was decided that it was possible to supply the city by air by means of special air corridors. The airlift lasted for 321 days and in total there were 278,228 flights. 2,326,406 tons of food and supplies were delivered, including more than 1.5 million tons of coal. The blockade was lifted on 11th May 1949.

THE WORLD 1950
In 1950 World War II was still fresh in people's minds but the world was changing. The British Empire was in terminal decline; India was now independent and the dominions of Canada, Australia, New Zealand, and South Africa no longer felt such strong ties to the motherland. France still controlled Vietnam, but Holland had lost all of its Indonesian colonies. Britain, France, Spain, Portugal, and Belgium continued to control large areas of Africa, but within the next few years these would gain independence, as would most other colonial territories throughout the world.

BERLIN AIRLIFT
June 1948 – May 1949

- Radio location beacon
- Air corridors (US)
- Air corridors (British)

THE WORLD 1950

- Major city
- British possessions
- French possessions
- German possessions
- Italian possessions
- Portuguese possessions
- Russian possessions
- Spanish possessions
- United States possessions

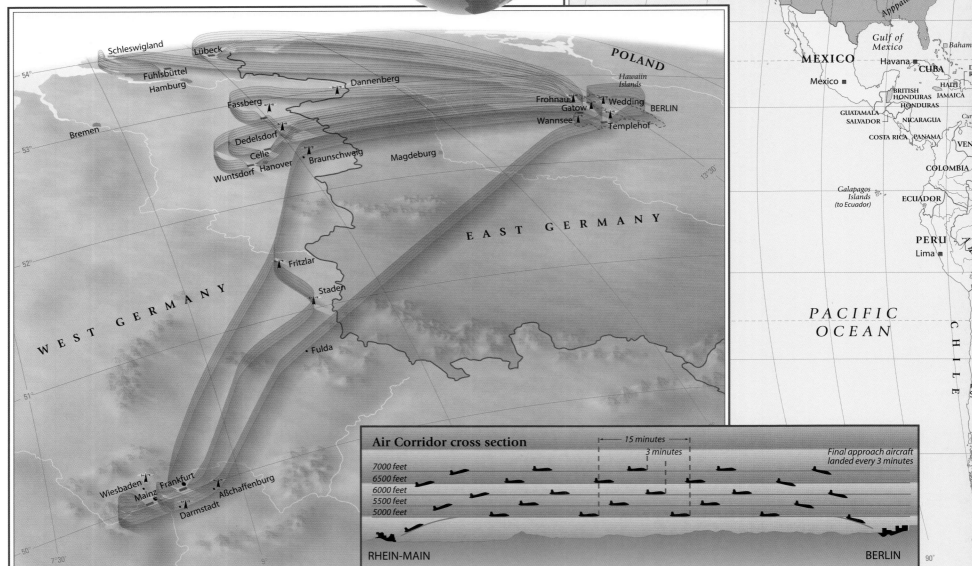

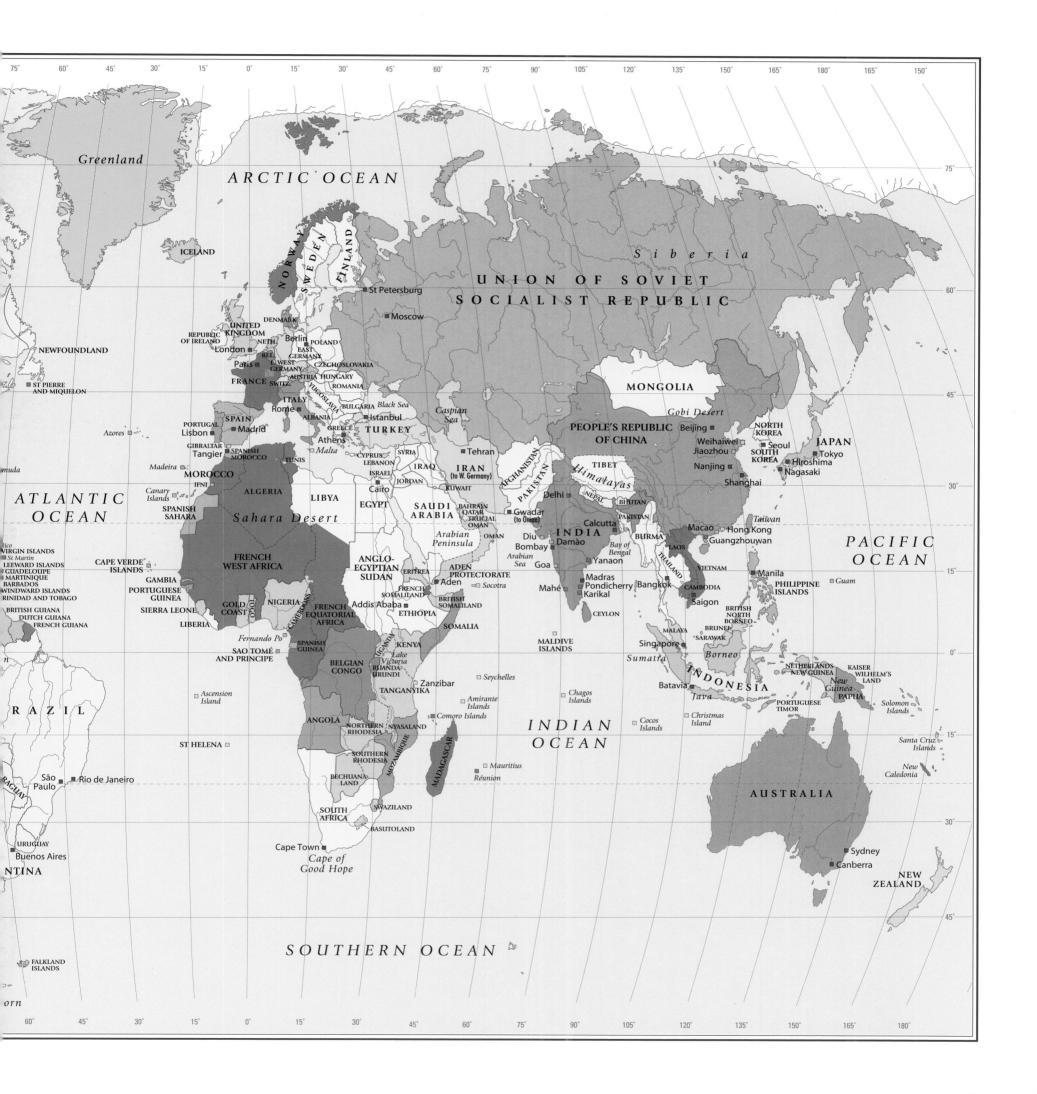

END OF EMPIRE

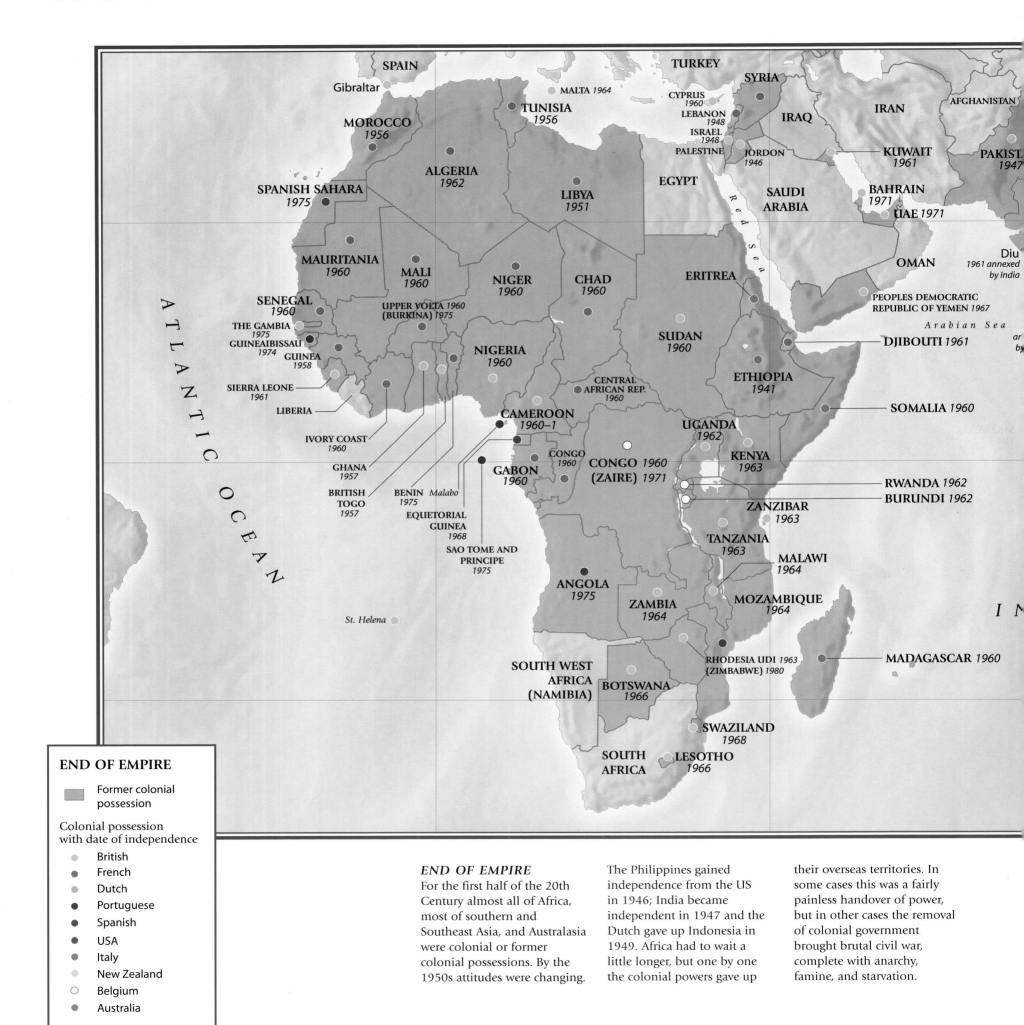

SPAIN

Gibraltar

MALTA *1964*

TURKEY

SYRIA

CYPRUS
1960

LEBANON
1948

ISRAEL
1948

PALESTINE

IRAQ

IRAN

AFGHANISTAN

JORDON
1946

KUWAIT
1961

PAKISTA
1947

TUNISIA
1956

MOROCCO
1956

ALGERIA
1962

LIBYA
1951

EGYPT

SAUDI
ARABIA

BAHRAIN
1971

UAE *1971*

SPANISH SAHARA
1975

OMAN

Diu
*1961 annexed
by India*

MAURITANIA
1960

MALI
1960

NIGER
1960

CHAD
1960

ERITREA

PEOPLES DEMOCRATIC
REPUBLIC OF YEMEN *1967*

Arabian Sea

SENEGAL
1960

UPPER VOLTA *1960*
(BURKINA) *1975*

SUDAN
1960

*ar
by*

THE GAMBIA
1975

DJIBOUTI *1961*

GUINEAIBISSAU
1974

GUINEA
1958

NIGERIA
1960

CENTRAL
AFRICAN REP.
1960

ETHIOPIA
1941

SIERRA LEONE
1961

SOMALIA *1960*

LIBERIA

CAMEROON
1960-1

UGANDA
1962

IVORY COAST
1960

CONGO
1960

CONGO *1960*
(ZAIRE) *1971*

KENYA
1963

GHANA
1957

GABON
1960

RWANDA *1962*
BURUNDI *1962*

BRITISH
TOGO
1957

BENIN
1975

Malabo

ZANZIBAR
1963

EQUETORIAL
GUINEA
1968

TANZANIA
1963

SAO TOME AND
PRINCIPE
1975

ANGOLA
1975

MALAWI
1964

ZAMBIA
1964

MOZAMBIQUE
1964

St. Helena

I
N

RHODESIA UDI *1963*
(ZIMBABWE) *1980*

MADAGASCAR *1960*

SOUTH WEST
AFRICA
(NAMIBIA)

BOTSWANA
1966

SWAZILAND
1968

SOUTH
AFRICA

LESOTHO
1966

*A
T
L
A
N
T
I
C*

*O
C
E
A
N*

Red Sea

END OF EMPIRE

Former colonial
possession

Colonial possession
with date of independence

- British
- French
- Dutch
- Portuguese
- Spanish
- USA
- Italy
- New Zealand
- Belgium
- Australia

END OF EMPIRE
For the first half of the 20th
Century almost all of Africa,
most of southern and
Southeast Asia, and Australasia
were colonial or former
colonial possessions. By the
1950s attitudes were changing.

The Philippines gained
independence from the US
in 1946; India became
independent in 1947 and the
Dutch gave up Indonesia in
1949. Africa had to wait a
little longer, but one by one
the colonial powers gave up

their overseas territories. In
some cases this was a fairly
painless handover of power,
but in other cases the removal
of colonial government
brought brutal civil war,
complete with anarchy,
famine, and starvation.

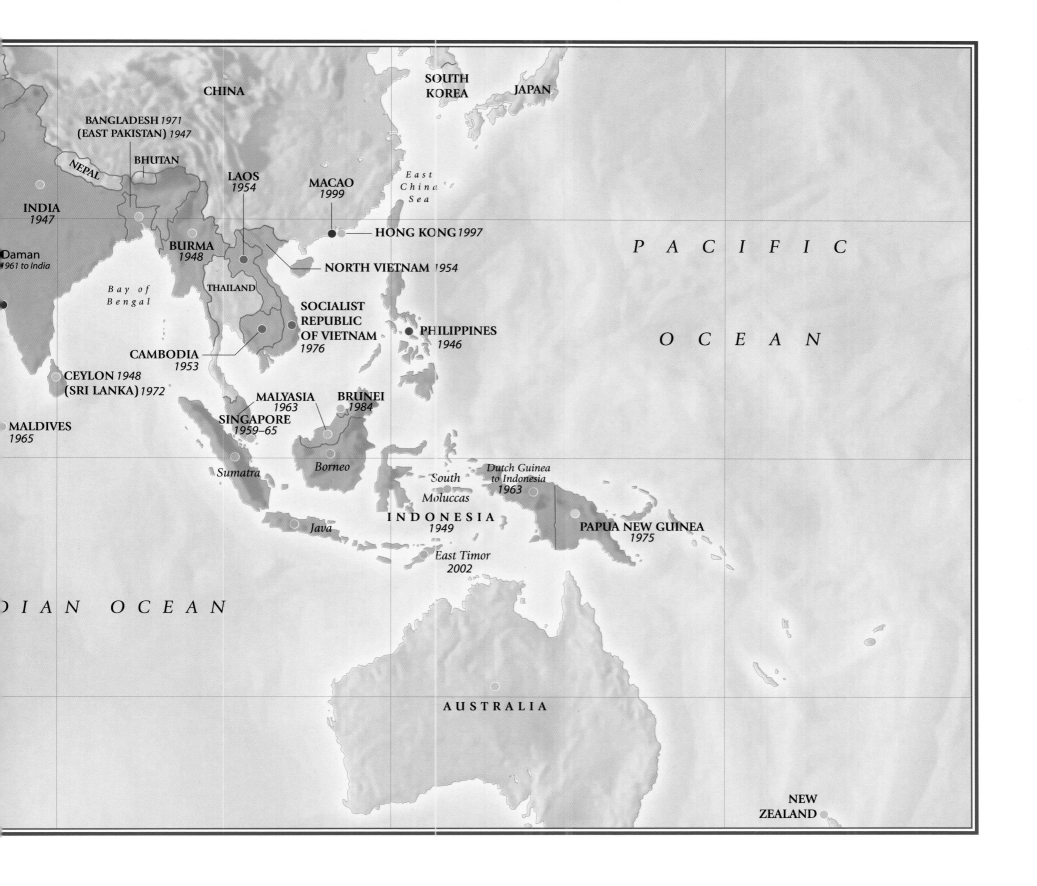

1945 – 1962 ORIGINS OF THE COLD WAR

ORIGINS OF THE COLD WAR, Europe After World War II 1945–1949

- Soviet Union from May 1945
- Western limit of Soviet occupation or influence mid-1945
- Occupied by western forces or pro-western in sympathy
- Soviet occupied or control
- Soviet zones of Germany and Austria
- Franco's Pro-western Falangist regime isolated
- Yugoslav–Soviet rift 28 June 1948 becoming non-aligned
- Civil war 1946–49 Pro-western Forces gain control
- Original members of NATO 4 April 1949
- Colonial territories
- Neutral

1. From Germany to Poland 1945
2. From Germany to USSR 1945
3. Returned to Czechoslovakia from Hungary 1945
4. Returned to Romania from Hungary 1945
5. From Hungary to USSR 1945
6. From Romania to USSR 1945
7. To USSR 1940, lost 1941, retaken 1944
8. To USSR 1940, lost 1941–44, returned 1947
9. To USSR 1947
10. Federal Republic of Germany formed Sept. 1949

ORIGINS OF COLD WAR
The Cold War was the result of deep distrust between the USA and the USSR. Although the USA and USSR had both outwardly been allies during the war, there had always been mutual suspicion. When the West refused Stalin's demand to "destroy Germany's capacity for another war," he set about creating a chain of "buffer states" to protect his western borders. Suspicion degenerated into open hostility and the result was a polarization that divided Europe along lines of allegiance. With Europe now split between East and West, both superpowers entered an arms race in preparation for conflict.

KOREAN WAR (PHASES 1, 2 , 3 AND 4)

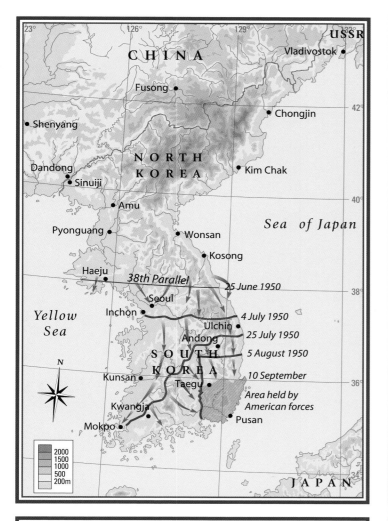

KOREAN WAR
The Korean War began as a civil war on the Korean Peninsula. After World War II Korea had been divided into Soviet and American occupation zones and the War began when North Korea attacked South Korea on 25 June, 1950. The North was principally supported by the People's Republic of China, while the South was supported by United Nations forces, principally from the United States, but many other nations were involved. The war ended with the signing of a ceasefire on 27th July, 1953, but no peace treaty has ever formally acknowledged this.

KOREA PHASE 1
North Korea attacks
25 June – 10 September
1950

→ Main axis of attack

▨ Pusan perimeter

KOREA PHASE 2
United Nations
counter attack
15 September –
25 November 1950

→ UN counter attack

▨ Pusan perimeter

KOREA PHASE 3
Chinese attack
26 November 1950

→ Chinese attack

KOREA PHASE 4
UN counter attack
January 1951 –
27 July 1953

→ UN campaign

1962   # THE CUBAN MISSILE CRISIS

THE CUBAN MISSILE CRISIS

The Cuban Missile Crisis occurred at the height of the Cold War in the early 1960s, and it was as close as both superpowers came to open conflict. The US had installed ballistic missiles in Turkey that were 16 minutes flying time from Moscow. The Soviets countered this by sending missiles to Cuba, whose leader, Fidel Castro, had become very close to the Soviet Union. The Americans threatened to invade Cuba, and it seemed for a time that the world stood on the brink of a cataclysmic conflict. In the event, after intense diplomatic activity, both sides withdrew their missiles and the crisis was over. To help prevent similar incidents in the future a "hot line" was installed between the leaders of the USA and USSR.

THE CUBAN MISSILE CRISIS September – November 1962

MRBM site	
IRBM site	
Position of Soviet cargo ship *Marcula*	
U.S. troop concentration	
Air patrol	
Picket ship	
Aircraft carrier	
U.S. naval site	

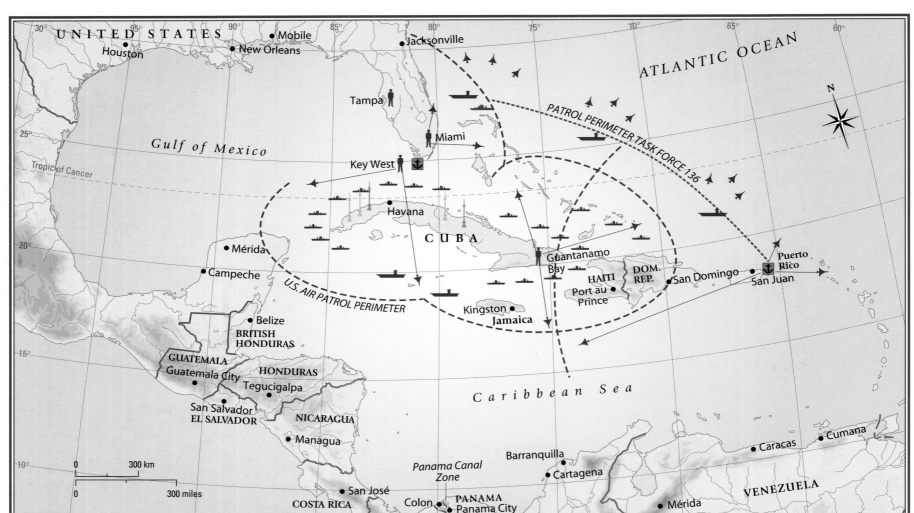

1959 – 1975 — VIETNAM WAR; COMMUNIST SUPPLY ROUTES

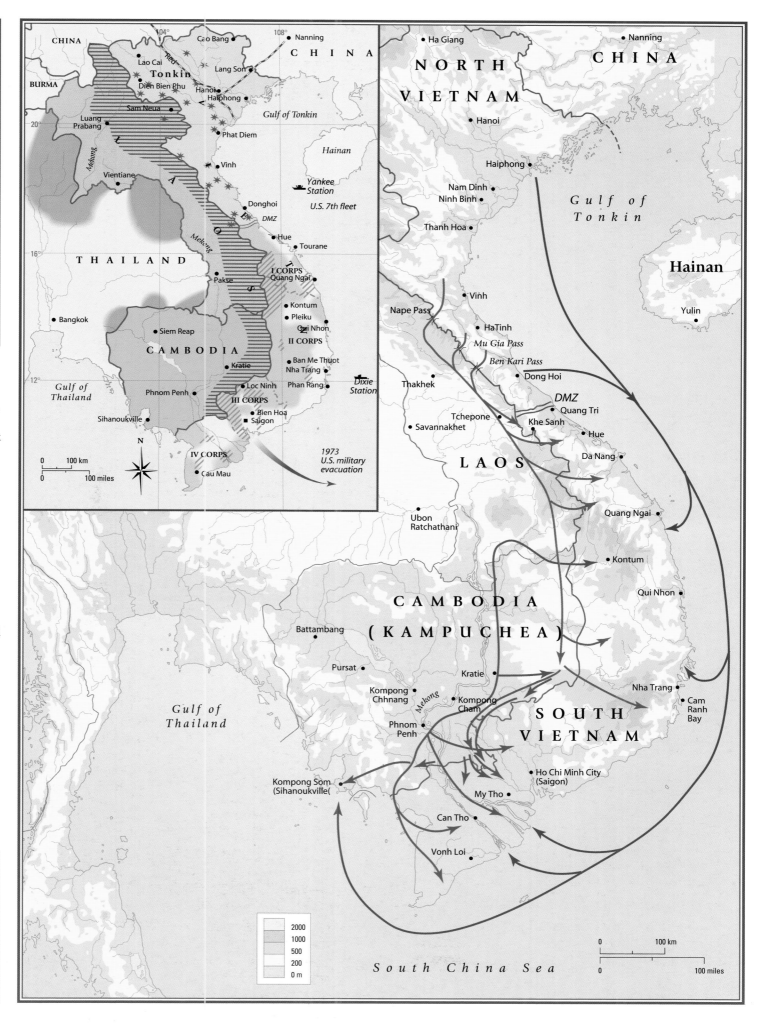

VIETNAM WAR 1959–75 (Inset)

- Communist-held area January 1973 "ceasefire"
- ‑ ‑ ‑ U.S. Corps command area
- ✳ North Vietnam subject to air attack
- Communist-controlled area in Laos and Cambodia 1950–75
- Controlled by Khmer Rouge c. 1975
- Controlled by Pathet Lao c. 1975
- Area of Communist guerrilla activity c. 1975

THE VIETNAM WAR

This war between North and South Vietnam began in 1959. The Communist North was supported chiefly by the Soviet Union and China, while the South was chiefly supported by the United States. By the late 1960s huge numbers of US combat troops were in Vietnam. The North fought a mainly guerrilla war and its troops were kept supplied largely by what was known as the Ho Chi Minh Trail. This was a complex maze of mountain truck routes, paths for foot and bicycle traffic, and river transportation systems. The war ended with the fall of Saigon in April 1975.

COMMUNIST SUPPLY ROUTES

- ➤ Ho Chi Minh Trail
- ➤ Sihanouk Trail
- ‑➤ Sea supply routes
- ▨ Communist-held area 1959–60

SUEZ AND SINAI CAMPAIGN;
THE SIX-DAY WAR; INVASION OF LEBANON

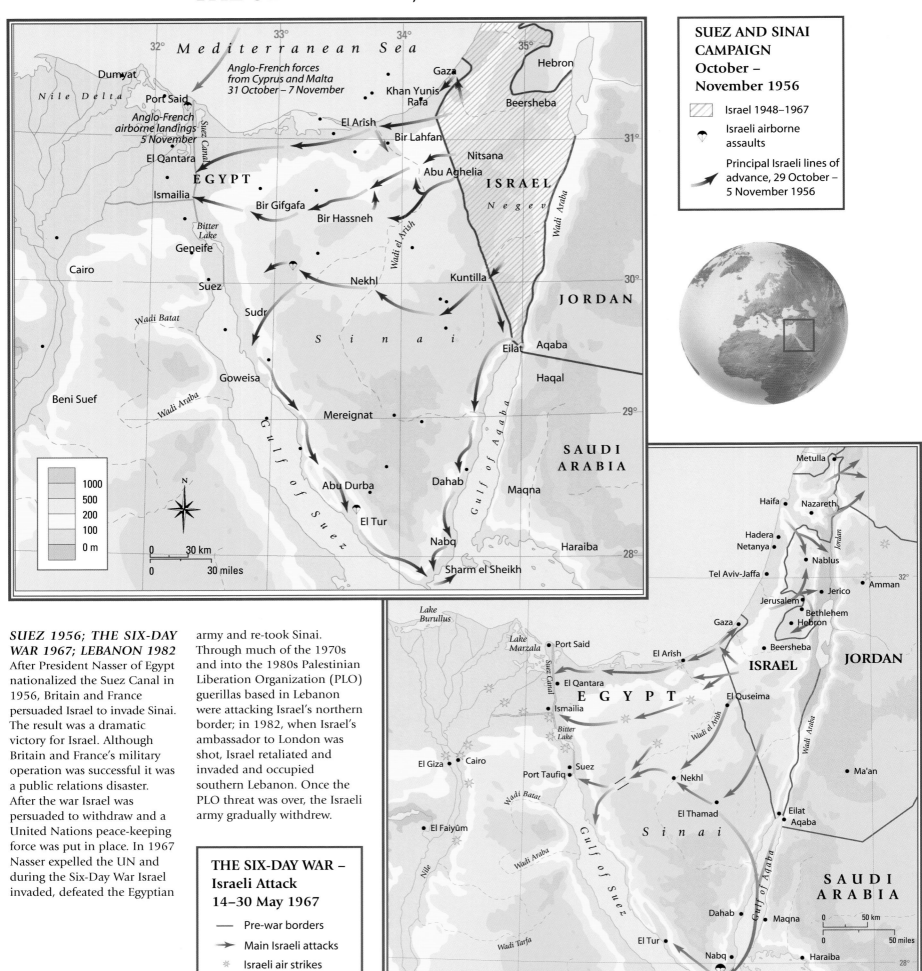

SUEZ AND SINAI CAMPAIGN
October – November 1956

- Israel 1948–1967
- Israeli airborne assaults
- Principal Israeli lines of advance, 29 October – 5 November 1956

THE SIX-DAY WAR –
Israeli Attack
14–30 May 1967

- Pre-war borders
- Main Israeli attacks
- Israeli air strikes
- Airborne landing

SUEZ 1956; THE SIX-DAY WAR 1967; LEBANON 1982
After President Nasser of Egypt nationalized the Suez Canal in 1956, Britain and France persuaded Israel to invade Sinai. The result was a dramatic victory for Israel. Although Britain and France's military operation was successful it was a public relations disaster. After the war Israel was persuaded to withdraw and a United Nations peace-keeping force was put in place. In 1967 Nasser expelled the UN and during the Six-Day War Israel invaded, defeated the Egyptian army and re-took Sinai. Through much of the 1970s and into the 1980s Palestinian Liberation Organization (PLO) guerillas based in Lebanon were attacking Israel's northern border; in 1982, when Israel's ambassador to London was shot, Israel retaliated and invaded and occupied southern Lebanon. Once the PLO threat was over, the Israeli army gradually withdrew.

THE NEW WORLD ORDER

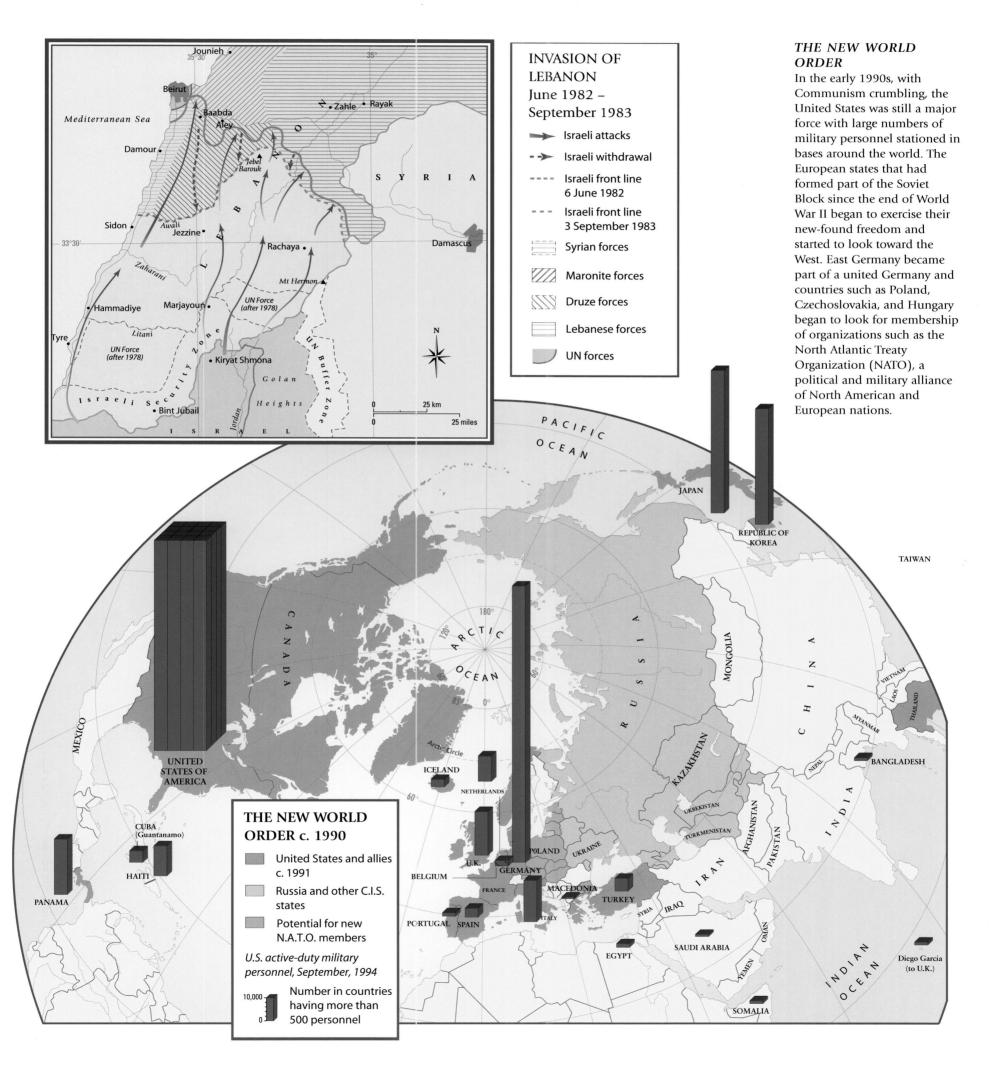

INVASION OF LEBANON
June 1982 –
September 1983

→ Israeli attacks

⇢ Israeli withdrawal

---- Israeli front line
6 June 1982

- - - Israeli front line
3 September 1983

Syrian forces

Maronite forces

Druze forces

Lebanese forces

UN forces

THE NEW WORLD
ORDER c. 1990

United States and allies
c. 1991

Russia and other C.I.S.
states

Potential for new
N.A.T.O. members

U.S. active-duty military
personnel, September, 1994

10,000

Number in countries
having more than
500 personnel

0

THE NEW WORLD
ORDER

In the early 1990s, with
Communism crumbling, the
United States was still a major
force with large numbers of
military personnel stationed in
bases around the world. The
European states that had
formed part of the Soviet
Block since the end of World
War II began to exercise their
new-found freedom and
started to look toward the
West. East Germany became
part of a united Germany and
countries such as Poland,
Czechoslovakia, and Hungary
began to look for membership
of organizations such as the
North Atlantic Treaty
Organization (NATO), a
political and military alliance
of North American and
European nations.

AFGHANISTAN; GLOBAL TERROR

GLOBAL TERROR

In the past 30 years it is estimated that there have been some 80,000 terrorist attacks around the world. Many have been suicide attacks, most have involved explosives of some kind, and many have resulted in considerable loss of life. Terrorism today is truly global and transport systems, whether air, land, or sea have always been popular targets. Recent high profile attacks include the Madrid train bombings of 2004 and the suicide attack on the London transport network in 2005. Other terrorist plots have involved buildings, the most devastating one being the 2001 attack of the World Trade Center in New York which killed just over 3,000 people.

WORLD TERROR
1970 to present day
🌿 Terrorist attacks

AFGHANISTAN

The Marxist regime of Afghanistan had been receiving economic support from the USSR. When Mujahideen insurgents began fighting to overthrow Communist rule, a request was made to the Soviet Union for military assistance. This was given, but since the US had been supporting the rebels, the West saw it as an invasion. It was a very difficult war for the Soviets to fight. They were not used to fighting in such terrain and their equipment was often ineffective or vulnerable. The result was a military stalemate. Casualties were high in this very unpopular war. It was impossible to win and is often known as "Russia's Vietnam."

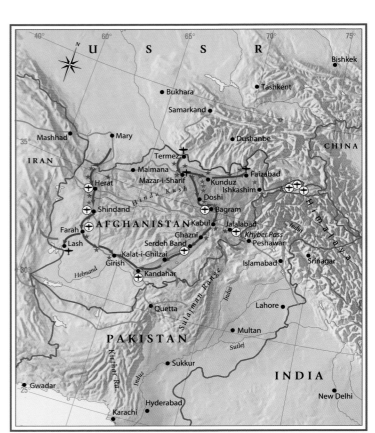

AFGHANISTAN
1978–84
➤ Soviet advance from 1979
▢ Main area of conflict
★ Main Soviet base
✛ Soviet airfield
⊕ Airfield constructed or enlarged after 1980 by USSR
➤ Refugees
— Major road

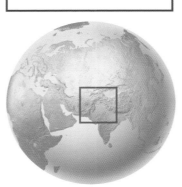

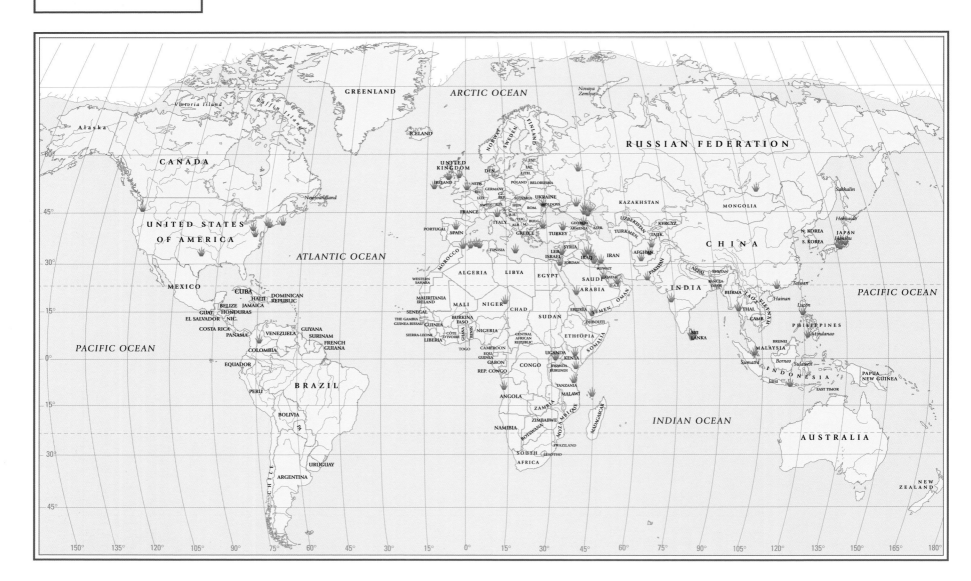

THE GULF WAR (PHASES 1, 2 AND 3)

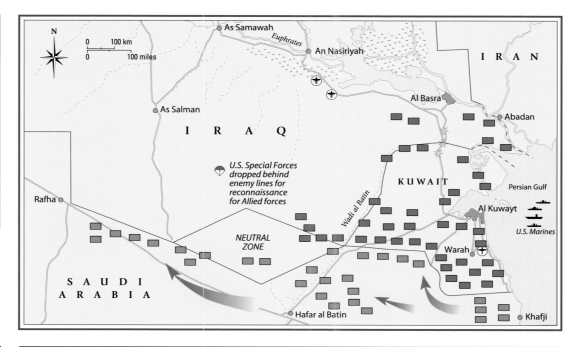

**THE GULF WAR
PHASE 1
17 January to
23 February 1991**

- Allied units
- Iraqi units
- Allied movements
- Iraqi airbase destroyed
- Bridge destroyed

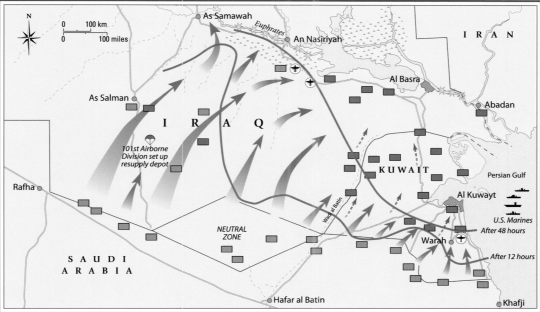

**THE GULF WAR,
PHASE 2
24–26 February 1991**

- Allied units
- Iraqi units
- Allied movements
- Iraqi airbase destroyed
- Bridge destroyed
- Advance lines with timing
- Iraqi retreat

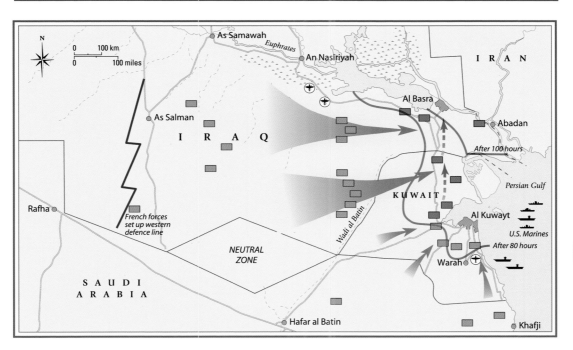

**THE GULF WAR,
PHASE 3
27 February 1991**

- Allied units
- Iraqi units
- Allied movements
- Iraqi airbase destroyed
- Bridge destroyed
- Advance lines with timing
- Iraqi retreat

THE GULF WAR

The Allies, led by the United States, began their military build up in the Gulf following Iraq's invasion of Kuwait on 2nd August, 1990. The United Nations immediately introduced economic sanctions against the aggressor and authorized a coalition of approximately 30 nations to liberate Kuwait. Armed intervention began in early 1991 and involved Kuwait's general encirclement. Aerial and ground conflict was confined to Iraq, Kuwait, and bordering areas of Saudi Arabia. It resulted in a decisive victory for the coalition forces, driving the Iraqi forces out of Kuwait with a minimal number of coalition deaths.

157

GLOBAL CLIMATE (THE FINAL FRONTIER?)

GLOBAL CLIMATE CHANGE (THE FINAL FRONTIER?)
Along with global terrorism, the major problem facing the world today is climatic change, known widely as "global warming." There is no doubt that the Earth is heating up, though there is some dispute about the cause of this. Some scientists attribute the rise largely to a natural cyclical process. However, while this may be a factor, there is now a growing consensus in the scientific community that human activity is the most significant cause of global climate change. An increase in temperature of only a few degrees will speed up the melting of the polar ice caps, leading to a rise in the levels of the oceans and the risk of flooding in low-lying areas. The influx of cold water is also likely to upset delicate local weather patterns.

GLOBAL CLIMATE

Climate zones

- Ice cap
- Tundra
- Sub-arctic
- Cool continental
- Maritime
- Mediterranean
- Semi-arid
- Arid
- Tropical
- Humid equatorial

Ocean currents

- Warm
- Cold

Prevailing winds

- Warm
- Cold

Local winds

- Warm
- Cold
- Seasonal, can be either warm or cold

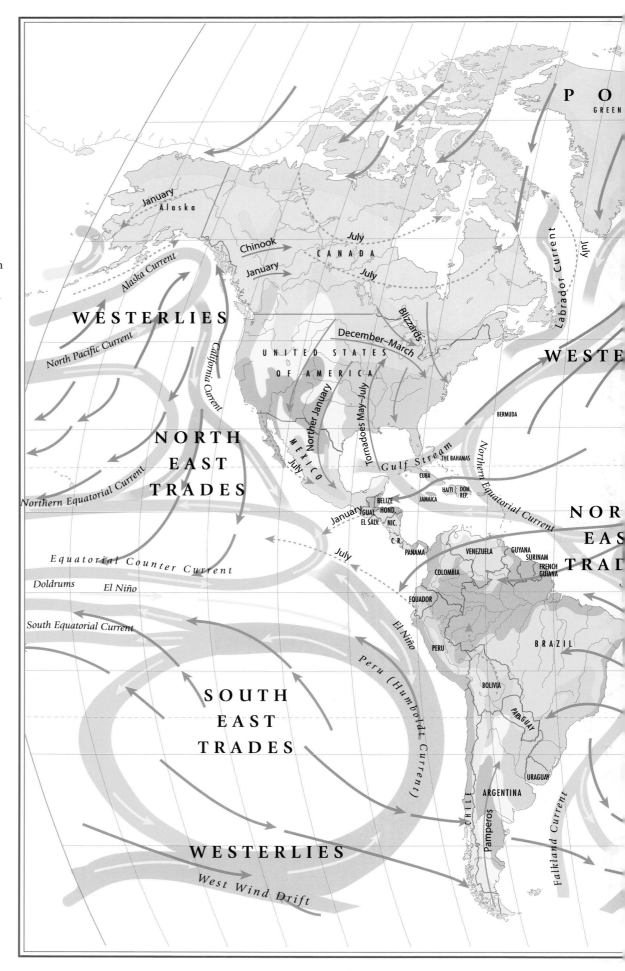

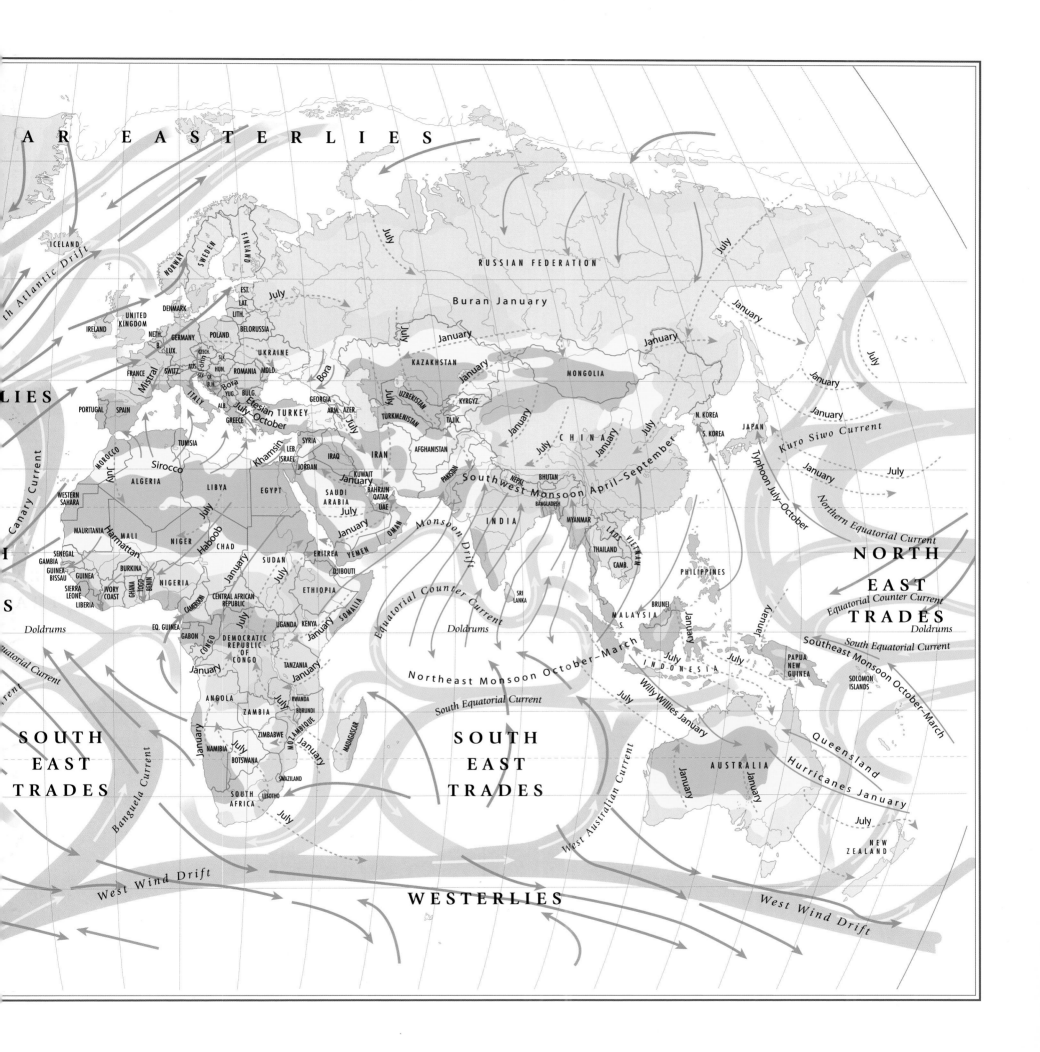

AR EASTERLIES

ICELAND

North Atlantic Drift

NORWAY SWEDEN FINLAND

EST.
LAT.
LITH.
DENMARK
IRELAND
UNITED
KINGDOM
NETH. GERMANY POLAND BELORUSSIA
B.
LUX. CZECH.
FRANCE SWITZ. SLV. HUN. ROMANIA MOLD.
AUS. Föhn
Mistral ITALY B.H. YUG. BULG.
Bora
ALB.
PORTUGAL SPAIN GREECE
July-October

Canary Current

TUNISIA

MOROCCO
Sirocco
WESTERN
SAHARA
ALGERIA LIBYA

MAURITANIA
Harmattan MALI NIGER
SENEGAL Haboob CHAD
GAMBIA BURKINA
GUINEA-
BISSAU GUINEA
SIERRA IVORY GHANA NIGERIA
LEONE COAST TOGO
LIBERIA BENIN CAMEROON CENTRAL AFRICAN
REPUBLIC
Doldrums EQ. GUINEA
GABON CONGO DEMOCRATIC
REPUBLIC
OF
CONGO
January

Equatorial Current

SOUTH
EAST
TRADES

ANGOLA
ZAMBIA
Benguela Current
NAMIBIA
BOTSWANA ZIMBABWE
MOZAMBIQUE
SWAZILAND
SOUTH LESOTHO
AFRICA

West Wind Drift

RUSSIAN FEDERATION

Buran January

July

July

January

KAZAKHSTAN

MONGOLIA

July UZBEKISTAN
GEORGIA KYRGYZ.
ARM. AZER. TURKMENISTAN TAJIK.
Etesian TURKEY July
July
LEB. SYRIA
ISRAEL IRAQ IRAN AFGHANISTAN
Khamsin JORDAN
January PAKISTAN
EGYPT KUWAIT NEPAL BHUTAN
SAUDI BAHRAIN QATAR
ARABIA UAE BANGLADESH
July OMAN
January
YEMEN
SUDAN Monsoon Drift
ERITREA INDIA
DJIBOUTI
ETHIOPIA
SRI
UGANDA SOMALIA LANKA
KENYA
TANZANIA
RWANDA
BURUNDI
January
MADAGASCAR

Southwest Monsoon April–September

CHINA
N. KOREA
S. KOREA JAPAN

Kuro Siwo Current

Typhoon July–October

Northern Equatorial Current

January

January

July

NORTH

EAST

TRADES

Equatorial Counter Current

Doldrums

South Equatorial Current

Equatorial Counter Current

Doldrums

South Equatorial Current

Northeast Monsoon October–March

SOUTH
EAST
TRADES

PHILIPPINES

BRUNEI
MALAYSIA
INDONESIA

MYANMAR
THAILAND
CAMB.
Apr VIETNAM

PAPUA
NEW
GUINEA
SOLOMON
ISLANDS

Southeast Monsoon October–March

Willy Willies January

West Australian Current

AUSTRALIA

Queensland
Hurricanes January

NEW
ZEALAND

WESTERLIES

West Wind Drift

MAPS AND RECONSTRUCTIONS

Part 1: Human Origins

Human Origins 24

The Migration of Homo Sapiens 120,000- 10,000 BC 24-5

Land bridge to the Americas c.18,000 Years Ago 26-27

Peopling of Australia 50,000- 10,000 BC 27

Spread of Agriculture 7000- 2000 BC 28

The Beginnings of Agriculture c.5000 BC 28-29

The Old Kingdom 30

Civilisation in the Indus Valley 31

The Babylonian Empire 32

The Hittite Empire 33

The World 2500 BC 34-35

Indo European Migration 5000-900 BC 36

Shang China 37

Shou China 37

The Middle East c. 900 BC 38

The World 1250 BC 38-39

Egypt: The Middle Kingdom 40

Egypt: The New Kingdom 41

Solomon's Empire 42

The Struggle for Egypt 674-663 BC 43

Nubia Ascendent 43

The Persian Empire 550-330 BC 44-45

Eurasia 750 BC 46

Part 2: The Classical World

Tiryn's Citadel 48

Mycenaean Greece 1500-1200 BC 48

Minoan Crete c. 1500-1250 BC 49

Early Greece 1200-400 BC 50

Early Attica 4th and 5th Centuries 51

The Phoenicians and Greeks colonise the Mediterranean 9th-6th century BC 51

Etruscan Expansion 600- 337 BC 52

The Rise of Macedonia 53

The Empire of Alexander the Great 336-323 BC 54-55

The Hallstatt Culture 753- 260 BC 56

The Celts 56

The Rise of Rome 57

Punic Wars 264- 146 BC 58

Rome 50 BC 59

The Roman Empire 55 BC 59

The First Jewish Revolt AD 66- 68 60

The Roman Empire 60-61

Feuding States of China c. 350 BC 62

Expansion of the Ch'in 316- 209 BC 62

The Han Empire AD 2 63

The Silk Road c. 112 BC- AD 100 63

Mauryan Empire 322- 297 BC 64

The Gupta Empire AD 320- 535 65

The World AD 500 66-67

The Empire Divided 68-69

Enemy at the Gates 70

Germanic Kingdoms c.500 71

The Empire of the East 72

Part 3: Divided Regions

The Maya 300 BC-AD 300 74

The Maya AD 300-900 74

The Maya AD 900-1500 74

The Toltec States 75

The Central Area of Teotihuacán 75

Vikings in the North AD 985-c.1020 76

Atlantic Routes of the Vikings c. 1000 AD 77

Viking Heartland 77

Kievan Russia 78

Europe 1095 79

Ch'ang An During the Sui and Tang Dynasties 80

A Century of Disunity c. 979 80

The Tang Empire c. 700 80

Sung China c.1000 81

Southern Sung and Chin

Empires 1142 81

Muslim India c. 1100- 1400 82

The Taika Reforms in Japan c. 646- 710 83

Warrior Japan c. 794-1185 83

The World AD 1000 84-85

Native American Southwest Culture 86

Adena, Hopewell, and Mississippian Mounds 86

East Coast Economy 87

Sapir's Thesis: Six Basic Indian Languages 87

African Languages AD 1000 88

Ghana and Mali Empires 89

Almoravid Empire 1059 89

Fatimad North Africa to c. 1000 90

Mameluke Sultinate 1171- 1517 90

Spread of Islam to c. 1500 91

The Crusades 1096- 1204 92-93

Muslim Spain c. 1030 94

The Christian Reconquest 94

The Empire and the Papacy 95

The Vatican City 95

Songhay Empire c. 1540 96

Desert States c. 1600 97

The Horn of Africa to 1500 97

Europe 1500 98

Expansion of the Ottoman Empire 1328-1672 99

Mongol Conquests 1206-59 100-101

The Empire of the Great Khan 1260-c.1300 102-103

The Battle of Mohi 1241 104

Part 4: Exploration and First Contact

Route of Marco Polo 1271 106

Routes of Columbus 1492- 1504 106

French Exploration 1524-1690 107

English Exploration 1497-1776 107

Voyages of Discovery 1499-1502 108

World Exploration 1487-1780 108-109

English Settlements and Colonial Grants 1603-35 110

The World 1600 110-111

European Explorers in the Caribbean 112

Treaty of Tordesillas 112

Explorers in Africa 1840-89 113

The Stamp of Spain after 1550 114

Audiencia System 114

Part 5: The Age of Empire

Colonial Frontiers 1700-1760 116

Predominant Immigration Groups c. 1750 117

Hispanic America c. 1780 118

British North America 1764-1776 119

The Ottoman Threat 1328-1672 120- 121

The Siege of Vienna 1683 120

Africa to c.1600 122

Africa's Black Gold 1500-1870 123

Indian Ocean 1800- 1900 124

Russian Expansion into Asia 1581- 1900 125

The World 1800 126-127

India, Invasions and Regional Powers 1739- 60 128

British Conquest of India 129

The American Civil War Campaigns of 1863 130

The American Civil War Campaigns of 1864-1865 131

The Sino-Japanese War 1894-95 132

Part 6: Globalisation

Manhattan 1880-1884 132

The World 1900 132-133

World War I 134

The Russian Revolution 135

Europe in 1914 136

Europe in 1919 136

Revolution and Invasion in China 1912-39 137

The Depression in Europe 138

Unemployment and Relief by State 1934 138

The Fascist States 1922-36 139

The Axis Expansion 1938-42 140

The Axis Collapse 1942-45 141

World War II in Asia 1941-43 142

World War II in Asia 1943-45 143

The Berlin Airlift June 1948-May 1949 144

The World 1950 145

End of Empire 146-147

Origins of the Cold War, Europe After World War II 1945-1949 148

Korea (Phases 1, 2 and 3) 149

The Cuban Missile Crisis September to November 1962 149

Vietnam War 1959-75 150

Communist Supply Routes 150

The Battle of AP Bac 151

Rolling Thunder 2 March 1965-31 October 1968 151

The Six Day War-Israeli Attack 14-30 May 1967 152

Suez and Sinai Campaign October-November 1956 152

Invasion of Lebanon June 1982-September 1983 152

The New World Order c.1990 153

Afghanistan 1978-84 154

World Terror 1970- present day 154

The Gulf War (Phases 1, 2 and 3) 155

Global Climate 156-157